Communication and the Mentally Ill Patient

of related interest

Child Psychiatric Units
At the Crossroads
Edited by Rosemary Chesson and Douglas Chisholm
1 85302 329 9

Psychosis
Understanding and Treatment
Edited by Jane Ellwood
1 85302 265 9

Working with Schizophrenia
Gwen Howe
1 85302 242 X

Deafness and Mental Health
John C Denmark
ISBN 1 85302 212 8

Collaboration in Health and Welfare
Working with Difference
Ann Loxley
ISBN 1 85302 394 9

Communication and the Mentally Ill Patient

Developmental and Linguistic
Approaches to Schizophrenia

Edited by Jenny France and Niki Muir

Jessica Kingsley Publishers
London and Bristol, Pennsylvania

First published in the United Kingdom in 1997 by
Jessica Kingsley Publishers Ltd
116 Pentonville Road
London N1 9JB, England
and
1900 Frost Road, Suite 101
Bristol, PA 19007, U S A

Library of Congress Cataloging in Publication Data
A CIP catalogue record for this book is available from the Library of Congress

British Library Cataloguing in Publication Data
Communication and the mentally ill patient : developmental
and linguistic approaches to schizophrenia
1. Schizophrenia 2. Schizophrenia – Treatment 3. Schizophrenia
– Psychological aspects 4. Linguisitics 5. Schizophrenics –
Language
I. France, Jenny II. Muir, Niki
616.8'982

ISBN 1-85302-414-7

Printed and Bound in Great Britain by
Biddles Ltd, Guildford and King's Lynn

Contents

List of Figures

List of Tables

FOR ALEXANDER
1967–1995

CHAPTER 1

Introduction

About Communication and the Mentally Ill Patient

Jenny France and Niki Muir

> Our mastery of communication affects our efficacy as clinicians every bit as much as our technical skill and our theoretical knowledge do. (Professor Anthony Clare 1993)

The origins of this book arose from the attendance of several speech and language therapists at the fifth Leeds Psychopathology symposium. It was held in May 1993 and was entitled 'Speech and Language Disorders'. In his introduction to the book resulting from that symposium, Sims (1995) stated that communication and its study is an established part of psychiatry, that it is widely recognised that psychiatric patients have problems communicating and that there are considerable differences in the abnormalities of speech in the major psychiatric diagnostic groups. Abnormalities in the speech of schizophrenia were identified over half a century ago by Kraepelin and Bleuler. Since then, interest in all aspects of schizophrenia has resulted in continuing research, publications and clinical involvement by many diverse professions. The speech and language therapists who attended the Speech and Language Disorder Symposium were founder- and core-members of the National Speech and Language Therapy Special Interest Group in Psychiatry. This was set up as a supportive and educative network for any speech and language therapists with an interest in psychiatry, many of whom were already delivering a service in mental health settings nation-wide.

The Leeds Symposium demonstrated the need for the speech and language therapy profession to inform the more traditionally accepted members of the psychiatric community of their presence and of the central role that their specialist contribution makes to speech, language and communication in the diagnosis and rehabilitation of mentally ill people. The convening of a two-day symposium on communication and the mentally ill patient was the speech and language therapy profession's response to the Leeds Symposium and was an attempt to open a multi-disciplinary dialogue in order to establish a forum to bridge the knowledge gap, as well as to highlight the present involvement in mental illness.

Dr Fiona Caldicott DBE, President of the Royal College of Psychiatrists (1995–1996), opened the symposium by stating that good listening skills are paramount and that, for a variety of reasons, doctors do not always listen to patients and psychiatrists alone do not have all the answers to mental health problems – highlighting the importance of working within multi-disciplinary teams. Dr Caldicott went on to stress the need for mental health professionals to take into account all aspects of the patient's communication processes, both verbal and non-verbal, in order to reach a diagnosis and to highlight and review patients' needs. She concluded her address by making reference to the increased demands for clear and accurate communication in mental health generally, given the need to implement the community care policy in the most effective way for service users and to negotiate in an informed way with purchasers. In Chapter 14, Dr David Abrahamson takes this idea of extended communication into the broader area of social networks and their development in the community. It is likely that transfer to, and maintainance in, the wider community is going to rest as much on the patients' communicative skills and their interpersonal networks as on their self-care competencies. He discusses and reviews attitudes to the social networks of long-term patients during the institutional era and in the current transition to community care, and presents assessments of the networks of residents on long-stay wards and in supported and independent community accommodation, and argues that mutually supportive relationships are an important, but neglected, aspect of care. Abrahamson also offers his views on the reasons for impoverished community networks and the efforts that should be made to enrich them through building design and developments in social and clinical services. He underlines the importance of promoting improved communication skills for the patients as well as within the team itself, supporting the view of a speech and language therapist as a specialist in human communication.

Language and our communication represent the broadest of our cognitive and psychosocial abilities and extend across the range of human activities and interpersonal relationships. The impact of any handicap can be both social and intellectual and its effects on self-esteem cannot be over-impressed. The purpose of the symposium, and of this book, is, first, to look at the language of one of the major mental illnesses – schizophrenia – in greater depth from the aspects of linguistic and communicative analysis and current thinking and research findings. Second, to discuss evidence as to whether it is neurodevelopmental – as in Chapters 7 and 8 – and, third, to present, in the concluding chapters, some information on the role and skills of the speech and language therapist in psychiatry, in specific aspects of clinical work, or as part of a team like David Abrahamson's, aiming to enrich and support the social networks in the community. This is a very broad remit and is reflected as such in the individual chapters of this volume with some differing approaches to the topic and through differing styles. It should be noted that the use of both the terms *client* and *patient* is retained as a reflection of this diversity and of the relative appropriateness within the given clinical settings of the individual authors.

Much has been said in the literature regarding schizophrenic patients frequently presenting with 'incoherent' and 'bizarre' speech, leading to difficulties in communicating with other people. The language disorder has been described as including deficits such as reduced syntactic complexity (e.g. Fraser *et al.* 1986; Morrice and Ingram 1982) and reduced numbers of ideas for the number of words spoken (Allen 1983), but its exact nature remains elusive. The conversational skills of some people with schizophrenia differ markedly from normal spoken interaction (Andreason 1979a; Rochester and Martin 1979) but such skills have received little attention from a therapeutic point of view (Holmes, Hansen and St. Lawrence 1984). Although judgements on language, speech and communication are used to reach a diagnosis (D.S.M. 1V 1994), management after that point still remains significantly rooted in pharmacologi cal- and activity-based models of care. From observations, it appears that some schizophrenic people show a level of awareness of their difficulties in conversing and become frustrated by this, posing the question as to whether focusing specifically on these skills will foster change.

In a sample of patients with schizophrenia, about 16 per cent will be rated as having incoherent speech (Andreason 1979 b) and, in Chapter 2, Professor Chris Frith suggests that the essence of such speech is that the listener cannot understand what the speaker is talking about. A much larger proportion will show less obvious problems, such as poverty of content of speech or loss of goal. These disorders seem to reflect lack of ideas, difficulties with planning a discourse and a tendency to perseverate on certain themes. He suggests that all these signs, including incoherence of speech, reflect defects of language use rather than language competence. In other words, schizophrenic patients have problems with communication, not language. As an example, Frith cites patients with 'delusions of reference', who falsely believe that people are trying to communicate with them and he discusses auditory hallucinations from the point of view of them typically involving patients hearing voices trying to influence their behaviour. This leads him to propose that all these abnormalities of communication arise because schizophrenic patients have difficulty in making inferences, particularly about the mental states of others. Inferential thinking is said to be a function of the right hemisphere of the brain (Cutting 1991), along with ability to process metaphor, humour and other verbal and non-verbal implied meaning(s), and there has been some discussion within speech and language therapy as to whether social use of language deficits, that is to say semantic pragmatic disorder (Leach 1983), is a right hemisphere syndrome (Shields 1991). A model of semantic pragmatic disorder is addressed in Chapter 11.

In Chapter 3, Professor Elaine Chaika presents another dimension of semantic pragmatic disorder by looking at the deviant speech of those with schizophrenia and stating that attentional dysfunction has long been posited as a cause of deviance in schizophrenic speech. However, her belief is that such a dysfunction does not explain the variety of errors that comprise what is usually termed schizophrenic speech. She considers recent research in the consequences of lapses of attention in normals and their effect on routinised behavioural sequences and suggests that we do find analogues to the peculiar combination of features of schizophrenic speech. Chaika looks at these in the light of the intention of the speaker and poses the following questions about schizophrenic speech: how is it pathological? Why does it take the forms it does? How do we understand it? Can we understand it? How can therapists help people control it from a linguistic perspective? She states that, no matter how deviant the speech of schizophrenia is, the patient does not mean to create a new language; these apparently diverse deviations in speech can be explained by attentional deficits and the severity of these is what we are dealing with in the language of schizophrenia. Chaika stresses that she now feels that the crucial element of the disruption of speech competence in the schizophrenic patient is not caused by a language deficit but by this attentional deficit and she postulates that intention is an integral part of meaning and speech. She indicates how attention devotes some part of its resources to inhibiting unwanted associative activities, therefore, when attention is disrupted, unwanted associations and behaviours proliferate. Finally, she discusses research into the executive function of the brain and slips of the tongue, which confirms the role of attentional dysfunction in schizophrenic speech.

Dr Philip Thomas, in Chapter 4, suggests that linguistic science might provide a new approach that would both complement and augment traditional psychopathological descriptions of thought disorder. He proposes that 'thought disorder' might be a term more usefully replaced by that of 'communication disorder'. Thomas discusses the 'Thought Language and Communication Scale' of Nancy Andreason (1980) and its possible applications to addressing the limitations of the current clinical term 'thought disorder', which fails to clarify the relationship between thought, language and speech, and he discusses pragmatics as a way of applying a psycho- or sociolinguistic model to the communication disorder resultant from the inferred thought disorder of schizophrenia. Mention is made of the four conversational maxims of quantity, quality, manner/clarity and relation/relevance (Grice 1975) and Thomas gives examples of each of these from discourse obtained from clients with schizophrenia.

He suggests that a study of linguistics as the science of language could be a valuable addition to the training of psychiatrists, as language constitutes the major investigative and therapeutic tool. Speech and language therapists have an important part to play in developing psycholinguistic approaches which will increase the explanatory power of cognitive neuropsychological models in order to help develop new methods of assessment and therapy based on linguistic theory.

Further research will be needed in order to move forward from repeated experiential anecdotes by measuring efficacy and validating the significance of the role of the speech and language therapist in mental health. Research into the area of linguistic and communicative function in schizophrenia, and strategies for its management, should be a task which speech and language therapists need to be encouraged to undertake. As a research therapist, Sarah Kramer presents the outline of one such project in Chapter 5. This will look at the language disorder and auditory hallucinations in schizophrenic patients and at a method of describing the language disorder by analysing natural language samples according to a theoretical model of discourse analysis (Frederikson *et al.* 1990). Discourse analysis allows the determination of the exact level at which language processing breaks down for the purposes of assessment and diagnosis. Kramer hypothesises that use of discourse analysis may contribute to the, presently, small amount of evidence providing empirical support for clinical observations of the value of language therapy in schizophrenia (France 1991). She suggests that, as in Lesser and Milroy (1993), this furthermore enables hypothesis-driven therapy to target the exact level of difficulty that the subjects experience in their discourse. She also discusses the implications for a therapy addressing language and auditory hallucinations (Hoffman and Satel 1993), indicating the need for the developing role of the speech and language therapist with this client group.

Current evidence to support the notion of the value of a greater role is provided by Thomas, Fraser, Joyce and Duckworth in Chapter 6, where they present a completed study undertaken by a multi-professional research group. The study directly looks at interviewing skills and how the descriptive frameworks for communication employed by speech and language therapists influence their techniques when compared with those of other professionals trained in human interaction.

A neurodevelopmental perspective is introduced by Dr Timothy Crow and Dr John Done in Chapter 7, who propose the need for an evolutionary theory of schizophrenia and suggest that the aetiology of schizophrenia is a disorder of the human capacity for the use of language that could be linked to a single-gene theory in terms of hemisphere asymmmetry and selection dominance in schizophrenia, which, if identified, would be of great significance. Crow and Done make reference to the work of the National Child Development

Study (Done *et al.* 1994), which is a longitudinal developmental study, in which there is particular reference to academic impairment and behaviour disturbances – including communication – found amongst the children in the group, who now, as adults, have been diagnosed as suffering from one or other form of mental illness, including schizophrenia. Crow and Done present the findings of parts of this study thus far, pertaining to the children when they were seven and eleven years of age. They also give some preliminary information from a study looking at assessment findings of relative hand skill in children and relate this back to the theory of hemispheric dominance referred to previously, demonstrating that it is indicative of deficits in verbal ability. This is tied-in to the theory of hemispheric dominance in the findings of brain studies of people who had been suffering from schizophrenia, which showed significant anomalies of asymmetry. These findings suggest that a failure to develop asymmetry would lead to a resultant failure to develop hemispheric dominance.

In Chapter 8, Stott, Burden, Forge and Goodyer present the current research into the psychiatric aspects of language delay being undertaken for the Department of Psychiatry at the University of Cambridge, with data being collected as part of an epidemiological project. In this cross-sectional and longitudinal study, the nature, course and outcome of language difficulties in a sample of three-year-olds is being investigated. The aims are to look at the co-variation between language difficulties and emotional/behavioural problems over a period of time, added to the importance of data on the familial aspects of language delay and related psychopathology. Stott *et al.* present detailed assessment of language, behaviour, temperamental and socio-emotional characteristics, early cognitive development and family background which has now been carried out with the four groups of children in the Cambridge project. It is this wide-ranging level of assessment that speech and language therapists commend. Pre-morbid levels of linguistic and communicative functioning have perhaps been given too little emphasis – certainly the preliminary results of the Cambridge project support the hypothesis that the profile of linguistic skills will differentiate children with or without behaviour problems and that there are indications of a suggestion that non-phonological difficulties are associated with an increased risk of behaviour problems.

People with a major mental illness have the highest incidence of speech and language disorders, yet the essential componants of their problems are seldom treated by speech and language therapists. This may be partly due to the limited understanding of the role of speech and language therapy and partly due to the perceptions of mainstream mental health professionals, all of whom could justifiably claim to work with 'communication'. A study within the mental health unit of Frenchay Hospital in Bristol (Emerson and Enderby in print) found that 78 per cent of the clients they screened had some sort of speech and language problem, ranging through hearing loss, dysfluency, severe receptive and expressive language deficits, voice and articulation problems and dysarthria and that these findings were *without* screening for functional communication deficits. Care-planning may make mention of language, speech or communication problems in the general sense but it is often difficult for medical, nursing and other therapy staff to set goals and administer targeted regimes of therapy because of the complexity of analysing and specifying individual targets. It is, perhaps, this measure of specificity that the speech and language therapist can add to the assessment and care-planning undertaken by the multi-disciplinary team.

Chapter 9 takes up the final theme of the symposium, that of presenting the clinical role of the speech and language therapist in psychiatry. Jenny France and Niki Muir present a look at the way in which face-to-face engagements with clients are managed. The chapter offers an overview of assessment and therapeutic interventions, as undertaken with particular reference to schizophrenia, and gives anecdotal and reported views of patients' own perceptions of their experiences and their responses to treatment.

Irene Walsh discusses conversational skills and schizophrenia in Chapter 10 by looking at conversational disability in pre-schizophrenic children and describing the results of a follow-back approach into the pre-morbid precursors of schizophrenia with regard to speech and language functioning (Murray 1994; Jones *et al*. 1994). It is interesting to note from Walsh's study that, of the five files she examined, only two had specific reference to the childrens' communicative abilities in the notes made by psychiatrists, thereby confirming the belief that, in the main, little emphasis is placed on looking at these behaviours in the kind of depth that might yield productive avenues for further research or for clinical management. Walsh's study, albeit brief and, to her mind, incomplete, nonetheless points to the need for detailed assessment of those children who may be at risk of developing a mental illness such as schizophrenia. She comments that such studies of pre-morbid development pose the question of whether a specific conversational disability, apparently pre-morbidly, may be some part of the insidious development of schizophrenia that is taking a neurodevelopmental perspective. This is a comment echoed by many of the speech and language therapists who work in both child and adult psychiatry.

Walsh also expands on the conversational skills of people with schizophrenia, outlining the implementation of an informal conversational skills programme which she devised and currently runs for people with chronic schizophrenia. The programme is targeted at increasing awareness of conversational skills and at promoting the use of those skills in a more appropriate and effective way, for example through encouraging self-monitoring skills.

In Chapter 11, Niki Muir contends that speech and language therapists' training creates an ideal platform for a major contribution to work in mental health – given that the most recent developments in speech and language therapy have been in the understanding and use of assessment and therapeutic techniques and materials relating to cognitive neuropsychological and semantic pragmatic models of communication – and she presents a model for looking at semantic pragmatics after Roth and Spekman (1984). She also offers a modular representation of the componant parts of the language, speech and communication 'chain' to illustrate the role of the speech and language therapist in mental health as the clinical specialist who can help make the diagnostic distinction between those componants, particularly between receptive and expressive language function. She indicates how to use targeted therapeutic strategies to improve patients' communication by addressing the specific pragmatic elements, which include attention and self-monitoring skills.

Carmel Hayes, in Chapter 12, specifically details the utilisation of the principles and techniques of Personal Construct Psychology (Kelly 1955) in communication skills groups. She states that there seems to be tacit agreement among cognitive psychologists that the meaning of a person's thoughts are understood within a context of personal relatedness. The way we think on one occasion is related to the way we think on another, whether in the past, present or future. She outlines Personal Construct Psychology as one comprehensive account that allows for identification of personal contexts, with its attendant methodology, with particular reference to Kelly's proposal of a model of man as an active construer of the world with the cognitive capacity for enhancement and change. Hayes describes how she has applied the principles and techniques of Personal Construct Psychology, in the context of rehabilitating communication skills in a small group setting, for people with chronic mental health problems in varying processes of resettlement. She demonstrates how it helps them, through a structured communication programme, to influence their view of their construed world and proposes that this experiential modality, which is often employed by speech and language therapists with people who stutter (Heyhow and Levy 1989), can have a powerful effect in helping long-stay clients explore, state and make change, and that it can be a non-confrontational alternative to other 'talking' therapeutic interventions.

In chapter 13, Laurie Macdonald provides a brief introduction to NeuroLinguistic Programming (O'Connor and Seymour 1990) which, when used as a psychotherapeutic methodology, enables patients to gain insight into their own cognitive processes. This understanding of how they develop their beliefs about themselves, and the world they live in, enables change to occur within their cognitive processing and, consequently, in their behaviour. Macdonald encourages the need to view semantic pragmatic disorder within an holistic approach to rehabilitation, incorporating psychotherapeutic and social models, showing that NeuroLinguistic Programming offers both a method of linguistic analysis of conversational speech and an indication of the linguistic forms that the therapist might employ in order to facilitate change for the patient.

In a closing address at the symposium, Dr Pam Enderby, Chair of the Royal College of Speech and Language Therapists (1994–1995), made further reference to the study undertaken at Frenchay Hospital as being an attempt to gain an overview of the range of detectable speech and language problems in the psychiatric population in order to gauge the perception of these problems held by other clinical professionals. She expressed concern that this client group is often marginalised, allowing significant disturbances of language, speech and hearing to go undetected or unspecified. She was emphatic that speech and language therapists have a significant role to play in diagnosis and management and that, at the very least, could make a contribution to the informing and training of others in areas where resources are scarce and no immediate service provision is contemplated. Dr Enderby concluded by saying that, as people in the business of communication, speech and language therapists should make it their intention to maximise their own communication by making strenuous efforts, in all specialisms, to undertake research and publish papers and books in order to inform others, particularly as the profession is a relative newcomer having celebrated the Golden Jubilee of the College in 1995. This book marks the starting point in the fulfilment of her exhortation for speech and language therapy in psychiatry, as yet a small group in a small profession.

During the process of printing this book, Dr. Enderby has been appointed the first professor of community rehabilitation at Sheffield University.

CHAPTER 2

Language and Communication in Schizophrenia

Christopher Frith

Description of the Phenomena

In a sample of patients with schizophrenia, about 16 per cent will be rated as having 'incoherent speech'. The essence of such speech is that the listener cannot understand what the speaker is talking about. A much larger proportion (about 40%) will show less obvious problems, such as 'poverty of content of speech or loss of goal'. These disorders seem to reflect lack of ideas, difficulties with planning a discourse and a tendency to perseverate on certain themes. Approximately 29 per cent of this group will demonstrate 'poverty of speech' which involves a lack of spontaneous, self-initiated speech. About 24 per cent show examples of 'perseveration' with persistent repetition of words or ideas. (Andreason 1979b)

The following language samples (Numbers 1, 2 and 3) are offered to illustrate these specific speech disorders:

Example 1 (from Wykes and Leff 1982):

> Where did all this start could it possibly have started the possibility operates some of the time having the same decision as you and possibility that I must now reflect or wash out any doubts that that's bothering me and one instant what's bothering me an awful lot in my wisdom the truth is I've got the truth to tell you with mine signing here and as I am as G-d made me and understand my position and you'll listen with intelligence your intelligence works lit again and is recorded in my head.

From this it can be seen that incoherent speech is unintelligible speech, with a lack of proper connections between words.

Example 2 (transcript of a description of a farming scene by a chronic schizophrenic patient) (Frith 1992):

> Some – farm houses – in a farm yard – time – with a horse and horseman – time where – going across the field as if they're ploughing the field – time – with ladies – or collecting crops – time work is – coming with another lady – time work is – and where – she's holding a book – time – thinking of things – time work is – and time work is where – you see her coming time work is on the field – and where work is – where her time is where working is and thinking of people and where work is and where you see the hills – going up – and time work is – where you see the – grass – time work is – time work is and where the fields are – where growing is and where work is.

In this sample, poverty of content arises because the patient uses rather few words and repeats them in very striking repetitions (Frith 1992).

Example 3:

E: How're you doing generally at the moment, Mr D?

D: All right

E: You're OK. How're... How've you been feeling in your spirits this past week?

D: Not so bad.

E: You're feeling all right. Do you have any spells of feeling sad or miserable?

D: No

E: No? Nothing like that? That's good. Now tell me, Mr D, do you have any special ideas about life in general?

D (shakes head)

E: No. Do you feel people stare at you and talk about you in some way?

D (shakes head)

E: No. No, you didn't get bothered with that at all. Do you feel in any way that people are against you and trying to do you harm?

D (shakes head)

E: No. You didn't get that either. That's good. Now I'd like to ask you some questions about your thoughts, Mr D. Do you ever feel that your thoughts or your actions are influenced in some way?

D (minimal head shake)

E: You didn't get that. You didn't get that. That's fine. Now could I
       ask you a routine question that we ask everyone? Do you ever…

In this sample, the patient answers all questions but never volunteers new
information or spontaneously elaborates his answers. Thus, although the patient
is compliant and will answer even difficult questions, the poverty of his speech
is noteworthy.

The Contention is that the Problem with Schizophrenic Speech Lies in Communication Rather than Language

Many studies of language disorder in schizophrenia have involved looking for
defects at different levels of 'language'. This can be defined as a repre-
sentational system governed by rules. In contrast, 'communication' is a process
by which one person changes knowledge and beliefs in the mind of another.
In most studies, specific defects in lower level processes have not been found.
The general consensus is that only the highest levels of language processes are

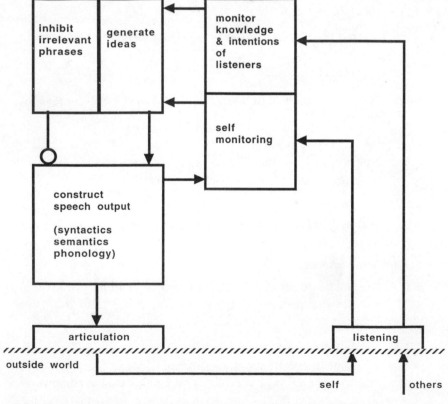

Figure 2.1 A flow diagram illustrating the various processes required for successful
     communication. The speaker must generate ideas, present them in a way that takes account of
     the knowledge of the listener and monitor the speech produced for errors.

impaired in schizophrenia. This does not mean that there will be no errors at the lower levels, for example lexical, syntactic, semantic, etc. Rather, it means that, in schizophrenia, errors at these levels can be explained as the consequence of higher level processing failure.

A central issue is to identify the high level processes that are impaired in schizophrenic language. The abnormalities of schizophrenic language appear not to lie at the level of language competence but of language use. The problems arise when the patient has to use language to communicate with others. These problems apply not just to speech but to all the non-verbal modes of communication as well.

These problems in the communication of schizophrenic patients can be illustrated by looking at a flow diagram of the processes involved in communication and language. Figure 2.1 implies that schizophrenic patients could have problems with making inferences about the knowledge and intentions of their listeners and in using these inferences to guide their discourse plans. These problems would be reflected in the symptoms of schizophrenia, which mostly involve communication.

These can be divided into four distinct groups:

- Failure to develop plans; poverty of speech, poverty of content of speech

- failure to control plans; incoherent speech; flight of ideas

- failure to self-monitor; thought insertion; auditory hallucinations

- failure to monitor others; delusions of reference; delusions of persecution.

Many patients with schizophrenia characteristically show a poverty of action in all spheres: movement, speech and affect. They can perform routine acts elicited by environmental stimuli but have difficulty in producing spontaneous behaviour in the absence of external cues. Thus, they frequently demonstrate poverty and slowness of speech, a poverty in the content of their speech and a poverty of expression and gesture (Frith *et al.* 1995).

However, this problem with willed action can also lead to positive behavioural disorders when there is a failure to control plans. In such cases, patients are not only unable to generate the appropriate behaviour of their own will but also fail to suppress inappropriate behaviour. Recent actions are repeated in perseverations and responses are made to irrelevant external stimuli, so action plans cannot be carried through to completion. This leads to incoherent speech. Furthermore, routine actions may be elicited by environmental stimuli when they are inappropriate as in non-social speech and flight of ideas.

A defect in self-monitoring can explain many of the experiences classified as first rank symptoms. Patients with these symptoms are no longer aware of the 'sense of effort' or the prior intention that normally accompanies a deliberate act. They can only fully monitor their actions on the basis of peripheral feedback, that is by observing the actual consequences of their actions after they have been carried out. In the absence of an awareness of their own intentions, patients will experience their actions and thoughts as being caused, not by themselves, but by some alien force. Thus, patients experience thought insertion, thought echo and thought broadcasting as well as auditory hallucinations.

Disorders in monitoring the intentions of others give rise to both paranoid delusions and delusions of reference. Patients with paranoid delusions believe that other people are intending them harm; patients with delusions of reference incorrectly believe that other people are intending to communicate with them.

Experiments on Communication

Failure of Willed Action

We have, in these observations, the beginnings of a cognitive model for behavioural signs. The explanatory power of this model can be examined by looking at a controlled experimental paradigm: fluency tasks. These tasks require the subject to generate responses with minimal specification by the experimenter, for instance 'name as many animals as you can'. With this verbal fluency task, the subject must find a series of different words within a given time limit. The task is not to generate completely novel words but to find and say appropriate words that already exist in his mental lexicon.

Three types of speech abnormality can all be seen as consequences of the impairment in the 'willed' route to action. What happens when it is not possible to generate a spontaneous new response? There are three possibilities.

1. nothing is done (poverty of speech)

2. the previous response might be repeated, even though it is now inappropriate (perseverative speech)

3. there may be an inappropriate response to some signal in the environment.

The sort of abnormality that will emerge depends on the specific task the subject is trying to perform, but this could include words from different categories or peculiar examples (incoherence). This is demonstrated in data from chronic hospitalised patients (Allen and Frith 1983) as well as data from patients in the community, as shown in a study by Allen, Liddle and Frith (1993). Current imaging techniques are now enabling the investigation of how these processes are reflected in the brain.

The above ideas have been corroborated using a sentence completion test in which subjects have to suggest a word that would *not* fit at the end of the sentence (e.g. The dog chased the cat up the ... idea). Schizophrenic patients, particularly those with incoherent speech have great difficulty with this task and tend to choose words that do fit (Nathaniel–James and Frith 1996). They cannot prevent themselves producing the obvious word even though they know it is inappropriate.

Failures of self-monitoring

Historically, an output theory was adopted with reference to hallucinations. At its crudest, this says that the patient is talking to himself but perceives the voices as coming from somewhere else. It can be examined very directly. Gould (1949) investigated a schizophrenic patient who heard voices almost continuously. When the patient's sub-vocal activity was amplified with a microphone, it was found to be whispered speech which was qualitatively different from the patient's voluntary whispers. On the basis of the content of this speech, and the patient's reports, Gould concluded that the sub-vocal speech corresponded to the 'voices'. This has been replicated in a number of studies.

If hallucinations are the consequence of sub-vocal speech, it should be possible to suppress them and reduce auditory hallucinations, but this has not been uniformly successful. Looking at other hypotheses, the problem with self-monitoring would suggest a possible difficulty with self-repair. This involves the speaker recognising an error and correcting it. Leudar, Thomas and Johnston (1992; 1994) used a task in which there was some evidence of problems in self-repair.

The ability to self-monitor has been examined from a different perspective in an experiment in which the subject's own voice was distorted in pitch. In contrast to those in remission, patients with delusions and hallucinations reported that they could hear someone else speaking whenever they spoke. The distortion in pitch led them to experience their own voice as coming from someone else. There is evidence from both animal and human studies that there are areas in the left temporal cortex where the distinction is made between the sound of our own voice and that of other people. The function of this area may be abnormal during acute episodes of schizophrenia (McGuire *et al.* 1995).

Monitoring the intentions of others

The ability to take into account the intentions and beliefs of other people has been extensively studied by developmental psychologists in recent years (Astington and Gopnik 1991). This ability, which is crucial for the development of a 'theory of mind', has been found lacking in children with autism (Baron-Cohen, Leslie and Frith 1985). Without this ability, the autistic child cannot handle the possibility that another person may have a different belief. This is subsumed in a deficit in the mechanism that permits us to have a 'theory of mind' (Premack and Woodruff 1978) or to 'mentalise'. Both these terms refer to our belief that other people have minds different from our own and also to our ability to infer the beliefs, wishes and intentions of other people in order to predict their behaviour. In Uta Frith's (1989) theory, this is used to explain many signs of childhood autism. If autistic children cannot mentalise, they cannot understand the behaviour of their mother when, in the course of pretend play, she talks into a banana. This behaviour is only explicable if the child can infer the mother's mental state: that she is pretending that the banana is a telephone. Without mentalising, the child's communication will be abnormal because he will not be able to take into account the beliefs and knowledge of the person to whom he is speaking. Finally, he will be in a world in which people are no different from objects. He will be alone because he is denied contact with other minds.

An impaired ability to represent mental states will also affect interactions with other people, as we see in people with a semantic pragmatic disorder. Communication cannot occur successfully simply on the basis of knowing what the words mean, since words mean different things in different contexts. The most important context is the beliefs and intentions of the persons saying the words (including their beliefs about the beliefs and intentions of the person to whom they are speaking).

People with schizophrenia resemble people with autism in that they too have impairments in the mechanism that enables them to mentalise. However, in most cases, this mechanism was functioning adequately until their first breakdown. Given these very different developmental histories, this defect will manifest in different ways. Autistic people have never known that other people have minds. Schizophrenic people know well that other people have minds but have lost the ability to infer the contents of these minds: their beliefs and intentions. They may even lose the ability to reflect on the contents of their own mind. Thus, whilst the autistic child does not try to infer the mental states of others, adult schizophrenic patients will continue to make inferences about the mental states of others but will often get these wrong. They will 'see' intentions to communicate when none are there (delusions of reference). They may start to believe that people are deliberately behaving in such a way as to disguise their intentions. They will deduce that there is a general conspiracy against them and that people's intentions towards them are evil (paranoid delusions).

This lack of ability to mentalise can be studied experimentally in stories such as that of 'The False Belief Story': John has five cigarettes left in his packet. He puts his packet on the table and leaves the room. Janet comes in and takes one of John's cigarettes without John knowing. In a memory question, the experimenter asks: 'How many cigarettes are left in John's packet?' Then, the subject is asked a mentalising question: 'When John comes back for his cigarettes, how many does he think he has?' Schizophrenics in remission perform like controls and are able to mentalise. Paranoid patients respond correctly to the memory question but answer incorrectly to the mentalising question. Once they know something, they infer that everybody else knows it too. Schizophrenics with incoherent speech are unable to answer either of the two questions.

Thus, in the opinion of the author, the theory of mind can be used to explain certain speech disorders in schizophrenia. A failure of the schizophrenic to take into account differences in knowledge between himself and the listener would result in speech disorder, which would concord with the statement 'People listening to me get more lost than I do' (McGhie and Chapman 1961). It would also explain the lack of referents reported by Rochester and Martin (1979), the lack of cohesive ties noted by Wykes and Leff (1982) and the confused discourse plan described by Hoffman (1986). Thus, the phenomena enumerated at the outset of this chapter, and subsequently demonstrated in controlled experimental paradigms, can be explained by a unified theory concerning deficits in the theory of mind.

CHAPTER 3

Intention, Attention, and Deviant Schizophrenic Speech

Elaine Chaika

There are twin issues in researching schizophrenic speech: how it is pathological and why. Dependent on the explanations for these, we then face another set of issues: how to understand it and how to help the patient control it.

Many scholars have attributed the peculiarities of schizophrenic speech to attentional dysfunction – either claiming that the patient has a deficit in attention, pays too little attention, or, alternatively, pays too much attention to extraneous matters (McGhie 1970; McGhie and Chapman 1961; McGhie, Chapman and Lawson 1965a; McGhie, Chapman and Lawson 1965b; Maher 1983). Although all of these presentations have merit, none explains the connection between attentional disorders and the peculiarities of the combination of schizophrenic deviations.[1] This chapter explores the role of attention in the syndrome of deviations in schizophrenic speech disorder. In a previous work, I suggested that this combination of dysfunctions stems from inhibitory dysfunction in schizophrenia (Chaika 1982). This chapter will also explore the role of attention in inhibitory dysfunction. I will show that attentional dysfunction may well be the cause of apparent inhibitory dysfunctions – ostensibly rendering my 1982 hypothesis doubtful, but not if we consider deficits in inhibitory functions as a product of attention malfunctioning. Moreover, lapses in attention (Reason and Mycielska 1982; Reason 1984) can be shown to accord with the specific variety of schizophrenic deviations[2] and also shed light on the relationship of attentional disorders to inhibitory dysfunction in schizophrenia.

---

1 It must be emphasised that not all diagnosed schizophrenics evince deviations in their speech. These are those traditionally called *non-thought disordered*. The merits of this terminology are discussed extensively by many scholars (Chaika 1974; Rochester and Martin 1979; Chaika and Lambe 1985; Chaika 1990).

2 Self-monitoring dysfunction, both before and after the utterance is made, is clearly also implicated in deviations in language production in schizophrenics.

Producing even the simplest utterance is an enormously complex affair requiring multitudinous choices of sounds, words, syntax and discourse strategies. Language is a set of intricately interrelated skills and knowledge that is fashioned to be infinitely creative. Language is multi-layered, going from a set of phonetic rules to morphemic rules to syntactic and semantic rules and rules of discourse. To these are added a lexicon and complex sociolinguistic strategies which dictate what we say, when, and how. In addition, much of what is said in ordinary conversation does not directly say what it means. 'It costs an arm and a leg' does not mean that one pays in body parts. 'Ooh chocolates' means 'Give me some of those chocolates.' Throughout language, there is metaphor; there is implication. We imply and we infer. Considering these complexities, it is no wonder that one result of psychosis is likely to be disruption in speech production, although not necessarily in language competence itself. An examination of the characteristics of schizophrenic speech, as presented below, indicates that schizophrenic speech is not necessarily caused by a language deficit.[3] Before determining the locus of dysfunction in speech disordered schizophrenia, we must first examine the syndrome of features of such speech.

In line with my previous practice, the characteristics of schizophrenic speech are here categorised in terms of their structural deviations (Chaika 1974; 1982; 1990) The samples below include the categories of *gibberish, neologising, perseveration, erroneous lexical choice, glossomania*, and *disruptions in syntax*, all well-known features of schizophrenic speech. These are all failures on the level of the word and sentence. Since most words and sentences, schizophrenic or other, occur in discourse, the samples in (II) to (V) are presented with snatches of the original discourses in which they were embedded. The glossomanic samples in (VI) are each complete as reported by Cohen (1978), although it must be noted that glossomanic chains do occur in longer discourses which are not entirely associative in character. Fuller samples of discourse are presented in (VII). These show failures in mechanisms of maintaining cohesive ties between sentences, lack of use of mechanisms for introducing, maintaining, and changing topics and faulty use of mechanisms for creating relevance between sentences in a discourse – including inappropriate framing (Chaika 1990; Ribeiro 1994). Moreover, these samples include dysfunction both in lexicon and syntax as well as in discourse.

The samples to be discussed are:

I.   Gibberish:

    (1) *gao, itivare, ovede* (Forrest 1976, p.286)

---

3   One argument against the proposition that schizophrenic speech results from a permanent linguistic deficit is that its characteristics largely disappear when the psychotic episode is over.

(2) (speaking about a pet) He still had *fooch* with *teykrimes* (Chaika 1974)

(3) dededededede colololololololololo (Ribeiro 1994, p. 277)

II. Neologising:

(4) …you still have to have a *plausity* of amendments to go through for the children's code and it's no mental disturbance of puterience (Vetter 1968, p.189)

(5) …with syndicates organised and *subsicates* in the way that look for a civil war (Herbert and Waltensperger 1982, p.226).

III. Perseverations (Inappropriate Repetitions):

(6) (in German) …sie haben es *von* dem *Vor*eltern, *von* der *Vor*welt, *von* der Urwelt, *Frank*furt-am-Main, das sind die *Franken*, die *Frank*furter, die *Frank*furter Wurschtchen, *Franken*thal, *Franken*stein (Maher 1972, p.9)

(7) Mill Avenue is a house in between avenues U and avenue T I live on Mill Avenue for a period of for now a period of maybe 15 year for around approximate 15 years I like it the fam– I like every family on Mill Avenue I like every family in the world I like every family in the United State of America I like every family on Mill Avenue I like Mill Avenue… (Chaika 1990, p.34)

(8) You know that you knew everything everything that I wanted. You are the one who knows. It's the mother, it's the mother, it's the mother, it's the mother, it's the mother, it's the mother, it's the mother, it's the mother, UHM. It's the mother of her. (Ribeiro 1994, p.276)

IV. Erroneous Lexical Choice:

(9) Dr: Dean, come here.

     Pt: What? You said go already?

     Dr: No, I didn't say *go*. I wanted to sit near you, Dean.

          (patient leaves room) (Laffal 1965, p.84)

(10) He says well what the heck give it to her [nooee]. Sh-she's a little daughter. (He has seen child on video. She is not his daughter)

(11) The cash register man handled the financial matters. (referring to his ringing up money for an ice cream cone.)

(Chaika 1990, p.202)

V. Word Salads and Other Disruptions in Syntax:

(12) After John Black has recovered in special neutral form of life the honest bring back to doctor's agents must take John Black out through making up design meaning straight neutral underworld shadow tunnel (Lorenz 1961, p.603)

(13) I am being help with the food and the medicate...to speak and think in a lord tongue...the memory knowledge... I still not have the thought pattern (Chaika 1990, p.24)

VI. Glossomania:

(The following were responses to being asked what colour Munsell Disc #2 is, a salmon pink colour.)

(14) A fish swims. You call it a salmon. You cook it. You put it in a can. You open the can. You look at it in this colour.

(15) Pancake make-up. You put it on your face and they think guys run after you. Wait a second! I don't put them on my face and guys don't run after me. Girls put it on them.

(16) Looks like clay. Sounds like gray. Take you for a roll in the hay. Hay-day. Mayday. Help. I need help. (Cohen 1978, p.29)

VII. Discourse:

((17) and (18) were both produced in response to being asked to tell about a video they had seen. The video was about a little girl who went to a shop to buy some ice cream.)

(17) I was watching a film of a girl and um s bring back memories of things that happened to people around me that affected me during the time when I was living in the area and she just went to the store for a candy bar and by the time ooh of course her brother who was supposed to be watching wasn't paying much attention *he was blamed for* and I didn't think that was fair the way the way they did that either so that's why I'm asking you *could we just get together and try to work it out all together for one big party or something ezz it hey if it we'd all in which is in not* they've been here so why you just now discovering it. You know they've been men will try to use you every time for

everything he wants so ain't no need and you trying to get upset for it. That's all. That's all.

(18) You want me to talk about – um – last week's experience I had? 'n it was funny 'is experience seems to sum up all of what's been goin' on because I've been walkin' around recitin' things. I've written to people and people been listening but then when you get down to it *you've got to scrub your own dishes* or else nobody's gonna and I've been so totally against *the idea of people feelin' they have a ticket to carry them along because it's a ticket is not an easy trip along by no means is probably harder* if you understand what I mean. (Chaika 1990, pp.221–222)

(This is a passage from a long intake interview with a schizophrenic patient. The original contained diacritics indicating pauses of various lengths, intonation, and voice quality as well as details of body motions. (3) and (8) above come from the same interview.)

(19) (Doctor has repeatedly tried to get patient's attention with limited success, although patient occasionally incorporates doctor's words, or responses to them. Her monologue is interspersed with stretches of gibberish and perseverations of entire phrases. The following is in response to 'so tell me your full name')

No, only *if you have. Do you have?* Oh mama! Mama, mama. She says *she has mama.* She says we can leave. Mama… Then ask to be excused my child. It's like this that we ask. So much curiosity ['hhh]. They *wanted to have*, didn't they child, ['hhh] to know about you, right child. Just because ['hhh] they saw you barefooted out…of doors, right child, ['hhh] *they thought you had* (gibberish).

How are such diverse deviations related? How can they proceed from attentional dysfunction? Is that dysfunction one of too little attention or too much paid to the wrong elements in the linguistic elements of the discourse?

Typically, a stretch of speech will contain more than one category of error. For instance, the patient who says 'dededededede' in (3) above has produced gibberish, but also perseveration. Other samples of gibberish may not show perseveration. Some perseveration consists of normal phrases, such as in (8) in 'It's the mother, it's the mother, it's the mother…' Similarly, disruptions in syntax, occur on the morphemic level in (13) but on the phrasal level in (12). Another example of syntactic disruption is the discourse presented in (17). Here the object of the preposition *for* is omitted[4] in 'he was blamed for and I didn't think that was fair...' Similarly, in (19), the object of the verb *have* is consistently omitted. (17) also contains word salad: '*ezz it hey if it we'd all in which is in not.*' Note that the patient does use cohesion markers like *and, so,* and *who* correctly, yet the passage as a whole is not coherent although it is comprehensible, as are many deviant utterances. Such diversity of deviations within a given passage should be expected, if, as will posited here, all the kinds of deviations themselves are caused by the same attentional dysfunction.

Before discussing these samples of schizophrenic speech in greater detail, there is one other important fact about language usage to consider: intention. Intention governs what we say and how we say it, and we interpret what others mean by assuming what their intentions were in saying what they did. The words and syntax that we produce are subordinated to our intentions in speaking. Thus, to evaluate their meaning and propriety, we must consider intention. This, in turn, entails accounting for context of utterance.

We will briefly examine each sample with reference to the thoughts they seem to be expressing in light of the patients' apparent intentions, where these can be ascertained. At all times, however, we must bear in mind that the thoughts and the language expressing them may not be equally deviant. Indeed, much of the pathological speech presented here and elsewhere in the literature seems to encode quite ordinary thoughts. Conversely, pathological thoughts are sometimes expressed in quite ordinary speech (Chaika and Lambe 1985).

We cannot say anything about the conditions under which the items in (1) were produced because Dr Forrest did not report them. They have been included because of their diversity, and because each of these non-words could be words in English. They conform to English sound system, as do the samples in (2) which are embedded in recognisable lexical items. Ribeiro's samples are from a Portuguese patient and are possible syllables in that language as well. This would seem to indicate that, at least on the level of phonotactics, schizophrenic speech may be unimpaired, although the paucity of studies of schizophrenic gibberish do not permit a definite conclusion at this time. Schizophrenic phonetics seems to be a very under-researched area.[5]

---

4   In my study of schizophrenic and manic narration (Chaika and Alexander 1986), I found that only schizophrenics failed to provide objects of prepositions and direct objects. These constitute failures to complete basic constituent structures of sentences. Manics never made this kind of error. Although she doesn't remark on it, Ribiero's (1994) transcript of an interview with a schizophrenic also shows several instances of failure to provide direct objects of verbs, as in (19).

5   I have never found samples of schizophrenic gibberish in the literature, or in my own patients, which do not conform to the phonotactics of English. I have never interviewed non-English speaking patients. This is not to say that samples of gibberish which do not conform to the phonotactics of the patient's language do not exist. There are few phoneticians, if any, who have analysed schizophrenic gibberish. There are no spectographic analyses of such gibberish of which I am aware, although such analyses abound for aphasics with known lesions.

The samples in (II) to (VII) usually start out as an attempted response to what someone else has said or to something in the environment. What is most notable is that, with the exception of (1), (3), (4), (5), (8), (12) and (19), the patient displays evidence that he or she intends to answer the questions asked of them. Four out of the seven apparent exceptions – (1), (4), (5) and (12) – might have been intended responses but, due to their being presented without context, we simply cannot tell. Ribeiro (1994, p.8) gives a plausible but unprovable explanation for (8) which shows that it, too, might be an effort at a response to the psychiatrist's question. Her explanation is that the mother is the one who knows everything and the doctor, like the mother, knows everything. Her explanation is reinforced by the patients' repetitions, throughout the interview, of an equation between the doctor, the mother and knowing everything.

Wherever a context is provided, most of the patients' utterances start out with a recognisable attempt to answer their interviewer and then become progressively more deviant, a fact noted and discussed by Chaika (1982) and Maher (1983) on different, but not conflicting, grounds.[6] That is, the speech disordered (SD) patient seems to intend to respond co-operatively but becomes derailed in some way as the utterance continues. In glossomania, for instance, the associated chaining occurs as the patient keeps talking. Although the first utterance may be correct, as in (16), in discourse, as in (17) and (18), the narration becomes progressively off the point and syntactic and lexical errors occur. This reality must be accounted for in any explanation for the etiology of SD schizophrenia.

Since Forrest gives no context for (1), we have no idea whether or not the gibberish he presents was embedded in clear enough language to tell if it was in response to another's utterance or to the general context. We don't even know if these 'words' were spoken by the same person or several people, nor if they were displayed in the same discourse. They stand only as examples of the kinds of gibberish schizophrenics might produce.

Three of the possible exceptions, (3), (19) and (8), were produced by the same patient in the same interview. Ribeiro does show that occasionally the patient's statements do incorporate the physician's words or give clear responses to them, showing an intention to respond but without the skill to do so normally. We can have no idea of what, if anything, was meant by (3) since it is total gibberish. Ribeiro does theorise that (8) could be a response to a question about the patient's son. She explains that the bizarre response in (8) refers to the rather usual circumstance that a patient feels that the psychiatrist knows everything, and that mothers do too, but, plausible as this may be, it is hard to justify the patient's response as a valid, or even nearly valid, response

---

6   This is generally true of schizophrenic speech, not just those samples provided here.

to a question about the whereabouts of the patient's son. Her response seems to have no connection to the question. Perhaps this is because transitions are missing and the repetitions are inappropriate (Chaika 1990, pp.235–237). These are discourse failures. The other levels of language are intact in (8), although – as we saw in (3), part of the same interview – the patient does evince speech deteriorated to the point of gibberish.

Vetter (1968) and Herbert and Waltensperger (1982), who, respectively, provided (4) and (5), do not provide the contexts for these utterances, so we cannot determine whether or not either or both were attempted rejoinders to previous utterances. These might have been intended responses. We just have no way of knowing at this point in time. Note, however, that the neologisms in (4) and (5) are embedded in otherwise comprehensible phrasing which appears to be conveying some information. This argues for the position that these statements were probably intentional and were attempts either to answer questions or comment on a remark.

In contrast, for the other twelve speech samples, we know what elicited the responses, responses which manifest clear intention to answer what had been said by the co-conversationalist. There may be speech disability in the responses but the responses themselves show quite normal attempts to co-operate in the situation. For instance, (7) was produced in response to the question about where the patient lived and what it was like. Throughout his monologue, which is more extensive than the sample presented here (Chaika 1990, p.34), the patient has clearly responded to the interviewer.

In (9), although Dean apparently both hears and speaks antonyms to the target words, a condition Dr Vetter calls *opposite speech*, his actions and statements are evidently in reaction to the doctor's statements. He is simply doing the opposite of what the therapist is commanding. That is, he understands antonyms as meaning their opposite – a condition I found in a patient as well, one who told me that many sets of antonyms mean the same thing (Chaika 1977).

In (10), (11), (17) and (18), the patients are obeying a request to tell what they had seen on a videotaped sequence and all responses referred to the video, with greater or lesser accuracy. (10) and (11) are accurate in their reference but not their word choice. In (10), *girl* would be expected, not *a little daughter*. The 'little daughter' he speaks of is not the patient's daughter. In (11), *handling financial matters* is too elevated a term to refer to ringing up a sale of an ice cream cone, which is what he was talking about. In both instances, related but inaccurate phrases were uttered.

All three samples under Glossomania, (14), (15), and (16), were responses to the question of what colour Munsell disc # 2 is. In fact, all accurately described the colour, so the patients clearly intended to answer the question. The glossomania in (14) actually starts out with an answer, albeit a highly unusual one, which clearly responds to the original question. Here, rather than equating the colour with the colour of a salmon, the patient retrieves a corollary answer about a fish and then identifies it as a salmon, which is the colour of the disc. He then continues, although he has provided the answer, and works his way to the associated fact that the fish is one often seen in a can. This passage evinces two problems: one of word finding, hence 'A fish swims', and another of not being able to stop associations to the answer. In (15), the patient starts out with the correct answer, that the colour is like that seen in pancake make-up, but then the speaker continues with associations to that fact that are not relevant to the task. In (16), the patient again starts out with the correct answer, that the disc is clay-coloured, but then continues both rhyming associates (which are phonological repetitions of final sounds) and, finally, semantic ones.

The syntactic deviations in (13) are embedded in a usual enough comment on how the patient is doing, although his syntax has gone awry – especially on the morphemic level – so that, for instance, the verb *medicate* doesn't have the ending *-tion* on it.

In my earlier explanations for data such as these, I posited that schizophrenic speech suffers from a lack of path control. That is, the speaker seems to be reaching for words to express something. He or she may start out accurately enough but does not filter out or block related words, expressions or ideas, so that associations are accessed in a basically uncontrolled manner. In instances like (11), in which the patient refers to purchase of an ice cream as 'financial matters', and (14), where the patient starts to answer the question about colour with the statement 'A fish swims. You call it a salmon.', the patient is answering the question properly but seems to have difficulty in controlling the path to the right word. In fact, this is an extreme example of an experience we've all had when we can't think of the word we want but can think of related ones. Again, after answering the question about colour, albeit with poor path control, the utterances get further and further afield, although the associational connections between them are obvious.

The discourse segments in (17) and (18) both show clear difficulties with blocking out extraneous memories or thoughts. In the latter, for instance, the patient obviously feels very strongly about people who get a 'free ride' so he cycles into this when he is recalling the past week (He was supposed to be telling me the story on the video he'd seen the week before). Instead of the idiomatic term 'free ride', he accesses an association of *ride*, a *ticket* and, of course, a *trip* in order to convey his opinion. Again, he has apparently not been able to stick to the path which would get the exact words for his intentions. Gibberish can be seen as an especially severe form of the same disability – one in which only the sounds making up words get accessed, not the words themselves.

In (19), the patient's response to being asked her name is most problematical. If the omitted object of *have* is what the psychiatrist must have before the patient will provide her name, then this would accord with the other examples – being an intended response which goes awry as the discourse proceeds. Ribeiro notes that the part beginning 'Oh mama!' indicates that the patient has stepped into the frame of being a child talking to her mother. Of course, we don't know what the omitted object of *have* is, so we don't know if this really starts out as an attempted response to the question, but the stepping into a new frame certainly shows the lack of path control that the other discourse samples do. This patient's speech is clearly highly disorganised and descending into gibberish.

To blame path control for the varieties of error evinced in (1) to (19) does not explain what causes the path control. What normal phenomenon gone awry can cause this?

The work of researchers like Baars, on normal slips of the tongue, and of Reason, on attention and intention, casts light on this matter. Research in these areas has concentrated on normal errors, both in speech and in action. Baars (1992) and others have concluded that slips of the tongue are caused by a lapse between volition and performance and are ultimately caused by a temporary malfunction of the executive function of the brain. That is, a gap occurs between what one intends and what one does because the executive controller which directs one's actions and speech malfunctions.

Research on attentional errors explain how and why these lapses occur. James Reason (1984) points out that attention is separate from intention. Attention is a more limited resource than intention and all activities, mental and physical, make some demands on the total resource. In other words, we can't pay consistent attention to carrying out our intentions because our attention is needed for many things at once. Reason's research shows that attention is actually quite fleeting, even in normals. We pay attention just long enough to set routines in motion. Attention then goes to some other matter while the routine is being carried out. Another of Reason's findings is that once the routines are set in motion, they may activate unwanted associated behaviours, so some part of attention is always engaged in restraining them, at least under usual conditions. Consequently, even normal people find themselves carrying out activities ancillary to the one originally intended – like putting instant coffee in the teacup – or we forget entirely – as when we walk purposely into a room and wonder why we went there. If attention is severely impaired, or especially fleeting, then unwanted associated behaviours would proliferate. This sounds suspiciously like schizophrenic speech production. The patient starts out with an intention to say something, usually something pertinent to the context, but, on setting the speech routine in motion, attention is quickly lost and speech becomes a set of random accessing to syllables and words.

Similarly, in an attentional deficit, syntax fails to constrain the sentential and discourse constraints on word production and placement. We have known for decades that we self-monitor our speech both internally, blocking inappropriate linguistic segments from utterance, and externally, correcting many of the slips of the tongue that manage to foil the internal monitoring when choosing linguistic forms. Under conditions of attentional lapses, often caused by excitement, despair, old age and general distracted states, self-monitoring also malfunctions. Baars (1992) and other slip of the tongue researchers have found that as cognitive interference increases, so do slips of the tongue. Reason (1984) and Reason and Mylcieska (1982) have found the same kinds of dysfunction both in action and in speech when attentional resources malfunction because of distraction, cognitive strain and the like. Schizophrenic speech disturbances seem to be another instance of attentional malfunctioning due to the cognitive strain and stresses caused by the illness.

The kinds of errors that Baars and Reason have elicited are very like schizophrenic error, but the schizophrenic ones are far more persistent and much more disorganised than normal error.

Of what import is understanding that schizophrenic speech is caused by a failure in executive control and attention? Such an understanding certainly changes our attitude to, and treatment of, a patient, for otherwise we might think that he or she is deliberately speaking as he or she does.

In interpreting what a patient says, we can recognise that circumlocutions like 'they have a ticket to carry them along' or 'a fish swims' are an attempt to express ideas or information appropriate to the context. This certainly constrains the interpretations we make of such speech. We can also recognise that Glossomania is an extreme example of loss of path control. Here the initial phrases are most likely to carry the intended meaning, the rest being produced by chance associations not controlled by the executive.

Also, we can get a window on a patient's memories or thoughts, as in (17). Even if these have been accessed by a lapse in control, it still gives us important information to work with. Most importantly, recognising that the patient's speech is likely to become further and further away from the situation at hand the longer it goes on, one can try to control attention by asking direct questions. This, of course, won't work too well in a patient so distracted that he or she doesn't answer questions, like Ribeiro's, but Hallowell and Smith (1983) have reported considerable success with what they call 'squiggles', in which the therapist gives a verbal opener and the patient responds with a short line. For instance:

THERAPIST: They said I am a hopeless case

Pt: Not I, a member of the human race, in disgrace

Th: I wish they wouldn't say that

Pt: In a non-joking way

Th: It makes me

Pt: Suspicious

Through these squiggles, Dr Hallowell often manages to get a patient to express rage, fear and so on. I think this works because it does constrain attention.

To sum up, the diverse manifestations of schizophrenic speech seem to be grounded in deficits in attention and the executive functions of the brain. The attentional deficits lead to accessing of related words and phrases which do not necessarily fit the intended response. Thus the associated, but inappropriate, material often uttered by schizophrenics is the result of a deficit, not of a surplus of attention. Understanding how language works normally, and how it can go wrong, allows us to understand better what patients mean.

CHAPTER 4

What Can Linguistics Tell Us About Thought Disorder?

Philip Thomas

Introduction

Language plays a central role in the way we perceive the world. It reveals the perspective that we ourselves adopt in describing what we see happening in it. If we make faulty assumptions about the positions of others, it is not surprising that the outcome is confusion. The underlying theme in this chapter is that our talk, or *discourse*, about thought disorder comes from a particular perspective, one which is detached from recent developments in cognitive science, linguistics and philosophy. I shall argue that the traditional clinical notion of thought disorder, so important in psychiatry, is unhelpful when compared with the insights to be gleaned from linguistics and philosophy. In order to show this, we must consider why thought disorder is important, and what problems are associated with the concept, before we consider the advantages to be gained from a linguistic approach.

Why is Thought Disorder Important?

Historically, psychiatrists have regarded thought disorder as a *sine qua non* for schizophrenia. This can be traced back to Kraepelin (1896) and Bleuler (1911), both of whom regarded the symptom as important in diagnosing schizophrenia. Kraepelin described a variety of abnormalities of communication which he considered to be an important feature of the illness. These included *akataphasia*, or a disorder of thought as expressed through speech. Bleuler went further. He believed that a disturbance in thinking (a disturbance in association) was one of the four fundamental symptoms of schizophrenia. It is not surprising that psychiatrists in America and Europe have regarded thought disorder as one of the most important symptoms of schizophrenia. Willis and Bannister (1965) investigated the diagnostic habits of over 300 senior British psychiatrists. Over

70 per cent rated thought disorder as the single most important symptom in diagnosing schizophrenia. Edwards (1972) found that over 80 per cent of American psychiatrists rated thought disorder as the single most important symptom in diagnosing the condition.

More recent studies of thought disorder have been undertaken by three groups: Harrow in Chicago (Harrow *et al.* 1982), Holzman in Harvard (Hurt, Holzman and Davis 1983) and Andreasen (1979a) in Iowa. Harrow stresses the importance of looseness of association and illogicality observed in subjects' responses to Gorham's proverb test, whereas Holzman's approach uses subjects' responses to the Rorshach ink-blot test. Andreasen's Thought Language and Communication Scale (TLC) is slightly different. She makes no *a priori* assumptions about the nature of thought disorder and chooses instead to describe a number of abnormalities of verbal behaviour commonly observed in psychiatric interviews. These three systems have been used extensively in recent research into the nature of thought disorder. One important finding to emerge is that thought disorder is not specific to schizophrenia. Both Andreasen (1979b) and Harrow (Harrow *et al.* 1982) have found that so-called 'schizophrenic' thought disorder occurs in other conditions, especially mania and depression. I shall return to Andreasen's scale later, but at this stage we must consider a number of serious problems associated with the concept of thought disorder.

The Problems of Thought Disorder

The problems of thought disorder relate to the following areas: assumptions concerning the relationship between thought, language and speech; method of assessment; reliability; diagnostic specificity. Each of these will now be considered in some detail.

The relationship between thought, language and speech

Rochester and Martin (1979) have pointed out that to say whether someone is thought disordered is tautological. Thought disorder is inferred on the basis of disordered speech but, when the patient's speech is disordered, the clinician decides that the patient's thinking is disordered. This is a circular argument. Chaika (1982b) too has argued convincingly for the separation of thought and speech. Not all speech conveys thought. The main purpose of much of our utterance, such as greetings and introductions, serves the process of social bonding. She considers that language is self-contained and has an independent structure of its own with no reference to thought or the outside world. Speech errors arise from errors in the application of linguistic rules without reference to thinking processes. This is important given that thought cannot be observed directly whereas speech can. The independence of linguistic rules from thought is exemplified by Lewis Carol's poem Jabberwocky:

> 'Twas brillig and the slithy toves,
> Did gyre and gimble in the wabe.
> All mimsy were the borogroves,
> And the mome waths outgrabe.   Verse 1, 1–4

In this poem, nonsense words are used in such a way as to imply meaning. '*Slithy*' suggests an adjective and '*toves*' a noun. This is because these meaningless words follow the rules of morphological transformation. Equally, the converse applies in that it may be difficult to decompose a single sentence into a single thought. For example, the sentence '*The Government is to blame for our country's economic problems*' can be decomposed into a number of different thoughts.

To utter such a sentence presupposes that there is a country, that the speaker is a member of it, that the country has a government, that there are economic problems in the country, that the government is responsible for the economic problems and so on. In addition, there maybe a variety of complex speaker intentions in making such an utterance which are not manifest in the content of the sentence. Chaika argues that, if thought and speech are identical, one must be able to correlate the concept of one thought with one particular speech structure.

The opposite point of view, that thought disorder underlies speech disorder, has been proposed by Lanin-Kettering and Harrow (1985). They consider that the abnormalities of speech found in schizophrenia are part of a sub-set of abnormalities of behaviour which includes disordered thinking. They claim that there is an intricate link between the use of symbols, words and meaning (language) and thought, and that, in schizophrenia, the disturbance is best regarded as a conceptual-linguistic problem and not just a speech problem. Historically, this view extends back to the work of Von Domarus (1944), who suggested that there was a specific disorder of logic in schizophrenic thought. Over the years, this idea has been highly influential and underlies both Harrow's and Holzman's work. In its simplest form, it posits that there is a specific identifiable failure in the logical process of thought. Despite this, there have been few attempts to examine the factors that might influence disordered logic in schizophrenia. Harrow and Prosen (1978) tried to do so using a technique that required schizophrenic subjects to review their own idiosyncratic or bizarre responses a week later. They found that the most significant factor influencing bizarre responses was subjects' tendency to intermingle material from their personal lives into their responses to the test. There was little evidence to support the idea that disordered logic was important in determining bizarreness. De Bonis *et al.* (1990) used a single case study approach to examine logical reasoning in a schizophrenic subject. This study consisted of two parts. First, they asked over thirty experienced psychiatrists to rate the transcript of a clinical interview for nine varieties of disturbances in logical thought. The psychiatrists' ratings varied significantly and there was little consensus as to the type of disturbance found in the transcript. In the next part of the study, they asked a logician to examine the most disordered segments of text using a reasoning analysis. The logician concluded that there were logical relationships between the statements made by the subject. Overall, there was no evidence to support the idea that there was a specific disorder of reasoning or logic in this subject.

Maher (1972) has pointed out that most theoretical approaches to the phenomenon of schizophrenic language assume that a disturbance of thinking is primarily responsible. These approaches adopt a set of implicit assumptions about the nature of the model appropriate to describe the relationship between language and thought. He compares this model to a typist copying from a script. The copy may be distorted because the original script is disordered, although the transcription process is working effectively. Alternatively, the script may be perfect but the typist, who may have had too much to drink the night before, may make many errors and thus distort the copy. Finally, both the original copy may be distorted and the typist, who had too much to drink the night before, may add further errors. The point here is that we can only observe the copy (language utterance) and not the script (thought). There is a fourth possibility: the person who reads the typist's copy may also have had too much to drink the night before and is thus unable to make sense out of it. The point here is that understanding a text involves two participants: the person who originates the text and the person who attempts to interpret it. Ebert (1991) has argued similarly that the investigation and study of speech and thinking disorders in schizophrenia has been hampered by investigators' failure adequately to distinguish between speech and thought.

Andreasen (1979b) concluded that clinicians and researchers should not refer globally to 'thought disorder' as if it were a homogeneous entity. The view proposed here is that 'thought disorder' is a multi-level disturbance involving abnormalities in thinking, language processing and social cognition. It is strongly argued that the term 'communication disorder' should be used to describe the group of phenomena which are generally subsumed under the category of thought disorder. Such a description makes no presuppositions about the focus of the disturbance, which can then be regarded from a variety of perspectives relevant to communication. These include cognitive and social interactional models.

Method of assessment

It follows naturally that the way in which researchers construe the relationship between thought and language will largely determine the way they go about trying to measure and assess thought disorder. Several techniques have been used to measure over-inclusive thinking. These include simple test batteries (Payne and Friedlander 1962) and proverb interpretation (Gorham 1956). Although these have been widely incorporated into the clinical practice of psychiatrists, they have their weaknesses. Forrest, Hay and Kushnew (1969) used the Gorham proverb test in schizophrenics and normal controls. Their results suggested that the ability to respond abstractly was more closely related to the subjects' intelligence than diagnosis. They concluded that the use of proverb interpretations to demonstrate the presence of thought disorder was of little value unless intelligence was taken into account. They also noted that a proverb's central meaning was more culture-bound than most psychiatrists realised. For example, a lady from the West Indies was interviewed when disturbed and said that she was 'the fifth wheel of the wagon'. When she was interviewed subsequently, she said this was a proverb she had been taught by her grandmother in the West Indies and it referred to the fact that she felt useless. Attributing deviance to such an utterance is dangerous without understanding the speaker's cultural and educational background.

There is empirical evidence to suggest that the nature of the experimental task may have a profound influence not only on how the subject performs, but how that performance may be judged by others. Gordon, Silverstein and Harrow (1982) examined associative thinking in schizophrenics in an attempt to establish whether deviant word associations actually had a greater degree of meaning than was apparent from the test. They found that the majority of 'pathological' schizophrenic responses to stimulus words became meaningful when the word was in a sentence created by the subject with the purpose of explaining their associations. The authors concluded that the subjects' experience of a stimulus word, and associations to that word, became much clearer when the word was placed in an appropriate context (a sentence) *rather than examined as an isolated semantic feature* (as in the word association test). The importance of this study is that it demonstrates that relying too narrowly on restricted aspects of linguistic features is problematic.

There is a more fundamental problem here. Classical approaches to thought disorder presuppose that the locus of the disturbance is in the speaker's thinking processes. But thought cannot be accessed directly. Such models disregard the fact that we can only make such judgements on the basis of the subject's speech. To overlook this results in the exclusion of the science of speech, that is linguistics and psycholinguistics. If you assume that the reason for your difficulty in understanding what a speaker is saying is to do only with what is going on inside his (or her) head, then it might seem reasonable to use proverb interpretations or Rorschach tests to assess the problem. Equally, it can be argued that there is as much to be gained from studying why it is that you become confused whilst listening to a particular speaker. Is there anything about the message that makes it difficult for you to follow? Is there anything about the nature of the communicative interaction that might influence the extent to which speakers and listeners are able to make sense of the messages that pass between them? The difficulty is that thought disorder disregards the possibility that these (and other) questions are of any value.

In ecological terms, human communication is an interaction involving two or more people. This communication takes place in an endless variety of contexts: social, professional, cultural, family, religious and so on. If we are to study communication disorders, we must take into account these interactions and contexts. It is essential that we use methodologies that take these factors into account. This applies to the way in which we sample speech – whether we use a proverb interpretation, a picture description or a conversation. It also applies to the way in which the sampling situation is set up, and, of course, to the way in which the speech samples are analysed. There is little point in studying speech and language used in the process of human communication if the setting in which the samples are obtained are artificial and non-naturalistic. Proverbs or word association tests provide very limited information about the nature of language and speech in real situations.

Reliability and diagnostic utility

Although psychiatrists believe they can easily recognise thought disorder, the evidence indicates that they have difficulty in doing so reliably (Kreitman *et al.* 1961). Neither Harrow's nor Holzman's systems have been widely used by workers in other centres, although Andreasen's TLC has been shown to have satisfactory inter-rater reliability in other centres. Hurt, Holzman and Davis (1983) have commented that the use of the Thought Disorder Index (TDI) requires some training (which) involves bringing the new rater up to acceptable levels of inter-scorer reliability, a process that may take a substantial amount of practice and experience. The team who originated it acknowledge that the scale is difficult to use.

Although Bleuler and Kraepelin stressed the diagnostic importance of thought disorder, not everybody agreed with this. Schneider (1939), whilst conceding that thought disorder may be theoretically important, considered the symptom to be of limited diagnostic value. Schneider correctly pointed out the difficulty of distinguishing thought disordered patients from those who may be intoxicated or 'merely scatter-brained'. Chaika's (1974) account of the linguistic errors of a single schizophrenic speaker was contested by Fromkin (1975) on the basis that the majority of these errors could also be seen in non-psychiatrically ill subjects. There is little evidence now to support the view that thought disorder is peculiar to schizophrenia. Both Harrow's work and that of Andreasen has shown that the type of thought disorder that was thought to be unique to schizophrenia, such as loosening of associations, can occur in mania as well. Studies using the TLC have consistently shown that communication impairment is not specific to schizophrenia and that the same sub-types of communication disorder occur both in schizophrenia and affective disorders (see also, for example, Oltmanns *et al.* 1985).

The Role of Linguistics

By now, many psychiatrists will be confused and disorientated: 'But we all know that there is something odd about the way some people speak.' Where do we go from here? The central thesis of this chapter is that linguistic science provides a number of ways of examining and understanding human communication that are of great benefit to the psychiatrist. In order to consider how, we first need to understand a little about the major branches of linguistics.

The major branches of linguistics

These include phonology, syntax, discourse and cohesion, and pragmatics. Phonology is the science of sounds and their relationship to words and the methods of speech production. It is the most quantitative, precise aspect of linguistics. Syntax is the study of the way in which words are structured into units such as phrases, clauses and sentences. Until 30 years ago, grammar simply described how these units were organised into sentences. Chomsky's transformational grammar (Chomsky 1957) revolutionised thought about language and its relationship to the mind. He argued that traditional grammar failed to account for the fact that sentences with different structures could convey the same meaning. The simplest example of this is to be found in active and passive sentences:

- ○ John sent the invitations (active)

- ○ The invitations were sent by John (passive)

The problem here is how can two sentences, with different structures, have the same meaning? Chomsky showed that sentence structure could be examined at two levels: a surface structure corresponding to the manifest organisation of words and clauses and a deep structure from which the surface structure was derived and which determined sentence meaning. He argued that sentence structure related directly to linguistic structures and processes within the mind. In mapping grammar onto the mind in this way, he opened up the field of psycholinguistics.

Discourse analysis and cohesion

Discourse analysis refers to a number of ways of examining speech and writing and, in particular, their relationship to the contexts in which they occur. Cohesion analysis has been used most often in psychiatry. If syntax is concerned with the organisation and structure of the units within a sentence, cohesion examines the way in which sentences are linked together to make a coherent whole. To make sense of what is being said, the listener must link what is being said now to what was said before or, occasionally, to what is about to be said. Cohesion is that aspect of language which makes this understanding possible. The speaker's ability to use cohesive ties successfully is essential if listeners are to understand the message. These ties are established when one element in the text is necessary to interpret another:

- ∘ John lost his umbrella.

- ∘ *He* left *it* on the train.

To understand the meaning of the pronoun 'it', it is necessary to establish a relationship with 'his umbrella' in the first sentence. This relationship is a cohesive tie. Halliday and Hassan (1975) described five varieties of cohesion, the most important of which, in relation to psychotic utterance, is pronominal reference. Other forms of discourse analysis fall more properly within the realm of sociolinguistics and describe the social and political features of the use of language by different groups within society.

Pragmatics

Pragmatics is concerned with the way speakers use language to convey meaning in social contexts. There are two main influences in pragmatic theory: one comes from the work of the philosophers Grice and Searle and the other, derived from anthropology, leads to conversational analysis through observations of speakers in natural situations. Although cohesion is important for coherence, it is insufficient to rely solely on the features of texts to explain coherence. Grice (1975) has shown the importance of speaker meaning and intention in understanding a text. He developed the notion of conversational implicature to account for the large discrepancy which can occur between what is said and what is meant:

HUSBAND: 'Have you seen my car keys?'

WIFE: (who is in bed) 'I am not getting dressed'

This exchange appears incoherent but, in responding, the wife may have drawn on contextual knowledge and assumptions accessible only to the speakers. It is only by taking this into account that we can understand more clearly the inference made by the wife as well as the significance of her response (that, for example, he is going to visit his mother, with whom his wife has fallen out). Such inferences are described by Grice as implicatures. Grice proposed that in conversation we use a co-operative principle, the main purpose of which is to ensure that our contributions are relevant and helpful. Co-operative responses are usually more helpful than direct ones. Grice elaborated the co-operative principle into four maxims: quantity (giving neither too much nor too little information), quality (be truthful), manner (be clear) and relation (be relevant). These he regarded as instructions for competent conversationalists. Participants work hard to ensure that maxims are not violated and to make sense of responses which might otherwise appear meaningless. The important point is that much normal utterance is impossible to follow, without assuming that co-operativeness and relevance are being observed.

A Linguistic 'Deconstruction' of Andreasen's TLC

The value of linguistics will become clearer if we examine a widely used clinical approach to thought disorder from a linguistic perspective. In this section we shall examine familiar examples of thought disorder taken from Andreasen's scale and categorise them according to the level of linguistic disturbance. All the examples and definitions are taken from Andreasen (1980). Table 4.1 compares the main items from clinical scales for thought disorder (The TLC, the TDI and Harrow) and categorises them according to the level of linguistic disturbance.

Phonemic/word level

Four TLC items represent disturbances at the sound or word level. These are word approximations, neologisms, clanging and paraphasias. Word approximations are, according to Adreasen's definition, 'old words which are used in a new and unconventional way, or new words which are developed by conventional rules of word formation.' She specifically excludes aphasic disturbances from this category. Examples given include a 'paperskate' (for a ball-point pen) and 'time vessel' for watch or 'food vessel' for stomach. Neologisms, on the other hand, represent new word formations whose derivation cannot be understood in terms of the rules of word formation for a given language:

- ° 'I got so angry I picked up a dish and threw it at the *geshinker*.'
- ° 'So I sort of *bawked* the thing up.'

Syntactic

Here the disturbance occurs at the sentence level. Only one TLC item involves a disturbance of sentence structure: Incoherence. According to Andreasen,

Table 4.1 Linguistic components of clinical rating scales for 'thought disorder'

Linguistic Domain	Andreasen	Holzman	Harrow
1. Phonemic/ Word level	Word Approximation	Idiosyncratic word usage	
	Phonemic and Semantic Paraphrasias	Queer word usage	
		Word finding difficulties	
2. Syntactic	Incoherence Fragmentation	Incoherence	
3. Discourse/ Textual	Derailment	Looseness of associations	Looseness of associations
	Loss of Goal		Abrupt Time Shift
4. Pragmatic	Poverty of Speech	Inappropriate Distance	
	Poverty of Content	Flippant Responses	Gap in Communication
	Pressure of Speech of Ideas	Vagueness	Vagueness
	Distractible Speech	Stilted Expressions	
	Tangentiality		
	Echolalia		
	Self Reference		
	Stilted Speech		
5. Other Linguistic	Clanging and Neologisms	Neologisms Peculiar Expressions	Private Meanings
6. Thought Disorder Blocking	Illogically and Blocking	Vagueness	Blocking
		Relationship Verbalisations	
		Idiosyncratic Symbolism	
		Autistic Logic	

Source: Thomas 1995

incoherent speech is incomprehensible because of a number of mechanisms. There may be parts of coherent sentences fragmented and mixed up in a larger, incoherent whole, words or phrases may be substituted and mixed up or 'cementing' words like *and*, *but* or *so* (conjunctions) may be omitted. For example:

INTERVIEWER: 'Why do you think people believe in God?'

PATIENT: 'Um, because making a do in life. Isn't none of that stuff about evolution guiding isn't true any more now. It all happened a long time ago. It happened in eons and eons and stuff they wouldn't believe in him. The time that Jesus Christ people believe in their thing people believed in, Jehovah God that they didn't believe in Jesus Christ that much.'

In this example, the first sentence consists of a subordinate clause without a main clause. A detailed syntactic analysis would show that the structure of the remaining sentences is deviant in a number of ways.

Discourse/textual

Two TLC items represent disturbances at the level of discourse: Derailment and Loss of Goal. Andreasen describes derailment as 'a pattern of spontaneous speech in which the ideas slip off the track onto another one which is clearly but obliquely related, or onto one which is completely unrelated.' The result is speech which sounds disjointed. Loss of goal occurs if the subject fails to return to the original topic or theme. Derailment and loss of goal are, therefore, closely related. In linguistic terms the description of such speech occurs at the level of textual coherence, which is an important aspect of discourse. Linguists make a distinction between texts and randomly organised sentences. In order that texts are coherent, there must be important links between sentences. These links may occur at different levels. We have seen that some are established through substituting nouns for pronouns. Other, occur through the hierarchical organisation of ideas represented within the text and the logical relationships between them. This is clearly demonstrated in the following example:

INTERVIEWER: 'You just must be an emotional person that's all.'

PATIENT: 'Well, not very much I mean, what if I were dead. It' funeral age. Well I um. Now I had my toenails operated on. They got infected and I wasn't able to do it. But they wouldn't let me at my tools. Well!'

Pragmatic

Almost half the TLC sub-scales fall within this category. These include: poverty of speech, poverty of content of speech, pressure of speech and distractible speech. The feature shared by these items is that they represent a failure to observe the rules that govern the interactional aspects of language use, or a failure of the speaker to recognise the needs of the listener.

Poverty of speech is a 'restriction in the amount of spontaneous speech'. Replies to questions are brief and unelaborated – they may even be monosyl-labic, or questions may remain unanswered. Such speech leaves the interviewer grasping the air for more information. It violates Grice's maxim of quantity: that speakers should provide neither too much information, nor too little. In distractible speech, the subject suddenly stops talking in mid-sentence and changes the subject in response to a nearby stimulus. This violates the maxim of relevance. For example:

> Then I left San Francisco and moved to…where did you get that tie? It looks like it's left over from the 1950s. I like the warm weather in San Diego. Is that a conch shell on your desk? Have you ever gone scuba diving?

Conclusions

We have seen that the symptom of thought disorder has played an important historical role, both in the diagnosis of schizophrenia and in attempts to explain the disorder. The concept is, however, beset with difficulties. There are tenacious assumptions concerning the nature of the symptom and its relation-ship to speech and language. It is unjustifiably regarded as a homogenous entity and can be difficult to measure reliably. When stringent definitions are used, there is no evidence to support the idea that it has any diagnostic utility. Despite this, there is no doubt that there is something unusual and distinctive about the speech of many patients suffering from acute psychoses. Linguistic science provides a new approach to understanding thought disorder. Its value is both descriptive and explanatory. An examination of a widely used clinical scale for rating thought disorder indicates that the term is probably best replaced by 'communication disorder'. This makes no a priori theoretical assumptions about the type of model most appropriate for characterising the utterance of psychotic subjects.

The full value of the application of linguistic science to psychiatry has been reviewed by Thomas and Fraser (1994) and includes a greater understanding of the psychological substrate of the major psychoses such as schizophrenia, as well as conditions such as Asperger syndrome and autism. It is striking that disturbances of communication figure prominently in all three. If we restrict ourselves to descriptions of thought disorder, we may overlook important insights into these conditions. There remains a serious problem: at present, theoretical linguistics, and practical assessments of human communication based in this, plays no part in the education and training of psychiatrists. Speech and Language Therapists have an important role to play in the future education of psychiatrists. Psychiatrists too should play a part in the education of Speech and Language Therapists. We can only expect to make progress in this important area if these conditions are met.

CHAPTER 5

The Language Disorder and Auditory Hallucinations in Schizophrenic Patients
Background to the Research Study

Sarah Kramer

Thought Disorder as a Key Symptom in Schizophrenia

Thought disorder is a major symptom associated with schizophrenia. Historically, it has always been considered a significant diagnostic factor and can be traced back to the early classification schemes of Kraeplin (1896) and Bleuler (1911). Kraeplin outlines a number of abnormal features of communication which he considers diagnostic of schizophrenia and Bleuler discusses these, describing a disturbance in thought – particularly in association – as one of the key/core features of schizophrenia.

Looking at the more recent literature, Rochester and Martin (1979) elucidate the difficulty with this definition by describing an imaginary conversation between a student and a textbook writer. In this conversation, the student seeks a description of the primary symptom in schizophrenia. This is considered thought disorder and he is told that it is inferred from incoherent talk. Incoherent talk is defined as language which is circumstantial and has loose associations, and loose associations refers to when the flow of thought is confused and bizarre. The student therefore concludes that thought disorder is when talk is incoherent, and talk is incoherent when the thought is disordered. This conversation illuminates some of the problems in referring to thought disorder as a key symptom of schizophrenia: What is the relationship between thought and language? What methods of assessment (and reassessment) are appropriate? Do we assess thought or do we assess language? How do we assess these? What is the reliability of our assessment?...

It might be expected that the above description is outdated and superceded by at least a somewhat more objective description, but looking at Professor Frith (1992), he describes a similar problem with circular definitions.

43

This leads to the questions: Why is there no better definition? Is there no adequate description of the language in schizophrenia? A few examples of language descriptions which have been formulated demonstrate what has been studied about this key symptom in schizophrenia: Reduced syntactic complexity and inappropriate syntax, reduced numbers of ideas for words spoken, and reference to subjective experiences. Thus, they cover a wide range of areas including syntax, semantics, and more cognitive difficulties. This can hardly be considered an objective description of language, let alone communication, in schizophrenia.

It is, therefore, important to look at some of the possible reasons why there remains no adequate description of schizophrenic language/communication so many years after Kraeplin and Bleuler identified this as a key symptom in order to understand this area better. Commonly, observations of verbal behaviour are cited together with accompanying explanations, but the actual explanations are only tangentially related to what is observed. Many assessments which are carried out do not reflect spontaneous language but are individual tasks which seem to be chosen because of ease in administration rather than their relationship to communicative abilities. Furthermore, slight differences in these tasks would mean that different abilities are being measured. A pertinent comment by Olson and Clark (1976) adds insight into the limited number of descriptions of schizophrenic language production: 'listeners are studied by experiment and speakers by naturalistic observation!', suggesting why many people prefer to look at comprehension rather than verbal expression. This results in a dearth of descriptions of the language production in schizophrenic individuals.

The above makes it clear why the language in schizophrenia is an important area for study. This is followed by the rationale for the methodology employed.

Rationale for a Description in Terms of Discourse

This study involves the analysis of schizophrenic subjects' discourse, where Crystal's (1991) definition of discourse is 'a continuous stretch of language larger than a sentence'. An explanation of the appropriacy for a description in terms of discourse will be followed by an outline of the three different types of discourse and how this study purports to assess them. Discourse functioning relates closely to functional communicative abilities. It is also a constituent interface between functional and cognitive neuropsychological models of disordered language, as suggested by Chapman et al. (1992) who wrote that discourse studies may provide the neurolinguistic sophistication necessary to clarify the scope of communication problems. This will be done using a theoretical framework as advocated by Ellis and Young (1988). They emphasise the need to examine language processes within the framework of a language model. Lesser and Milroy (1993) suggest a number of reasons why this is important.

Significance of a Description in Terms of a Language Model

A language model provides the vocabulary for a precise description of the language problem. It allows the formulation of important psycholinguistic questions for analysis and can suggest constraints on models which might sound intuitively correct. Thus, rather than a catalogue of surface manifestations, there is the possibility of breaking out of symptom descriptions with circular definitions. It is possible to formulate predictions about symptoms, to quantify the severity of the deficit(s) and to identify levels of expressive breakdown. This all means that intervention can be targeted more precisely at those levels and it is also possible to measure changes in performance between discourse tasks as well as over time.

After recognising the need for a model, it is necessary to choose the most appropriate model. This initially involves choosing between a discourse analysis model and a conversation analysis approach.

Discourse Analysis Versus Conversational Analysis Approach

A discourse analysis model was chosen because such models are semantically driven and, seeing that the literature on schizophrenia would suggest that semantic difficulties are very prominent, it seemed appropriate. In addition, historically, discourse analysis approaches have been devised in studies of people with unequal status and, although it would be nice to change the situation, the subjects involved in this study are largely people who generally regard themselves as being of unequal status when with conversational partners. Discourse models also tend to be more flexible and less reflective of theoretical stance, suggesting that these can reflect the data more accurately. A conversational analysis may reflect more closely the collaboration which is included in communication, but, by involving some rhetorical structure analysis, this aspect is included in the study.

The Particular Model Chosen for this Study

The next stage involves the choice of a specific model. Sinclair and Coulthard (1992) outline a system of analysis, but it appears applicable only to the kind of exchanges found in institutional interactions, as Sinclair himself said in 1992. The model proposed by Glosser and Deser (1990) is an analysis protocol that includes different levels of processing but, as soon as it reaches higher level functions, the analysis becomes a rating system. There are a number of other models available which are less suitable. Thus, Frederiksen *et al.*'s (1990) model was chosen for this study.

The Frederiksen, Bracewell, Breuleux and Renaud Model

To demonstrate how the theory relates to practical measures, a brief outline of the model's three main stages (Figure 5.1) will be followed by additional detail on one of these.

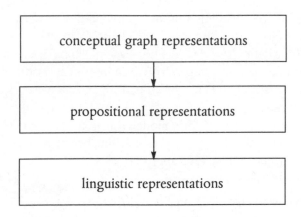

Source: Kramer 1995
Figure 5.1 The main stages of Fredericksen et al. *(1990) Model*

The first stage is entitled 'conceptual graph representations', where semantic representations of propositions are converted into the structure of meaning in the form of conceptual frames. In the next stage of 'propositional representations' syntactic trees and semantic markers in the lexicon enable the conceptual frames to be transformed into intermediate semantic representations/propositions. In the third level, properties of the linguistic representations allow for expressive alternatives in production.

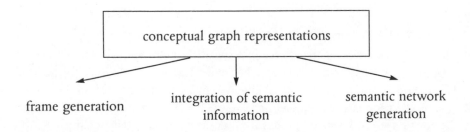

Source: Kramer 1995
Figure 5.2 Division of the First stage/level of Fredericksen et al. *(1990) into 3 strata*

Each of these levels can be further divided into strata (Figure 5.2). Thus, within the first stratum of conceptual graph representations, initially conceptual frames have to be retrieved or generated. Once the frame has been generated, descriptive semantic information is required to complete the specification of the frame, filling the superstructure with detail. The semantic information within any particular frame may then be linked to other semantic networks for elaboration or to provide continuity between topics. The semantic networks may either be generated or integrated. This involves decisions such as how much information needs to be stated explicitly, in which order topics should be introduced, and the resulting selection of sentence structures to express these.

Looking at some examples of the types of measures being used within this study explains how the strata within Frederiksen's model are being examined. This involves a number of measures in the area of frame generation, and integration of semantic information, as outlined below:

Frame generation

a) % evidence of ability to produce frame elements (uncued)

b) X frame types used in conversational discourse

Integration of semantic information

c) % non-self-corrected potential loss of integration of new topic/domain

d) % listener request for repair (inc. cues/prompts) to integrate/maintain topic

e) % paralinguistic anomalies in relation to social or emotional setting of topic/domain.

Key: X = gross number
% = percentage

NB: 'Domain' is used here to represent the area of experience/ knowledge covered by a particular set/network of semantic fields, e.g. food.

'Topic' (as opposed to comment) represents the entity/theme about which something is said, e.g. ingredients of a sandwich.

Source: Kramer 1995

Figure 5.3 Summary of Discoursive Analysis measures for first two strata of Fredericksen et al. (1990) Model.

The subject matter is given by the researcher in the study in a number of tasks, but the subjects are required to generate a suitable framework within which to put across the information. Thus, for example, within the tasks requiring that the subjects describe a sequence of events, it is expected that subjects follow a story grammar including a setting, development, complication, resolution and coda. Measurement at this level involves identifying the percentage of the frame components required to be covered by the speaker in order to fulfil the task. Where, however, a frame is not implicit in the task, as with free-field conversation, the types of framework employed by the speaker are noted as evidence that they are able to generate them. Within discourse speakers talk about various subjects, shifting subject matter to the listener linguistically or via suprasegmental cues such as by using an increase of vocal intensity. Where a speaker shifts subject without either linguistic or paralinguistic cues this is counted as a potential failure to integrate. The measure used within this study is the percentage of non-self-corrected potential loss of integration of subjects per total propositions. As communication is a two-way process, although there may be potential breakdowns at this level, the listener's actual requests for repair can confirm where breakdowns may be occurring. Thus, another measure used is the percentage of listener requests for repair of topic integration per total propositions. Due to the importance of suprasegmental information within discourse, the percentage of non-verbal anomalies in relation to overall semantic content/discourse situation per total propositions is also being measured.

Thus, using this model, it should be possible to suggest a more objective description of the communication in schizophrenia than that now available. Admittedly, many measures are being used but it is hoped that it will be possible to incorporate the most significant measures into a simpler protocol for clinical use.

So far, only the language in schizophrenia has been addressed – despite a title including the hallucinations in schizophrenia. Now, having laid the 'foundations', it is possible to describe a model of how language and hallucinations are connected, in order to explain why hallucinatory behaviour is included in this study.

Shallice (1988) explains that an environmental stimulus triggers one of a number of possible actions, where an action is a goal-directed response. Each action is triggered by an environmental stimulus. Via a method of mutual inhibition, all possible actions except that which is most appropriate are inhibited. A supervisory attentional system modulates these actions at a higher level (Figure 5.4).

Where the supervisory attentional system does not function adequately, only routine actions are produced and there may be poverty of speech when it is difficult to generate speech because it is not routine. Perseveration may be evident when routine actions are not terminated because they cease to be

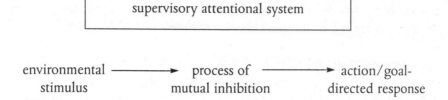

Source: Shallice (1988)
Figure 5.4 Supervisory Attentional System

appropriate. Finally, routine actions may be elicited by environmental stimuli when not appropriate and demonstrated by incoherent speech.

Ralph Hoffman (1986) suggests that there is a link between incoherent speech and hallucinations. Where the supervisory attentional system does not modulate routine actions effectively, many of the utterances do not fit in with the overall goals of the discourse. Hoffman suggests that, if there is a large discrepancy between the utterance or thought and the cognitive goal, it is experienced as unintended. When this takes the form of verbal imagery, this results in an auditory hallucination. Thus, incoherent speech and auditory hallucinations are the result of a similar underlying disorder.

Having described the background to this study, an outline of the methodology will explain how it is intended to research this information – which can then be connected to the underlying hypotheses. Twelve single case studies of schizophrenics will include video-taped data for future analysis. All subjects have a definite diagnosis of schizophrenia, as seen in their notes, and are resident on the same ward in a special hospital. This has many advantages: from an experimental point of view, there are fewer variables to control and it also allows me to get to know the patients and staff better, with obvious benefits such as getting to know better the people involved, obtaining better compliance, being more aware of variables which may be influencing my data, etc. Everybody included in the study is male, as using both male and female subjects would mean introducing more variables. Also, as this is a language study, everybody included in the study has English as a first language.

Although this study is a single case study design, it is necessary to look at control data as there is very little recorded data for the model chosen. This means that it is necessary to establish normative measures for all measures employed in the analysis. It is hoped that a prison population will be available for comparative data as the experimental subjects are all resident within a special hospital. There is reason to believe that educational background is probably quite similar and the institutionalisation would be a common factor as all the subjects would be living in a total institution. This is particularly significant as the literature suggests that this is a major influence on language. It will obviously be important to exclude prisoners with any psychiatric history – evidently there is a high prevalence of psychiatric disorder within this population.

With regard to the measures being obtained, these include the National Adult Reading Test (Nelson 1982), as an indication of premorbid IQ; the Weschler (Weschler 1981), as a measure of current IQ; the Right Hemisphere Language Battery (Bryan 1989), which is being used both as a standardised baseline set of measures and also to include measures which are not included within the language tasks devised. Regarding the language samples, an outline of the three sub-divisions of discourse allows an explanation of the measures proposed:

○ Narrative discourse can consist of the production of a story oriented around characters or events or the relating of an event.

○ Procedural discourse involves offering instructions or providing information.

○ Conversational discourse is any communicative interaction between two or more participants.

The samples of narrative discourse in this study include two six-picture sequences, one with the picture sequence in view of both the subject and researcher and one where it is evident that the researcher cannot see the pictures. The subject is also asked to speak about an important event in his life. An initial concern with procedural discourse related to the difficulty in finding an appropriate procedure for people who may have been institutionalised for many years. A pilot study showed that subjects found it very easy to describe how to make a sandwich. When considering conversational discourse, samples include varied conversational partners – including a member of staff, a fellow resident and the researcher. It was necessary to include 'a fellow resident' rather than a friend as it is not easy to find someone prepared to speak to the subject and with whom the subject is ready to speak, especially when this is video-taped. Observing the difficulty in convincing a member of staff to be video-taped whilst talking to a subject highlights the importance of considering how representative the various samples are of talk in these different environments.

Having briefly described the three types of discourse, together with how these are being sampled, it is relevant to outline some justification for including all three types within the study. Sherratt and Penn (1990) state that there are different patterns of discourse dysfunction, so that the same subjects demonstrate different difficulties across a range of tasks. Alverson and Rosenberg (1990) actually illustrate the problems which can arise when using one type of discourse and then generalising from these results, thereby making assumptions about other forms of discourse. Within the pilot study, this has been evident in the initial analysis. There are a number of reasons why this would be expected. When considering the different types of discourse from a pragmatic perspective, they involve very different communicative functions. In a narrative, the primary function is usually to entertain whereas with procedural discourse, the primary function is to inform or to instruct, so that one might, perhaps, expect that procedural discourse would require more clarity and explicitness. Looking at the information content, with a narrative this is typically oriented around characters or events whereas a procedure is typically action-oriented. Observing the cohesion in these types of discourse, a narrative is likely to involve large segments of text, because it probably involves the description of a character with continuous reference to the character for cohesion, whilst in a procedure, one might expect more local cohesion between adjacent sentences but very little over the length of the procedure. This is particularly significant when considering the emphasis on cohesion in studies of the abnormalities in schizophrenic communication.

This study involves looking at the language of twelve schizophrenic subjects, using a discourse analysis model, with the following hypotheses: First, that the language disorder in schizophrenic subjects can be described using objective terminology rather than what is currently available. Using Frederiksen's model should enable an analysis at different levels of language, resulting in a relatively comprehensive description rather than individual aspects of language. Second, that there is a relationship between overt language disorder and auditory hallucinations – an aspect which is not described in detail here but which is included in Professor Frith's presentation. Third, it is hoped that the incidence of auditory hallucinations, as well as language disorder, will be reduced by specific language therapy addressing the underlying deficit, as seen when applying Frederiksen's model to the language samples described.

Acknowledgements

This research part of a three-year study supported by a grant from the Department of Health, for which I am most grateful. I would also like to thank Mrs Jenny France for enabling this study to take place, Dr Andrew Horne for his help and accessibility, Ms Anne Kavanagh for her administrative assistance, Mr John Carol for his recording expertise and all the staff and patients who have participated directly, or indirectly, in the study. I am also indebted to Dr Karen Bryan and Professor Christopher Frith for their extensive academic and practical assistance.

CHAPTER 6

'By our frames, we are hung'

Clinician's Descriptions of Interviews

William Fraser, Philip Thomas, Joseph Joyce and Martin Duckworth

Clinicians' Limitations in Describing Communication

> 'I beg your pardon', the Doctor said, 'I am perhaps a little jealous since you use your language to communicate with yourself and not with us of the world'. (Green: 'I Never Promised You a Rose Garden' 1964, p.30)

Ronald Laing emphasised the need for greater awareness of the pragmatics of communication when quoting from Green at a Maudsley Bequest Lecture in 1966. Since then, several factors have reinforced the need for psychiatrists to update their knowledge about human communication:

1. Interviewing skills have developed greatly – particularly in transmitting information to patients – and excellent textbooks exist on this, for example Ley (1988). McGuire, Fairbuison and Fletcher (1989) have demonstrated the importance of teaching medical students basic practical interview skills. There is, however, less emphasis on teaching advanced communication-awareness skills, including the intricacies of pragmatics to the psychiatrist (although Wykes (1981) demonstrated that young psychiatrists can be taught how to discriminate between schizophrenic and manic utterances by understanding cohesion). More fundamentally, while it is unlikely that a speech therapist would have much difficulty differentiating between schizophrenia and dysphasia, Faber, Abrams and Taylor (1983) have demonstrated that both psychiatrists and neurologists have difficulty in distinguishing the two conditions.

2. Advances in pragmatics have specified how emotions can determine what we mean, as distinct from what we say. Speech Art Theory (Austin 1962; Searle 1969) seek to distinguish between the meaning

of an utterance (its propositional content) and the intention of an utterance (its illocutionary force). The interviewing psychiatrist has to be able to judge covert intentions and communication breakdown in a variety of situations. An impressive consequence of increased understanding of pragmatics is to be found in the sophisticated analysis of the discourse of people with aphasia made by Speech and Language Therapists (e.g. Lesser and Milroy 1993). This knowledge must be valuable in specifying the communicative failure of people with mental illnesses.

3. The clinical symptom of 'thought disorder' has been criticised by several authorities. Rochester and Martin (1979) have pointed out that the concept is tautological, as disordered thinking is inferred from disordered speech. The term 'thought disorder' carries with it particular assumptions which are untenable. We consider the term problematic because its narrow focus on disordered cognition in the speaker overlooks the fact that communication is an interactive process occurring between people in social context. There is as much to be gained in trying to establish why the listener is unable to make sense of the message as there is in trying to find out why the speaker failed to convey the sense in the first place. From this it can be deduced that an examination of the utilisation by psychiatrists of more modern technical frameworks and specific terminologies for language analysis – such as is taught to Speech and Language Therapists – might at least be worthy of scrutiny.

4. The development of the concept of 'Theory of Mind' (Leslie 1987), and its manifestation in language (e.g. the maxims of politeness and self repair of linguistic errors), is of great importance for a variety of psychiatric disorders – including the autistic spectrum disorders and schizophrenia. Such developments require greater precision from psychiatrists in their descriptions of the clinical features especially the linguistic features, of people with schizophrenia, autism and Asperger's syndrome.

More accurate description requires more precise terms. 'We dissect natures on lines laid down by your native languages', said Benjamin Lee Whorf, and his arguments, alone with those of Edward Sapir, led to the development of this position into the Sapir-Whorf Hypothesis (see Hymes 1962). Whilst this hypothesis may have distracted attention from more theoretical semantic issues, Whorf, particularly when he referred to fashions of speaking – 'frames of consistency' – alerted the professional to the selective effect of the culture upon the cognitive significance of behaviours. The segmentation of nature is fundamentally related to lexical items. The most widely quoted example is the Eskimos great competence in describing snow conditions being attributed to the Eskimo language's vast number of words for 'snow'. Nancy Andreasen's Thought, Language and Communication Scale (TLC) (1979) proffers a range of terms which enables more details and accurate observation of the communication of psychotic people, more useful, for instance, in linguistic descriptions of schizophrenic sub-groups and their neuro-imaging correlates – such as Positron Emission Tomogrpahy (PET) and Single Photon Emission Computerised Tomography (SPECT) imaging. Frith (1992) points out that there are many different ways of being incomprehensible and Andreasen's framework captures most of them by specifying communication terms which explicate 'thought disorder'. As frameworks based on traditional terms such as thought disorder are still in usage alongside more precise frameworks such as Andreasen's TLC scale and exact frameworks such as those used in Speech and Language Therapy, it is appropriate to investigate the skills of psychiatrists, psychologists and speech and language therapists (all trained in human interaction) in describing communication and examine the influence of such frameworks. It was hypothesised that:

1. There would be a measurable difference in the skills of psychiatrists, psychologists and speech and language therapists (all trained in human interaction) in describing encounters with mentally disabled people. (Analysis I)

2. Difference in terminologies acquired by professionals in their training would be reflected in descriptive skills. (Analysis II)

Method

The subjects in this study were 20 trainee psychiatrists, 15 students of speech and language therapy and 15 recently qualified clinical psychologists. The trainee psychiatrists all had at least two years experience in clinical psychiatry and were either preparing for the final membership examination of The Royal College of Psychiatrists (in the next month) or had obtained that examination within the previous two years. The speech and language therapy students were all in their final year of a four-year BSc (Hons) degree in Speech and Language Therapy. They had no formal training from the discipline of psychiatry. The clinical psychologist group comprised clinical psychologists who had completed their training in the past year in South Wales, North Wales or Liverpool. All these subjects were asked to view a videotape consisting of a compilation of six (3 minute) excerpts from interviews by psychiatrists with clients/patients who demonstrate a range of communication abnormalities. These abnormalities consisted of examples of discourse failure seen in psychotic and organically impaired subjects (and their interviewers) and varieties of pragmatic and grammatical disturbances commonly seen in people with autistic spectrum disorder and those with learning disability. The videotape was shown to subjects either in groups or individually and, after each excerpt, subjects had three minutes to provide a brief written description. One of the authors invigilated. Subjects were told they were not required to make a diagnosis. The answer book also stated:

> 'The purpose of this exercise is to compare the expertise of professionals in communication disorders. You are asked to view 6 brief video excerpts of encounters between therapists and subjects. We are sure you will find them interesting.
>
> After viewing each video clip please provide a brief written description, in about 3 minutes, on the basis of your training and experience, what are the problems present in the interview. There may be a number of appropriate answers to each excerpt. After the last video you will have an opportunity to revise your answers and then view the panel's model answers'.

The identifying feature on each answer paper was a number.

Analysis I

A rating scale was devised, based on model answers provided by William Fraser, Philip Thomas and Martin Duckworth with a scoring of zero to three. A zero score was given when there was no evidence of description of the dyad nature or influence of non-verbal factors in an interview. A score of 1 was given when there was a description of the interview, including note taken of the interviewer or non-verbal communication, and an attempt at terminology, a score of 2 when the dyadic nature of non-verbal aspects and terms were described correctly, and a score of 3 was given when three or more of the following were evident in the answer: interviewer mentioned, non-verbal communication noted, appropriate terminology and detailed accurate description of the encounter.

All the subjects' replies were rated blindly, separately by William Fraser and Philip Thomas. The inter-rater reliability (pearson product) was $0.79 p < 0.001$. In the few cases where there was a large difference, a consensus was agreed by reviewing the answers together. Each subject's answers were rated separately for each of the size excerpts and then the scores were added together, so the range of scores for any one subject could be between 0 to 18. The scores were then combined according to which professional group they were from and group averages calculated.

Analysis II

The written descriptions provided by the subjects were re-analysed by Joseph Joyce using a different method, again blind to which profession the individual subjects belonged. This second assessment consisted of counting the total number of times the subjects used terms from predetermined lexical lists in their descriptions of the six excerpts. The lists comprise three types of words as follows (Table 6.1):

> Type A words are traditional clinical terms as used by Psychiatrists from 1900 to 1970
>
> Type B words are precisely defined terms according to Andreasen (1979)
>
> Type C words included prosody, pitch articulation, consonant use and repeat (Speech and Language Science Terms).

Table 6.1 Lexical classes

Type A: Form of speech, formal thought disorders, asyndetic thinking, metonymic thought blocking.

Type B: Preservation, neologisms, derailment, distractible speech, incoherence, illogicality circumstantial, speech, poverty of content, echolalia, loss of goal, pressure, tangentiality, word approximations, phonology, sematics, syntax.

Type C: Prosody, pitch, volume, utterance, voice quality, grammar, articulation, gestures, non-verbal communication, listener's needs body language, facial expression, eye contact, gaze dysarthria, consonant use, conversation, rhythm, paralinguistic, stereotypes, ellipsis, reference, stress, repair, fluency, topics, maxims of co-operation, success, politeness.

Source: Fraser, Thomas, Joyce and Duckworth 1995

The code was then broken and the use of words of the three types were summed according to professional group.

Results

Analysis I

Psychiatrists were inferior to the other two groups in the panel's ratings of their descriptive skills. One-way analysis of variance showed this as highly significant ($F=38.2$; $p>0.001$) (Table 6.2).

Table 6.2 Panel's ratings of descriptive skills of the three professions

One-way	Psychiatrists (N=20)	4.9
Anova	Psychologists (N=15)	11.9
Independent Samples	Speech Therapsits (N=15)	12.5

	Between Groups	DF.2
		VAR 32.4 >0.0001
		f=38.2

Source: Fraser, Thomas, Joyce and Duckworth 1995

Analysis II

The means and standard deviations of scores in relation to the number of terms of each type (A B C) used by the three groups – psychiatrists, psychologists and speech and language therapy students – were determined. From these, Z scores and, subsequently, T points were calculated for each group. T points give an indication of performance of the three groups in relation to each other. The higher the point, the better the performance. The psychiatrists were most competent on clinical terms. The speech therapists, unsurprisingly, were most competent on linguistic terms and were devoid of clinical terms (Table 6.3).

Table 6.3 Frequency of descriptive terms according to type and profession

			Psychiatrists	Psychologists	Speech Therapists
TEST A	Traditional Terminology	Z	24.2	6.3	0
		T	292	113	0
TEST B	'Defined' Terminology	Z	39.1	12.9	17.2
		T	441	179	222
TEST C	Technical Linguistic	Z	20.2	19.8	57.3
	Terminology	T	251	248	623

Source: Fraser, Thomas, Joyce and Duckworth 1995

Discussion

The results in Analysis II offer a tentative explanation for the findings in analysis I, viz. that the poor performance of psychiatrists shown in Analysis I arises because of constraints in their framework, as suggested in Analysis II. What most distinguishes the psychiatrists (the poorest in the panel's ratings) was their high use of traditional terms.

While the capacity to describe a communication episode is not identical to the ability to communicate – which includes such complex factors as empathy, listening skills and experience (see Evans, Stanley and Burrows 1993) – the observational performance of these psychiatrists, who have completed their training, compared with the two other professions is worrying. The practice of all three professions studied here depends on well-managed clinical encounters. Psychiatrists are reliant upon their use of language and communication skills both for assessment and for treatment. The teaching of interview skills has rightly featured prominently in the training of psychiatrists. We even make attempts to *assess* our trainees' skills in this domain in their professional examinations. But all this effort appears to be of no avail as far as their ability to assess human communication. The answer, of course, is not simply to teach more technical terms (which experience tells us trainees will reject as jargon anyway and psychologists get by without). Rather we suggest the problem is more fundamental and has two components: first, psychiatrists demonstrate selective attention to, and abstraction of, clinical signs which they then fit into a pre-ordained framework. The principal influences on this framework are phenomenology and psychopathology, both of which stress the location of a disturbance within the individual's mind/brain. Whilst this approach has its strengths, we believe this study demonstrates its limitations and how the traditional 'clinical' interpretative and diagnostic mode exemplified in clinical linguistic terms from Bleuler to Cameron, and still perpetuated in these young psychiatrists' frames of reference, interfere with proper observation of discourse. This applies not only to clinical work but also to research in the field of psychosis and autism. This is not to deny the value of the narrow cognitive approach to understanding communication failure, but it is incomplete. Frith's (1992) account of the neuropsychology of schizophrenia shows how social cognition and social interactional models of communication are closely inter-woven with cognitive models in understanding the symptoms of the illness.

The problem was visibly and repeatedly demonstrated in one excerpt where the patient, who had difficulties in expressing what it felt like to have complex partial seizures which affected her search for words and grammar, was described by several psychiatrists as 'thought blocking with metonymic distortion'.

Harrison (1992) considers the psychiatrist is aware of the vague and indeterminate meanings of psychiatric terms. He says the use of a concept comes before a clear definition and that we learn our concepts by using them rather than by referring to definitions, the latter process of clarifying can occur later. Such clarification may, however, never occur. Berrios (1992) has described how terms such as 'positive and negative', in relation to symptoms of schizophrenia, remain fashionable whether or not this use adds anything to understanding. While accepting that broad and vague psychiatric terms and concepts are not simply linguistic bad habits, we assert that there comes a time when the terminology which we had traditionally, and still are taught, in the absence of specific further elaboration by teachers' knowledge about psycholinguistics confines, limits and forecloses the observational skills of psychiatrists in situations of communicative distortion and breakdown. We are arguing for a broader, ecologically and pragmatically valid frame of reference for psychiatrist's communications.

CHAPTER 7

Schizophrenia as a Disorder of the Human Capacity for Language
The Trajectory to 'Hemispheric Indecision'

Timothy J. Crow and D. John Done

Summary

From the cross-cultural constancy of incidence it is argued that schizophrenia is intrinsic to human populations. It must arise from some genetic variation associated with the human condition and, since a part of this variation is disadvantageous, the relevant genes must be associated with an important functional characteristic. This characteristic, it is proposed, is the function by which man has speciated, that is language. Developmental (e.g. cohort) studies have revealed a number of ways in which individuals predisposed (presumably by their genetic constitution) to schizophrenic illness deviate from general population means in terms of behaviour and academic performance and, in recent studies, linguistic ability. Such studies provide routes to an understanding of the disease process. The hypothesis is advanced that schizophrenia is associated with a deviation in the process of hemispheric specialisation, specifically with a failure to establish dominance in one hemisphere. Some symptoms may arise from anomalies of inter-hemispheric communication.

Epidemiological Background

The range of possible aetiologies of schizophrenia is narrow. Two epidemiological findings constrain the theories we may entertain:

1. When those factors which might lead to ascertainment errors are taken into account, the incidence of schizophrenia (at least as defined by restrictive criteria – Schneiderian nuclear symptoms) is constant across cultures which differ widely in their climatic, industrial and social environments (Jablensky *et al.* 1992). The disease must be

primarily intrinsic in origin, that is genetic. It seems that the psychoses, in a way that distinguishes them from common physical diseases, are disorders of humanity.

2. Onsets occur throughout the reproductive phase of life, a fact that acquires particular significance in that the psychoses are associated with a decrease in fecundity (MacSorley 1964). There is also a sex difference – onsets are earlier in males (with a mean sex difference of 3 to 4 years) and the diminution of procreativity is also greater in males (Penrose 1991). These facts require an evolutionary explanation. If the disease is primarily genetic in origin, why do these genes persist in spite of a significant biological disadvantage? The argument advanced in this chapter is that the origins of psychosis and the evolution of the human brain are closely linked. Specifically, it is suggested that psychosis and language share a common origin in a process of increasing hemispheric specialisation (Crow 1995a; 1995b).

Childhood Precursors of Adult Psychosis

Some answers to the above questions are suggested by precursors of illness in childhood; these provide clues to the nature of the genetic predisposition and to the time-course of its evolution. That there are such precursors has been suggested by retrospective studies of the childhoods of individuals who later developed schizophrenia. Lane and Albee (1964) found that the intelligence scores in the second, sixth and eighth grades at school of children who became schizophrenic were significantly reduced compared to their siblings. Offord and Cross (1971) found low IQ in childhood to be a predictor of early age of onset and longer duration of hospitalisation and Offord (1974) reported that the deficit in IQ and poor school performance relative to siblings applied particularly to males. Earlier, Gittelman-Klein and Klein (1969) had identified a group of schizophrenic patients with 'premorbid asociality' who also had academic problems and were likely to have a poor outcome. In a study of school records, Watt (1978) described pre-schizophrenic girls in their early school years as emotionally unstable, introverted and passive, and the boys as emotionally unstable and disagreeable, becoming more so in the later school years. Across studies, the picture that emerges is that individuals who are later destined to suffer from schizophrenic illnesses are distinguishable (at least on the basis of group means) from individuals not so predisposed 10 or 15 years before the onset of psychosis. The distinguishing features include impaired academic performance and difficulties in establishing interpersonal relationships. There is at least a suggestion that deficits in IQ are a predictor of poor outcome.

Unanswered questions are: the time-course of emergence of these impairments, the relationship between them and the meaning of the sex difference.

The UK Perinatal Mortality Survey and National Child Development Study

The Perinatal Mortality Survey included 98 per cent of all births in England, Scotland and Wales registered during the week 3–9 March 1958. Four subsequent attempts to trace all members of the cohort, to monitor physical, educational and social development (in 1965, 1969, 1974 and 1981), became known as the National Child Development Study (NCDS). Using the Mental Health Enquiry (a register of admissions to psychiatric hospitals and units that continued until 1986), we were able to identify all cases recorded in the NCDS who had been treated as in-patients for psychiatric reasons between 1974 and 1986, that is until the cohort were aged 28 years. From the casenote histories, Present State Examination Catego diagnoses (Wing, Cooper and Sartorius 1974) were derived to give groups of patients suffering from schizophrenia by broad (n=57) or by narrow criteria (the presence of nuclear symptoms, n=40), affective psychosis (n=35) and neurosis (n=79) (Done *et al.* 1991). We found that pre-schizophrenic individuals were not more likely than the rest of the sample to have experienced pregnancy and birth complications (Done *et al.* 1991), nor were their mothers more likely to have been affected by the 1957 influenza epidemic (Crow and Done 1992).

Behavioural assessments at the ages of 7 and 11 years
(Done, Crow, Johnstone and Sacker 1994a).

At the ages of 7 and 11 years the teacher of each subject in the NCDS cohort was asked to complete the Bristol Social Adjustment Guide (BSAG), a standardised psychometric test of social adjustment and maladjustment in which the teacher underlines which of some 200 descriptions of school behaviour are relevant to the child. At the age of seven, pre-schizophrenic subjects are rated as more anxious and hostile toward adults and children and more likely to engage in inconsequential behaviours – each of these differences being significant at the one per cent level or less. These differences were largely restricted to males. Moreover, the differences between patients and controls were mostly confined to the component of over-reaction; there were no differences with respect to unforthcomingness and withdrawal and the difference for depression was significant (for males) only at the 10 per cent level. The changes are, therefore, sex-specific and relate to those components of behaviour that one might be inclined to relate to positive rather than to negative symptoms. At the age of 11 years, pre-schizophrenic females, as a group, were rated as more withdrawn and depressed than controls and as more likely to write-off adult values. Males were rated as significantly more likely to be depressed, although not withdrawn, and there was a trend with respect to writing-off adult values. Even at this age, the female group showed little evidence of the over-reaction that was present in the male group four years earlier.

Academic performance (Done, Crow, Johnstone and Sacker 1994b)

Assessments of reading and mathematical ability were made in the NCDS cohort at the ages of 7, 11 and 16 years and a test of General Ability (GAT), that includes an assessment of verbal and non-verbal intelligence, was administered at the age of 11. The tests used differed at the different ages – at age seven a word recognition test (the Southgate group reading test) was used to assess reading skill, while at the later ages this was assessed by a reading comprehension test. Mathematical skill was assessed by tests appropriate to each age. Of potential interest are sex differences and trends over time. Although there was a trend toward a greater impairment in performance on the GAT in male pre-schizophrenics, and the impairment was greater in verbal rather than non-verbal ability, the Analysis of Variance (ANOVA) group by sex by ability interaction did not reach the five per cent level of significance. Scores on reading and mathematics attainments were standardised with respect to normal controls at each age. Deficits at age seven years (with the schizophrenic group 1.1 standard deviation below the mean for controls) were as great as at later ages, suggesting that the impairments reflect a constitutional limitation rather than the emergence of a disease process. Overall, the picture that emerges is of a group of individuals who are significantly impaired across a range of intellectual abilities from an early age – these impairments having a particular impact on their ability to communicate either in written or oral format. The sex differences in academic ability are less striking than in the case of the disturbances of behaviour.

Physical and neurological development

No significant differences were observed between patients and controls with respect to height or weight at the ages of 7, 11 or 16 years or with respect to head circumference assessed at the age of 7 years. The timing of puberty was assessed with ratings of pubic hair and genital and breast development at the age of 11 and pubic hair, the onset of menstruation and age of the voice breaking made at the age of 16. These assessments did not distinguish psychiatric patients from controls. A number of aspects of neurological function were recorded (by medical officers) at each age and some of these separated the pre-schizophrenics from controls. For example, at age seven, patients were more likely to have been recollected by parents as having been wet by day at age three years and by night at age five years. At seven, they were also recorded (p<0.01) as showing poor co-ordination and were rated as poor on a simple test of vision for both left and right eyes. By age 11, vision is recorded as normal and on indices of motor coordination (walking backwards, heel-to-toe standing) they were not now impaired. At this age they were still more likely than controls to be recorded as incontinent. At age 16 years, although coordinated in heel-to-toe standing and hopping on either foot, they were rated as significantly (p<0.01) clumsy. The implications of this study for theories of aetiology and pathogenesis can be summarised. The findings with respect to birth complications (Done *et al.* 1991) and the 1957 influenza epidemic (Crow and Done 1992) give no support to claims that these factors contribute significantly to the aetiology of psychosis. The absence of abnormalities of physical development fail to support theories, for example of Kretschmer (1921), that psychosis is associated with significant anomalies of somatic growth and the relative normality of indices of puberty adds no empirical support to hypotheses, for example that of Saugstad (1989), that there are substantial deviations in the timing of endocrine changes. The changes in behaviour suggest that psychosis reflects a disturbance of selected aspects of central nervous system function that are time-dependent and, in certain respects, sex-specific.

The UK National Survey of Health and Development

Findings comparable and, in some respects, complementary to those in the National Child Development study have been reported by Jones *et al.* (1994) from a cohort of 5362 individuals born in the week 3–9 March 1946 (referred to as the National Survey of Health and Development). Thirty cases of schizophrenia were identified and were found to have reached their developmental milestones more slowly. They were delayed in walking by a mean of 1.2 months and had more speech problems than controls. They had low educational test scores at ages 8, 11 and 15 years. At age 13 years these individuals rated themselves as less confident and at 15 years their teachers rated them as more anxious than controls. The sex difference was less marked in this cohort than in the NCDS but the findings are in general agreement and establish that differences between pre-schizophrenics and controls are present in the first two years of life.

Asymmetry as the Key

Crichton-Browne (1879) appears to have been amongst the first (although preceded in the notion of a functional separation of the hemispheres by Wigan (1844)) to suggest that cerebral asymmetry was relevant to psychosis: 'It seemed not improbable that the cortical centres which are last organised, which are the most highly evolved and voluntary, and which are supposed to be located on the left side of the brain, might suffer first in insanity' (p.42). One of the first asymmetries to be recognised was the greater length of the Sylvian fissure on the left (Eberstaller 1884; Cunningham 1892). This probably reflects the increased extent, in most individuals, of the planum temporale (which corresponds to Wernicke's area) on the left side (Geschwind and Levitsky 1968). In a post-mortem brain study of hospitalised patients with schizophrenia, Falkai *et al.* (1992) found that this asymmetry was lost – similar observations were reported by Crow *et al.* (1992). Other findings consistent with a loss of asymmetry have been reported in computerised tomographic (CT) scan (Crow *et al.* 1989; Daniel *et al.* 1989), and magnetic resonance imaging (MRI) studies (Johnstone *et al.* 1986; Bogerts *et al.* 1990; Barta *et al.* 1990; Rossi *et al.* 1992; Hoff *et al.* 1992; Shenton *et al.* 1993 and Bilder *et al.* 1994). What is the meaning of this anomaly of asymmetry? The fact that it is present early in the course of the disease suggests that it reflects an abnormality of development – either that there is an arrest of a normal process of asymmetrical growth or that, amongst a number of hemispheric growth patterns, individuals at risk of schizophrenia are amongst those with greater symmetry of development.

Evidence for Failure to Establish Unequivocal Dominance

If structural asymmetries reflect on the mechanism of the disturbance, they must have a functional correlate. In the National Child Development Sample, a single index of hand skill – number of squares ticked with the right and left hands – was recorded at the age of 11 years. In the population as a whole, a well-marked superiority with the right hand was present but in 22 individuals, who were identified as having been admitted to a psychiatric facility by the age of 28 years with features of nuclear schizophrenia, the superiority was significantly (p=0.005) less pronounced (Crow *et al.* in press 1996). It appears that these individuals are less lateralised. While it is not clear that there is an excess of left handers amongst populations of patients with schizophrenia, there may be a failure to develop unambiguous cerebral dominance. In spite of a lack of a consistent excess of either right- or left-handers as defined by hand preference (Taylor 1987), a number of studies emphasising relative hand skill have shown that schizophrenic individuals exhibit an increased incidence of non-right-handedness – a finding that indicates a deviation away from strong left cerebral dominance for language (Shan-Ming *et al.* 1985 and Clementz, Iacono and Beiser 1994). Green *et al.* (1989) have suggested that this trend towards mixed handedness could be accounted for by an increase in ambiguous handedness. Ambiguous handedness is defined as a failure to manifest a consistent hand preference within, rather than across, tasks. Whilst infrequent in the normal population (2–3%), this handedness phenotype is in excess (i.e. 19.4%) in patients with schizophrenia (Green *et al.* 1989). Annett (1985) proposed the hypothesis that hand skill is a predictor of cognitive ability, with individuals at the extremes of the relative hand skill distribution being disadvantaged relative to those in the centre. She accounts for these relationships on the basis of a 'heterozygote advantage' theory of the underlying genetic determinants of handedness. Although controversial (see, for example, McManus, Shergill and Bryden 1993), this theory derives support from the findings in the NCDS survey. On a variety of indices of academic ability, individuals at the right-hand extreme of the continuum of relative hand skill (defined by the square checking test administered at age 11 years) did less well than those who were less strongly right-handed. At the left-hand end of the distribution, however, it was not those who were strongly left-handed who were most disadvantaged but those who were at the point of equal hand skill. The findings are consistent with the view, first clearly enunciated by Zangwill (1960), that failure to develop clear dominance in one hemisphere or the other is a risk factor for certain pathologies, amongst which he included dyslexia. The observation that pre-schizophrenics differ from the mean of the NCDS population in the direction of an equivalence of hand skill gives support to the interpretation that the fundamental deficit is a failure of hemispheric differentiation.

Language and Schizophrenia

The key function is language. The capacity for complex communication is the ability that distinguishes *homo sapiens* from other primates and, presumably, is the characteristic by which speciation has taken place. It seems that some component of this function needs to be focused in one or the other hemisphere and that this specialisation is completed at a point in development close to sexual maturity. One can speculate that it is those in whom this process is delayed or incomplete who are at risk of psychotic illness. Individuals who, by their genetic (or other) endowment, are close to the point of 'hemispheric indecision' – of which equality of hand skill is an index – are at particular risk of schizophrenia. Decreases in syntactic complexity, more severe in those with an early age of onset, were described in patients with schizophrenic illness by Morice and Ingram (1983). Such decreases are reported as more marked in patients with negative symptoms and to increase in severity with progression of the disease (Thomas, King and Fraser 1987; King *et al.* 1990). Such findings appear to reflect an overall reduction in the capacity to generate syntactically complex sentences. Chaika (1990), on the other hand, considers that the fundamental defect lies at the level of discourse organisation. The key to understanding the nature of the language disturbance in schizophrenia lies in formulating the abnormalities in terms of the relationships between the processes of discourse generation and control and the underlying psychological mechanisms, for example working memory. A clue to this formulation comes from a study of essays written at the age of 7 years by the individuals in the NCDS cohort. Whereas in the above studies in patients with schizophrenia there was a reduction in the capacity to generate complex sentences, in pre-schizophrenic children there was evidence that they were attempting to generate sentences that were more complex than those generated by their peers. It was as if they had a capacity or a drive to achieve intricacy in language production that later in development would encounter inflexible limits and that this encounter would somehow spill over into the symptoms associated with the disease. Morice's (1995) concept of a trade-off between complexity and errors is relevant. Individuals with a predisposition to schizophrenia appear to be amongst those in whom there is a mismatch between the flow of information and the capacity of some channel through which this information has to pass, a mismatch which becomes critical at some late stage of development. Key questions are: what is that nature of the information flow? and what is the channel that imposes limits on its passage? A possible answer to the first question is the information content of a sentence or (if Chaika is right) of a discourse. On the basis of the above studies of hemispheric dominance in the NCDS cohort, a possible answer to the second question is the information channel between the hemispheres – that is the corpus callosum and related structures (Beaumont and Dimond 1973; Flor-Henry 1983; Nasrallah 1985; Jaynes 1990).

Conclusions

A number of characteristics in the childhood of individuals who later develop schizophrenic illnesses have now been established. Such children are likely to be modestly delayed in their milestones, are likely to do less well than their peers academically (the mean impairment for reading being approximately one-half standard deviation) and have a number of behavioural deviations from the mean of the general population. For example, at the age of seven years, males are more likely to be rated by their teachers as anxious and hostile toward other children and adults and, at age 11, both males and females are more likely to be rated as depressed and withdrawn. These are quantitative variations and few of these children are referred to child guidance or psychiatric clinics. They may indicate the dimensions of variation in the normal population that underly the genetic predisposition to psychosis. A clue to the origins of psychosis from morphological studies is evidence of loss of the normal asymmetries. These structural anomalies are paralleled by evidence of a failure of hemispheric specialisation, for example in the finding of an excess of individuals with 'ambiguous handedness', and in the development of hand skill in pre-schizophrenic individuals On the continuum of relative hand skill assessed at age 11 years, pre-schizophrenic individuals were closer to the point of equal hand skill (hemispheric indecision) than the population mean. The findings are consistent with the following conclusions:

- That failure to establish unequivocal cerebral dominance is the mechanism of development of psychotic symptoms.

- That the gene that (in association with a random element) determines cerebral dominance is the major determinant of susceptibility to psychosis.

- That the genetic variation associated with the evolution of language (the characteristic by which *homo sapiens* has speciated) is the origin of the predisposition of a relatively constant fraction of human populations to develop psychotic illness.

- That those predisposed to psychosis have a genetically determined mismatch between their capacity to generate linguistic structures (sentences or discourses) of a target level of complexity and an informational channel (possibly inter-hemispheric) through which this information passes.

CHAPTER 8

Cambridge Language and Speech Project
Preliminary Findings on Language and Behaviour

Carol Stott, Vivian Burden, Jenny Forge and Ian Goodyer

The Cambridge Language and Speech Project (CLASP) is a community-based, prospective investigation into the nature, characteristics and outcome of speech and language difficulty in a sample of three-year-old children born between April and December 1989 and living within the catchment area of the Cambridge Health Authority. The project has been carried out in two phases: first, a screening phase in which three-year-olds with speech and language difficulties were identified together with a matched group of controls; second, a longitudinal phase involving ongoing detailed assessment of the identified cases and controls at intervals during their primary school years.

Although children with speech and language difficulties absorb considerable health care resources, estimation of the real size of the problem for health care planning remains problematic. Prevalence estimates have varied widely, from as low as 3 per cent to as high as 17 per cent in some cases – a likely reflection of the range of definitions employed. As Dixon, Kot and Law (1988) point out, language delay is norm related, not absolute, meaning that prevalence figures must always depend on the somewhat arbitrary cut-off point decided upon at the time of assessment.

In addition to nosological uncertainties, predictions about the outcome of early speech and language difficulties for any individual child are problematic. There is continuing debate about the nature of the relationship between transient and more persistent problems, and the picture is further complicated by the influence of other developmental and/or psychiatric factors that may influence health and educational outcome (Bishop 1994).

For many years there has been discussion about early identification of children with delayed language development and its implications for service provision. At the beginning of the 1980s early recognition and treatment were advocated by most texts in developmental paediatrics (Silva 1980). Earlier,

Johnston and Magreb (1976) stated that '...the importance of early screening and diagnosis for early treatment cannot be over emphasised'. More recently, Whitehurst and Fischel (1994) point to the increasing differences of opinion amongst informed professionals as to the significance of pre-school language difficulties, stating that most pre-schoolers with specific language delay recover to within the normal range by five years of age. This is corroborated by Bishop and Adams (1990) and Scarborough and Dobrich (1990). The implication is that treatment for many of the children identified before school age might be neither necessary, nor wise, if spontaneous recovery is a possibility.

There is evidence to suggest that the profile of language deficit at three years may be predictive of later outcome and may, therefore, provide useful information in helping to target service provision. In a sample of children enrolled in the Dunedin Multi-Disciplinary Child Development Study, Silva (1980) found that whilst children with delays in only one aspect of language did have an increased risk of developmental delay at five years, the risk was not very high; children with delays in both receptive and expressive language were at very much higher risk for later problems. Whitehurst and Fischel (1994) suggest that poor long-term outcome is much more likely if the language delay persists to later pre-school years and if the delay is not specific to language and/or includes problems in understanding. However, the situation is far from clear cut. It is particularly difficult, for example, to determine what constitutes a subtle, but significant, pre-school difficulty. In practice, children in this category are likely to go unrecognised until literacy (e.g. Aram and Nation 1980; Silva, Williams and McGee 1987) or behavioural/emotional and other psychiatric problems (e.g. Baker and Cantwell 1982; Beitchman *et al.* 1986) arise in primary school years and previously undetected verbal difficulties are discovered (Cohen, Davine and Meloche-Kelly 1989; Cohen *et al.* 1993; Gualtieri *et al.* 1983).

The association between language impairment and behavioural disturbance is well documented. Stevenson and Richman (1978) reported behaviour problems at 14 per cent in a group of 705 randomly sampled three-year-olds. Of those children in the sample with language delay, 58 per cent also had behaviour problems. Stevenson, Richman and Graham (1985) carried out a follow-up study with a group from the same sample when the children were eight years old. They noted different behavioural outcomes for children obtaining high and low scores on scales measuring language 'structure' – children with lower scores faring less well behaviourally. This was still the case when behaviour scores at three years were controlled, indicating a specific association between early language difficulties and later behavioural deviance regardless of early behaviour status. The relationship also held good regardless of whether the child still had language difficulties at eight years old.

More recently, the literature has reported a clear association between speech and language difficulties and psychiatric disorder by studying the behavioural and emotional development of children with speech and language disorders (Baker and Cantwell 1987; Beitchman *et al.* 1986) or by studying the language abilities of children with psychiatric disorders (Cohen, Davine and Meloche-Kelly 1989; Gualtieri *et al.* 1983; Grinnell, Scott-Harntet and Glasier 1983). Beitchman *et al.* (1986) found that a group of speech and language impaired children were more likely than a control group to show behavioural disturbance according to parent and teacher reports. They were also more likely to be diagnosed as having a DSM-III classification disorder (DSM IIIR 1987), particularly Attention Deficit Hyperactivity Disorder (ADHD), and to suffer from a higher risk of psychiatric disorder.

An association between speech/language impairment and ADHD has been reported by many authors (e.g. Love and Thompson 1988). Clear evidence of the association comes from a series of studies by Beitchman and colleagues based on an epidemiological sample of five-year-old children with a variety of speech and language difficulties (Beitchman *et al.* 1986; Beitchman *et al.* 1989a; Beitchman *et al.* 1989b). More recently, Baker and Cantwell (1992) found that 78 per cent of a sample of children with ADHD also had some speech/language impairment. Benasich, Curtiss and Tallal (1993) found a significantly greater proportion of behaviour problems in a group of language impaired children than in a matched control group but also found that once factors suggesting neurodevelopmental delay had been partialed out, there was no evidence to suggest a relationship between language impairment and ADHD in particular or between language impairment and general behavioural deviancy. The authors suggest that the previously noted association between language impairment and behavioural psychopathology may often have resulted from a failure to differentiate between behavioural/emotional disorder and neurodevelopmental delay. Other studies (e.g. Gascon, Johnson and Burd 1986; Burd and Fischer 1986) have indicated that children with ADHD demonstrate significant difficulty on tasks used to assess central auditory processing skills. Keith and Engineer (1991) found that a sample of children with ADHD were functioning at a lower level than predicted by chronological age in areas of auditory attention, auditory processing and receptive language. The authors suggest that a core pathology in central auditory processing could be contributing both to the language impairment and ADHD.

Additional methodological limitations in some of the studies linking speech and language difficulties with behavioural deviance have been addressed by Tallal and her colleagues (Tallal, Dukette and Curtiss 1989; Benasich, Curtiss and Tallal 1993) who point out that many studies have not screened for hearing impairment, learning disabilities, autism '…and other associated disorders'. The authors suggest that this brings the specificity of the language impairment into question. The inclusion of children with learning disabilities and/or low intelligence quotient (IQ) is of particular concern given previous findings that different behaviour profiles are a function of IQ (Silva *et al.* 1984). Although it is generally accepted that children with IQs below 70 have a significantly increased risk of psychiatric disorder (Scott 1994), Goodman, Simonoff and Stevenson (1995) provide epidemiolgical evidence that childhood psychopathology is also influenced by IQ variation within the normal range. The Benasich, Curtiss and Tallal (1993) study used a longitudinal design to investigate the development of language impaired children and addressed questions pertaining to the interaction between neurodevelopmental delay, behavioural/emotional disorders, cognitive ability and language development. The authors found no evidence of an overall relationship between non-verbal IQ and behaviour after language ability and neurodevelopmental status had been taken into account. An interesting finding was an unexpected decline in non-verbal IQ between four and eight years of age for language impaired children. This decline was significantly related to behavioural outcome at age eight. The language impaired children with the largest drop in IQ received the highest behaviour problem scores. On the basis of this finding, the authors suggest that the previously reported increased incidence of behaviour problems in language impaired children may be related more to IQ than to linguistic deficit *per se*. Evidence of a non-verbal IQ decrement with increasing age in language impaired children has also been reported in other longitudinal studies (Naylor, Felton and Wood 1989; Silva *et al.* 1984). Tomblin, Freese and Records (1992) found a decline in performance IQ on the Wechsler Adult Intelligence Scale-Revised (Wechser 1974) between childhood and adulthood in a longitudinal study of young adults with a well-documented history of language impairment.

In addition to specifying the nature of the behavioural deficits often shown by speech and language impaired children, many studies have attempted to specify particular types and features of speech and language difficulty that relate to psychiatric and/or behavioural comorbidity. Several studies have shown that different impairments are not equally associated with behavioural problems. Baker and Cantwell (1982) reported a significantly greater prevalence of psychiatric disorder amongst children with language impairments than amongst children with mixed language and speech impairments. For children with pure speech impairments, there was a lower prevalence of psychiatric disorder than for those with language impairment or for those with combined language and speech impairment. Caulfield *et al.* (1989) found an increase in behavioural difficulties amongst children with pure expressive language disorders compared with controls, whilst Cantwell, Baker and Mattison (1980) found the highest rates of psychiatric problems in children with comprehension problems. The series of studies carried out by Beitchman and colleagues (1986; 1989a; 1989b) employed cluster analysis to classify speech and language impairment in a sample of 347 children. Their findings showed that a group of children identified as having 'low overall' language skills was more disadvantaged than other groups (high overall, poor articulation, poor comprehension) on measures of cognitive, developmental, demographic and audiometric functioning; the 'low overall' group showed the highest rate of behavioural disturbance. A clear association between linguistic impairment and ADHD was found, with 59 per cent of the children in the 'low overall' group receiving a diagnosis of ADHD following psychiatric assessment.

Benasich *et al.* (1983) looked at the relationship between the degree and course of language impairment and concurrent and predicted behavioural outcome. They found that, in general, degree of language impairment was associated with neither concurrent nor predicted behavioural/emotional status.

CLASP is well placed methodologically to address issues relating to the concurrent and predictive association between speech/language difficulties and behavioural/psychiatric problems. The children involved in the project comprise an epidemiologically ascertained community sample of potentially language impaired children. Recruitment of potential cases and controls took place during the month of each child's third birthday when initial assessments took place. Further assessment was carried out when the children were 39 and 45 months old. Two hundred and fifty-five children are taking part in the longitudinal stage of the project. These children have now taken part in full assessments of speech and language, behaviour, neuropsychological, cognitive and motor functioning, temperament, pragmatic skills and family demographics. Further assessment will take place at regular intervals during the childrens' primary school years.

This chapter contains a description of the initial response to a postal questionnaire sent to parents of all children within the target group in the Cambridge Health Authority during a nine-month period in 1991. It also provides details of assessments of speech/language, behaviour and developmental abilities carried out at 39 and 45 months and makes comment on the implications of these preliminary findings. Particular reference is made to the relationship between speech and language difficulties and problem behaviour.

Method

Overview

Full methodological details can be found in Burden *et al.* (1996). Briefly, a three-stage procedure was used. These stages are referred to as Net, Screen and Assessment. The Net stage involved asking parents to complete a postal checklist and a short interview. Net data was used to select a group of children at risk, together with a matched group of controls. The Screen stage involved face-to-face assessment of speech and language, and completion of a behaviour checklist by parents. Screen data was used to denote the presence or absence of potential speech/language and behavioural difficulties in children continuing to this stage. The Assessment stage involved face-to-face assessment of each child's speech, language, cognitive and developmental abilities, together with the collection of questionnaire data about behaviour, temperament, pragmatic skills and family demographics. Details of measures used to assess temperament, pragmatic skills, neuropsychological functioning and family demographics will be provided elsewhere. This chapter focuses on measures of speech/language, behaviour and developmental abilities.

Selection procedures and subject details

Two thousand, five hundred and ninety children (51.5% boys, 48.5 girls) born between April and December 1989 were identified by means of a community paediatric database held at Addenbrookes Hospital, Cambridge, which records all births on a monthly basis. The study adopted a standard age design in order to minimise the potential confound between age and developmental pace. Parents of the children identified were asked to complete a postal checklist during the month in which each child became three years old and a short interview during month 37. Subsequently, 277 children for whom Net responses indicated a potential difficulty, plus 148 matched controls, completed the Screen stage when the children were 39 months old. Any child whose language score fell at or below the tenth centile for the CLASP sample on any one Screen language measure (or between the 10th and 20th on any three) was deemed to have potential language difficulties and was asked to participate in the longitudinal phase of the project, regardless of behavioural status. In addition, a number of children whose language appeared to be developing normally, but whose scores on the behaviour checklist indicated a potential difficulty, were also asked to continue – together with a matched group of controls for whom on problems with language or behaviour had been indicated. Details of the development of criteria for potential impairment at Screen are given fully in Burden et al. (1996) but were close to clinically accepted guidelines for impairment provided by the International Classification of Diseases (ICD-10) criteria (World Health Organisation 1993). A total of 255 completed the Assessment stage at 45 months and thus comprise the longitudinal sample to be assessed at intervals during the childrens' primary years.

Procedures and materials

NET (36/37 MONTHS)

The Pre-school Language Checklist (PLC) was sent to parents at the beginning of the month in which their child became three years old. The checklist consisted of 12 items, eleven of which focused on the child's receptive and expressive language; a twelfth item asked if the child had ever had a hearing problem. Full details of the checklist can be found in Burden *et al.* (1996). Each of items 1–11 was framed in such a way that a negative response would flag a potential problem and would indicate that the child should continue to the next part of the Net as a potential case. If the only problem indicated was in response to item 12, the child was excluded from the next stage of the project. At this stage parents were also asked to provide details of any problems which they believed may have contributed to speech and language difficulties for the child in question.

Once checklists had been returned, a number of exclusion criteria were applied. Children were excluded if they met one or more regardless of speech and language status. Children were excluded if they had:

- ○ same age full siblings
- ○ a current diagnosis of learning disability (mental handicap)
- ○ chronic illness involving frequent or prolonged hospitalisation
- ○ profound hearing loss/deafness
- ○ other known, significant pathology
- ○ bi- or multi-lingual family background.

The second part of the Net was based on the Developmental Profile II (Alpern, Boll and Shearer 1980). This is an interview schedule with questions covering general developmental and linguistic progress. The information was obtained by means of a telephone interview with a parent (usually mother) when the child was 37 months old. Respondents without a telephone were visited at home. The DPII served as a check on PLC response and allowed the elimination of those children who were given negative responses on the PLC where further discussion indicated no cause for concern.

In summary, children with potential language difficulties continued beyond the Net stage if there had been an indication of potential difficulty on the PLC, they did not meet any a priori exclusion criteria and they were not elimated at DPII. A sex/geographically group-matched sample of children who had no problems on the PLC or DPII was selected to continue as a potential control group.

SCREEN STAGE (39 MONTHS)

Expressive language skills were measured using the Action Picture Test (Renfrew 1966) and the Bus Story Test (Renfrew 1969). These are standardised tests for three- to eight-year-old children designed to stimulate samples of spoken language that can be evaluated in terms of information provision, grammatical structure and mean length of utterance. In the absence of appropriate standardised instruments, measures of receptive language and phonological ability were developed by speech and language therapists on the CLASP team. Full details of reliability assessments of the CLASP-devised scales are given in Burden *et al.* (1996). The measure of receptive language was based on the Derbyshire Language Scheme's concept of information-carrying words (Knowles and Madislover 1982). Children were tested on items containing two, three or four information-carrying words and on concepts of size and position. The measure of phonological ability consisted of 15 words that should elicit sounds normally within the phonological repertoire of a child of 39 months. The child was asked to produce words in response to simple pictures. The phonology scale also included an item rating connected speech for intelligibility.

Parents were asked to complete the Pre-School Behaviour Checklist (PSBCL) (McGuire and Richman 1986). This is a 22-item checklist asking for ratings of the child's behaviour during the previous two-week period. Items cover a variety of behaviours related to conduct disorders, aggression and social/emotional factors. Two of the items on the PSBCL refer explicitly to the child's language ability, so, in order to avoid confounding behaviour and language related ability, these items were omitted when calculating overall behaviour scores. A total score was derived by prorating the two language items on the basis of scores obtained on the remaining 20 items – this allowed us to maintain the cut-off point for indication of problems at 12 or above, as suggested by the authors.

ASSESSMENT STAGE (45 MONTHS)

Expressive and receptive language abilities were measured using the Reynell Developmental Language Scales – Revised Edition (RDLS/E; RDLS/R) (Reynell and Huntley 1985). Articulation skills were measured using the Edinburgh Articulation Test (EAT) (Anthony, Bogle, Ingram and McIsaac 1971) and information about receptive vocabulary was provided by the British Picture Vocabulary Scale (BPVS) (Dunn, Dunn, Whetton and Pintilie 1982). In addition, parents were asked to complete the PSBCL again (Richman and McGuire 1986 – see above).

The Griffiths Mental Development Scales (Griffiths 1970; 1984) were used to assess each child's developmental progress. The Griffiths Scales consist of six scales covering aspects of the child's development in the following areas: locomotor, personal/social, hearing/speech, eye/hand co-ordination, performance and practical reasoning. Scores on each scale are represented by a sub-scale quotient. A general developmental quotient (DQ) is derived by calculating the mean of the six sub-quotients. The hearing/speech sub-scale score was not included in the computing of overall DQ for any analysis of the relationship between DQ, behaviour and language. In these instances, mean overall DQ was computed using a sixth sub-scale score prorated on the basis of scores on the remaining five.

Results and Conclusions

Speech and language

PLC RESPONSE AND SCREEN PERFORMANCE

There were 1936 (75%) returns for 2590 questionnaires sent. Of these, approximately 51 per cent were boys and 49 per cent girls. Four hundred and seventy-two of the respondents (24%) gave a negative response to one or more items on the PLC. Of these, 274 (58%) were boys and 198 (42%) were girls. Full details of exclusions, withdrawals and non-returns can be found in Burden *et al.* (1996). The overall picture shows that items relating to expressive language and vocabulary (items 1–4, 10 and 11) were most likely to be given a negative response, indicating a potential problem, whilst those relating to receptive language (5–9) were least likely to do so.

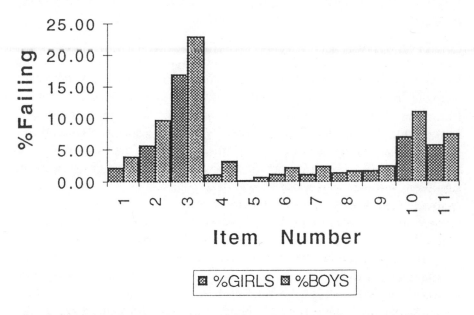

Figure 8.1 PLC responses

Following withdrawals and exclusions, 277 (72%) of the negative PLC re-sponders were involved in the Screen stage (173 boys and 104 girls). From the pool of 226 children not indicating a Net problem, 148 (87 boys and 61 girls) were selected as controls. In all, 425 children were involved in the Screen stage. The 277 children indicating a problem on the PLC and proceeding to Screen were grouped for analysis into three potential risk categories according to the number of negative PLC responses made:

- low risk (one negative response), n=140

- medium risk (two or three negative responses), n=89

- high risk (more than three negative responses), n=48.

This categorisation makes the assumption that the level of risk is related positively to the number of negative responses made; at this stage, no assumptions were made about the type of speech and language difficulties that may be represented by the pattern of negative responses. Response patterns within the low and medium risk groups reflected the overall response rate. An interesting finding, however, was that, although failure on receptive items was relatively infrequent overall, those children who did fail on these items tended to be in the high risk group – suggesting that failure of receptive items does not usually occur in isolation. One expressive item (item four: 'Can your child string three or more words together in a meaningful way?') also followed this pattern.

PLC RISK AND SCREEN PERFORMANCE

Raw scores from the 425 children who completed the Screen speech and language measures were subjected to a square root transformation and means were obtained for all measures. Significant differences were found between the PLC risk group mean scores on each Screen speech and language measure. A between-groups Analysis of Variance (ANOVA) looking at controls (i.e. no risk group) and various levels of PLC risk confirmed that children shown to be at any risk on the PLC obtained scores on all Screen speech and language measures significantly lower than those of the PLC controls. Furthermore, *post hoc* analyses (Tukey) of group means showed that children in the PLC high risk category achieved significantly lower scores on all language measures compared with subjects in the other two PLC risk categories (Table 8.1).

A total of 123 children failed at least one item below the 10th centile whilst an additional 11 children passed all items at the 10th but failed three or more between the 10th and 20th. A total of 134 children therefore met CLASP criteria for Screen failure. The 123 children with speech/language difficulties defined by the 10th percentile failure were divided into three levels of 'severity' according to the number of failed measures. The additional 11 children failing three or more items between the 10th and 20th percentiles, but none below the 10th, were assigned to the mild group. The following groups were defined:

- mild – failing on one Screen measure (n=56+11, 50% of Screen failures)

Table 8.1 Screen mean scores – (root transformed) by PLC risk

Screen Measure	Whole Sample	PLC RISK				
		No Risk	Low	Med	High	Any
n=425		148	140	89	48	277
APInfo 1	4.4	4.8	4.5	4.4	3.1	4.4
APMLU 2	1.9	2.1	1.9	1.8	1.4	1.9
APGrammar 3	3.0	3.5	3.1	2.9	1.6	3.0
BSInfo 4	2.7	3.2	2.7	2.6	1.4	2.8
BSMLU 5	1.8	2.0	2.0	1.8	1.1	1.9
Comprehension 6	3.1	3.3	3.1	3.1	2.5	3.0
Phonology 7	4.0	4.3	4.0	3.9	3.4	3.8

1. $F=38.08$, df. $(3,401)$ p <0.000, Tukey (high<medium=low<no risk)
2. $F=37.36$, df. $(3,401)$ p <0.000, Tukey (high<medium=low<no risk)
3. $F=41.80$, df. $(3,401)$ p <0.000, Tukey (high<medium=low<no risk)
4. $F=33.09$, df. $(3,374)$ p <0.000, Tukey (high<medium=low<no risk)
5. $F=37.52$, df. $(3,371)$ p <0.000, Tukey (high<medium=low<no risk)
6. $F=10.17$, df. $(3,391)$ p <0.000, Tukey (high<medium=low<no risk)
7. $F=38.08$, df. $(3,394)$ p <0.000, Tukey (high<medium=low<no risk)

(Tukey procedure of the multiple range test taken at the p=0.05 level)

Source: Own data.

○ moderate – failing on two or three measures (n=34, 25% of Screen failures)

○ severe – failing on four or more measures (n=33, 25% of Screen failures).

Fifty-six (46%) failed only one Screen measure at or below the 10th centile; 24 (20% of all failures) were on phonology alone.

The PLC risk categories (low, medium, high) were found to be positively associated with Screen severity groups (Chi square = 115.18, p <.000). A positive Spearman's correlation coefficient was also obtained between PLC raw score and number of Screen tests failed (r=0.48, p <0.01), indicating that increasing PLC scores are positively associated with increasing number of failed Screen tests.

Preliminary analysis, using Screen speech and language status as the outcome criterion, looked at the overall accuracy of the PLC as a predictor of language status at 39 months. Using a cut-off point of one failed item on the PLC, sample sensitivity was estimated at 87 per cent and specificity at 45 per cent with a 7.5 per cent false negative rate.

ASSESSMENT

It is important to note that the provisional CLASP criterion for speech and language difficulty at the Assessment stage is based on less stringent criteria than suggested by ICD–10. First, performance at one standard deviation below the age mean on any test was considered to constitute failure and, second, although all children in the CLASP sample fall within the normal range of DQ, no discrepancy between DQ and speech/language achievement was required for a child to be designated as having failed a particular language test. Further analysis, and the application of more stringent criteria, is required before precise diagnostic labels can be applied. Any conclusions made on the basis of current data must be considered to be preliminary and tentative. Measures were categorised along two separate axes: receptive/expressive and language/non-language. The Reynell scales provided measures of expressive and receptive language, whilst the EAT and BPVS provided measures of expressive and receptive 'non-language': 81 children met criteria for speech/language difficulty on at least one of the language measures – this represents approximately 4 per cent of the original sample. The full breakdown of scores for all 255 children completing the assessments is presented in Table 8.2.

EXPRESSIVE AND RECEPTIVE MEASURES

From Table 8.2 it can be seen that of the 81 children with speech/language difficulties, 61 (75%) had a problem involving some form of expressive difficulty and 51 (63%) had some expressive difficulty but no problems in other areas; 52 (64%) had problems involving pure speech; 30 (37%) had problems with speech alone; 19 (23%) had problems involving expressive language and three of these had problems with expressive language alone. We can also see that 41 children (51% of the assessment failures) had a problem involving some form of receptive difficulty and 32 (39%) of these had no problems in other areas; 25 (31%) had problems involving receptive language and seven of these had receptive language problems alone. Twenty-seven (33%) had problems involving vocabulary and seven of these had problems with receptive vocabulary alone.

LANGUAGE AND NON-LANGUAGE MEASURES

If we look at the profile of difficulty in terms of failure on language and non-language measures, we see that 33 children (41% of the failures) had problems involving one or other of the language measures and 28 (35%) of these had no problems in other areas; 66 (81%) failed one or other of the non-language measures and 59 (73%) failed non-language alone.

SINGLE AND MULTIPLE FAILURES

Of the 81 children meeting criterion for speech/language difficulty, 47 (58%) failed on only one measure and 30 (37% of all failures) were pure speech

Table 8.2 Speech language profiles at 45 months

Speech/language	Total	Percentage of total	Boys	Girls
Specific Language Impairment (SLI)	81			
Expressive Difficulties				
Speech and/or Expressive Language				
Any Expressive	61	75%	45	16
Any Speech	52	64%	38	14
Any Expressive Language	19	23%	17	2
Expressive Alone	51	63%	39	12
Speech Alone	30	37%	21	9
Expressive Language Alone	3	4%	1	2
Receptive Difficulties				
(Vocabulary and/or Receptive Language)				
Any Receptive	41	51%	29	12
Any Vocabulary	27	33%	15	12
Any Receptive Language	25	31%	22	3
Receptive Alone	32	39%	24	8
Vocabulary Alone	7	9%	2	5
Receptive Language Alone	7	9%	7	0
Language Difficulties				
Any Language	33	41%	28	5
Language Alone	28	35%	23	5

Source: Own data.

difficulties. The remainder of the single failures were: three (4%) expressive language, seven (9%) receptive vocabulary and seven (9%) receptive language. Twenty-nine (36%) of the 81 failed on more than one measure, 21 (26%) failed on exactly two measures, four (5%) failed on exactly three measures and four (5%) failed on four measures. For five children failing at least one item, missing data meant that we did not have information on how many measures were failed in total.

Speech/language and behaviour

SCREEN

Preliminary indications of a significant association between speech/language and behaviour was seen at the Screen stage, with speech and language difficulties being positively associated with an increased behavioural risk (chi-square 33.7, p<0.000001). Full data on speech, language and behaviour was available for 414 children – of these, 197 had no problems with speech, language or behaviour whilst 130 children had difficulties with speech and language (61% of these also had behaviour problems, compared with only 31% of the children without speech and language difficulties). When specific speech/language measures were looked at, significant associations were found between overall behavioural status and all but the phonological measures (see Table 8.3).

Table 8.3 Speech/language and behaviour (39 months)

Speech / language measure	Association between speech / language and behaviour		
	All	Boys	Girls
Action Picture Grammar	(**)	(**)	(**)
Action Picture Information	(**)	(**)	(**)
Action Picture MLU	(**)	(**)	(*)
Comprehension	(**)	(**)	(*)
Phonology	–	–	–
Overall speech/language (any measure)	(**)	(**)	(**)

Significant relationships between speech/language and behaviour status at $p<0.01$ (**) or $p<0.05$(*)

Source: Own data

ASSESSMENT

Preliminary analysis of assessment results provided further indication of a significant relationship between speech/language and behaviour. At this stage, full data on speech, language and behaviour was available for 214 children. Of these, 113 children (53%) had no problems with speech, language or behaviour, 43 (21%) had problems with behaviour alone, 33 (15%) had problems with speech/language alone and 25 (12%) had problems with speech/language and behaviour.

It should be noted that the sample of children to be followed longitudinally includes 67 children selected specifically because they met criterion for behavioural difficulty in the absence of any speech/language problems at 39 months. As 59 (88%) of these children continued to have normal speech/language at 45 months, their presence as a selected group is likely to mask overall behavioural risk effects when making direct comparisons between speech/language impaired and non-impaired children. Nonetheless, the data does show a significant association ($p<0.05$) between overall behaviour status and overall speech/language status for the sample as a whole and for boys on their own.

There appears to be no significant relationship between overall speech/language and behaviour status for girls.

When looking at specific areas of speech/language impairment, the presence of receptive difficulties, regardless of performance in other speech/language domains, increases behavioural risk for boys (see Tables 8.4 and 8.5). This association holds when receptive language difficulties occur in isolation, but not when receptive vocabulary is the only area of difficulty. Similarly, and again for boys, there is an association between overall behaviour status and difficulties on tests of language (expressive and receptive), as opposed to non-language measures, with an increase in behavioural risk in the presence of language difficulties regardless of whether the language difficulties occur in isolation. This association does not hold for expressive language difficulties occurring in

Table 8.4 Speech/language and behaviour (45 months)

Speech/language measure	No. of failures on Language Measures		
	All	Boys	Girls
Reynell Expressive	16(**)	14(**)	2
Reynell Receptive	19(**)	16(**)	3
EAT	44	32	12
BPVS	24	13	11
Overall speech/language (any measure)	68(*)	46(*)	22

Significant relationships between speech/language and behaviour status at p<0.01 (**) or p<0.05(*)

Source: Own data

Table 8.5 Speech/language and behaviour (45 months)

Speech/language domain	Association between speech/ language and behaviour		
	All	Boys	Girls
Any Expressive	–	(*)	–
Any Receptive	(**)	(**)	
Any Receptive Language	(**)	(**)	–
Any Expressive Language	(**)	(**)	–
Any Language	(**)	(**)	–
Receptive alone	(**)	(**)	–
Language alone	(**)	(**)	–
Overall speech/language (any measure)	(*)	(*)	–

Significant relationship between speech/language and behaviour status at p<0.01 (**) or p<0.05 (*)

Source: Own data

isolation. No significant relationships between behaviour and particular areas of speech/language impairment was found for girls, but it should be noted that the actual numbers of girls failing those measures which tend to be strongly associated with behavioural risk was very low.

SPEECH/LANGUAGE, BEHAVIOUR AND DEVELOPMENTAL QUOTIENT (IQ)

When looking at the relationship between developmental quotient, language, behaviour and sex (see Table 8.6) preliminary analysis suggests a significant association between mean adjusted DQ and overall language status and a slightly weaker, but significant, association between mean adjusted DQ and overall behaviour status. There were no significant relationships (or two/three-way interactions) between any of the variables and sex.

We also looked at the status of individuals on combinations of speech/language and behaviour problem status as follows:

- neither speech/language nor behaviour

- speech/language alone

- behaviour alone

- both speech/language and behaviour.

Analysis of the association between combined speech/language and behaviour status with mean adjusted DQ (see Figure 8.1, p.77) indicates that, although DQ decreases with the involvement of language and behavioural difficulties and there is a significant overall difference between mean DQ for all groups (F=df. p<0.00001), there is no significant association between DQ and behavioural status in the absence of language difficulties. In contrast, the association between language and DQ holds true when children with behavioural difficulties are excluded from the analysis (Table 8.6).

DEGREE OF LANGUAGE IMPAIRMENT

When severity of language impairment (defined by failures across domains) is taken into account, there is evidence of a significant relationship between the number of tests failed and behaviour status – the more speech/language domains involved, the greater the behaviour risk (Chi-square 15.6, df 4, p<0.00362). There is no evidence of a significant association between adjusted mean DQ and increasing severity, although the control group perform significantly better than children failing one, two or four measures (F=10.8218, df 4, p<0.00001). The lack of significance between controls and children failing three measures is likely to be due to the small number of children failing on exactly three measures. Again, there were no significant effects of sex.

Table 8.6 Speech/language, developmental quotient, behaviour and sex

DQ by Overall Speech/Language Status and Sex (ANOVA)
**DQ by Overall Speech/Language (F=31.916, p<0.0001)
  DQ by Sex non-significant
  Interaction non-significant

DQ by combined Speech/Language and Behaviour status and Sex (ANOVA)
**DQ by combined Speech/Language and Behaviour status (F=11.612,
  p<0.0001)
  (i.e. problems with: speech/language only, behaviour only, both, neither)

DQ by Sex non-significant
Interaction non-significant

DQ by Behaviour Status and Sex (ANOVA)
* DQ by Behaviour status (F=6.032, p<0.015)
  DQ by sex non-significant
  Interaction non-significant

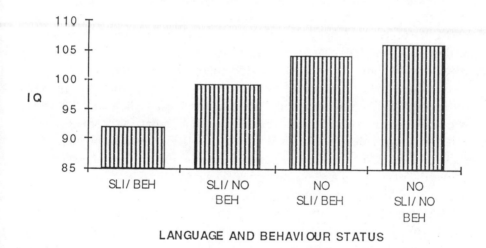

LANGUAGE AND BEHAVIOUR STATUS

Figure 8.2 Non-verbal IQ increases with decreasing involvement of language and behaviour

One of the first conclusions to be drawn from the analyses completed so far is that the Parent Language Checklist used at the Net stage of the project has the potential to become a useful adjunct to current surveillance procedures for early detection of speech and language difficulty. Broadly speaking, CLASP responses to the PLC – along with preliminary analysis looking at concordance between CLASP identification and Speech Therapy involvement – suggests that the overall CLASP screening procedure identified a number of speech/language impaired children that current surveillance has missed. Final analyses looking at the predictive accuracy of the PLC using outcome at Assessment as a comparative criterion are yet to be carried out, but the levels of sensitivity/specificity indicated at Screen are promising.

Problems indicated on the PLC tended to be in areas related to expressive speech/language and vocabulary. Failure of receptive items was relatively infrequent overall, but those children who did fail receptive items tended to fail other items as well. This pattern of relative infrequency of isolated receptive problems was repeated at the assessment stage when children were 45 months old and is in line with much of the literature. This suggests that the PLC is sensitive to the differences in early language profile reported elsewhere. The fact that item four (an expressive item involving more than pure phonology) also tended not to be failed in isolation is also worthy of note. An initial hypothesis might be that children with early language problems in receptive and/or expressive domains are more likely to have a broader range of deficit later. Detailed analysis of the predictive accuracy of Net and Screen performance, and the association between different Net/Screen profiles and eventual outcome as subsequent stages of assessment, will be provided elsewhere.

Analysis of data collected at 39 months suggests an overall relationship between speech/language and behaviour for boys and girls. Preliminary analysis of Assessment data suggests that this was repeated for the sample as a whole and for boys, but not girls, at 45 months. An important factor in the association may be the presence, or absence, of language (rather than speech) difficulties; receptive language difficulties in particular seem to be associated with increased behavioural risk. Preliminary CLASP data also provides evidence to suggest that the previously cited association between phonological status and behavioural status at 39 and 45 months and the lack of association between Griffiths DQ and phonology at 45 months, it is also likely that the mediating skills are not related to phonology.

As emphasised earlier, the suggestions made at this stage are tentative as full analysis of all assessment data is not yet complete. In addition, further analysis of comparative performance at the various stages of the project is currently being carried out and data on speech, language and behaviour, collected from parents and school teachers when the children were six years old, is being collated. Further assessment of language, behaviour, psychiatric status and cognitive-neuropsychological functioning will be carried out at regular intervals during the children's primary school years and reports provided when analysis at each stage is complete.

CHAPTER 9

Speech and Language Therapy and the Mentally Ill Patient

Jenny France and Niki Muir

> I've always thought everybody was like me. I've heard voices ever since I can remember. I don't think I will ever be well but I don't now have the acute physical pain that I experienced earlier on in my illness. It is still difficult to find words to describe how I felt.

This description of his predicament was delivered by a young schizophrenic patient in a psychodynamic psychotherapy group held in a hospital ward setting where groups have a mix of both mentally ill and personality disordered patients. The pre-condition for successful participation in most forms of psychotherapy is adequate communication skills. The ability to engage in, and benefit from, psychotherapy also necessitates the ownership of sophisticated linguistic skills from which, during therapy, emerge the accompanying paralinguistic skills supporting the evidence of developing psychological well-being and personal maturity (France 1995). For example, another schizophrenic patient in therapy remarked that he thought everyone was like him, that is had auditory hallucinations and racing thoughts. It was many years before he realised that he was in fact different to most other people. This explained much of his developing confusion when with others and reinforced his need to lead a solitary existence. This, in turn, produced further problems such as drug, alcohol dependence and deteriorating relationships with the family, violence and tragedy: 'I was desperate for someone to talk to, the only people who would listen were people like me – on the street and drunk'.

We know that both Bleuler (1950) and Kraepelin (1971) considered disturbances in speech to be core symptoms of schizophrenia and that research has been focused on traditional categories of thought disorder, but recent work examining schizophrenic speech has used approaches borrowed from the literature on normal speech production (Barch and Berenbaum 1994). France

(1995) reports that disorders of communication, speech, language and hearing greatly reduce intelligibility of communication and limit communicative exchanges of thoughts and feelings. This is often met with intolerance, ridicule and rejection leading to isolation, hostility and anger, engendering feelings of low self-esteem and self-confidence, worthlessness and uselessness. Therefore, the prime concern of a speech and language therapy service in psychiatry is the communication skills and welfare of the individual client/patient – where physical, emotional and social needs must be recognised.

Schizophrenia is stated as being the heartland of psychiatry and the core of its clinical practice (Kendall 1988). It is a relatively common condition which cripples people in adolescence and early adult life and probably causes more suffering and distress than most other illnesses. Blakemore (1988) states that one per cent of the world's population suffers from schizophrenia, that it is a disease of the brain and mind, causes global impairment and disrupts personality and that people with this and other major mental illnesses have a high incidence of speech and language disorders which are essential components of their problems, yet they are seldom treated by speech and language therapists. This may be partially due to the lack of knowledge and understanding of the role of speech and language therapy in mental health, particularly by other mental health care professionals – some of whom will be members of the multi-disciplinary team who also consider they work with patients and their communication problems.

Few mental health units have access to speech and language therapy services and most local services are over-burdened and will often be ill-equipped for the task of managing clients with major mental illness. So providing services to mental health settings demands a degree of sensitivity, particularly by the therapists! Misconceptions and myths as to the therapist's role need to be explored with care and, furthermore, blurring of professional roles needs to be accepted and understood.

Speech and language therapy is always seen within the context of a multi-disciplinary approach which aims to assist clients to lead as full and valued lives as possible. The service offered must be sufficiently flexible to meet individual needs, be delivered across a range of mental health settings to clients from all, or some, of the major mental illness diagnostic groups and be prioritised according to need.

Assessment

Speech and language therapy assessments in psychiatry may add information assisting psychiatric diagnosis, highlighting specific communication problems and providing diagnosis of any speech pathology, as well as assist in differential diagnosis. At this stage in the developing speech and language therapy services in psychiatry there are no standardised formal assessments available for speech, language and communication problems for those suffering from mental illness. Many of the tests used by speech and language therapists in other therapeutic settings can be adapted to help fulfil the overall assessment needs and it has been found that an holistic approach to assessment and treatment is essential (France 1993). In order to obtain a full communication assessment, a patient will need to be assessed and observed in as many different settings as possible as it is known that styles of communication changes occur with different people and in different environmental settings – for example, on the ward, in a work area, a social setting, the home or a formal psychiatric interview. Video and audio recordings are, perhaps, the most popular means of assessing patients; recording of clinical interviews is important for ongoing assessment and can also provide the therapist with samples of speech, language and communication behaviour that can be further analysed. Audio and visual tapes can be used as transcripts for comparison of pre/post-intervention levels of functioning. Furthermore, the recordings can demonstrate to members of the clinical team descriptions of communication, voice, language and articulation disorders and might, therefore, be helpful when diagnosis of speech problems are confused by symptoms of mental illness. The sharing and involvement with the patient during recording is usually enjoyed by all, particularly in group settings, and the pleasure and surprise witnessed when viewing or hearing the recordings and identifying difficulties and monitoring progress during therapy often produces quite accurate and perceptive observational skills by the patients. For example, 'cor is that me – don't I look funny – but I sound alright don't I?'

In the main, the central contribution of the speech and language therapist will be in the assessment, management and co-management of the following areas:

- communicative environment
- hearing
- attention
- perceptual and associative skills
- receptive language
- expressive language
- motor speech programming
- speech
- swallowing
- functional communication

   ° pragmatics.

In all these areas, treatment should begin at the point of breakdown. It is understood that this role will be undertaken as part of a team and that many other team members will have contributions to make in evaluating and treating environmental, attentional and perceptual needs and deficits but, in all skills related to speech and language function, it is the speech and language therapist who will have significant grasp of the specific neuropathology and psychopathology which will raise the level of description of the disorder and assist towards differential diagnosis. The results of language assessment can aid the team in making other distinctions between, for example, the onset of a dementia or specific dysphasia (Stevens 1985). Assessments such as verbal fluency tests and the Test for the Reception of Grammar TROG (Bishop 1983) have been demonstrated to show a characteristic difference in performance between elderly people with a dementia and those with a clinical depression – often a difficult area in which to make initial judgment. Assessment of the prosodic features of voice can be significant if there is doubt regarding the existence of depression.

Many sub-tests of currently standardised assessments for language, for example Aphasia Screening Test (Whurr 1974) or Psycholinguistics Assessment of Language Processing in Aphasia (Kay, Lesser and Coltheart 1992) can be used and will produce the beginnings of language profiles in both the dementias and the psychoses. Speech assessments such as the Frenchay Dysarthria Assessment (Enderby 1988) can identify even earlier onset of speech problems and signify types of dysarthria, whether due to drug side-effects or neurological co-pathology.

Voice change or difficulty with respiration and phonation is often part of the wide range of symptomatology in psychoses, neuroses and personality disorders. Assessment of voice using qualititative tools and questionnaires, for example Lockhart and Martin (1987), can help plan therapy. Functional communication profiles will also have their place (Skinner *et al.* 1984) as will carefully devised checklists. Familiarity with the major psychological test materials is recommended to encourage patients, if able, to undertake some self-rating. This can be helpful later in establishing base-lines which the patient feels he or she has, to some extent, chosen – as well as in demonstrating outcomes from the patient's own point of view. Compliance, concentration and fluctuation of mental state will affect performance and assessment results. Evaluation of the factors which may impede a patient's opportunity to communicate in many environments is necessary and might determine therapeutic options and opportunities. The patient's motivation to communicate positively may be minimal and this may either be related to pre-morbid personality, the effects of institutionalisation or living in an impoverished communicative environment.

Hearing assessments are essential and pure tone audiometry, or an initial screening, can identify hearing loss, whether pre- or post-lingual (Eastwood *et al.* 1986 and Thacker 1988). Vision and dentition are often overlooked in the broadness of the mental health diagnostic categories and these, and sensory impairments resulting from behaviours of withdrawal, confusion, aggression or incoherence, can become wrongly attributed to a worsening of mental state. Hearing aids, spectacles and dentures are often thrown away by the patient, leaving carers confused as to whether these items have ever been prescribed and/or used! Practical management strategies can be of significant value and will need to be provided both to patients and carers.

In the assessment and management of attention, association and perception, the speech and language therapist will collaborate with the psychologist, medical and nursing team, occupational therapist and others but will be specifically extrapolating the clinical information gained as to the effects of deficits of these skills on language processing and competence of communication interaction. The assessment of receptive language abilities extends into a higher level linguistic functioning of deeper processing and involves observations and remediation of abilities such as logical and inferential thinking, grasp of metaphor and humour and semantic memory capability and will involve both written and verbal pathways. It will test non-dominant hemisphere language functions, particularly those of the right hemisphere in relation to pragmatic skills (Bryan 1989). Assessments of expressive language functioning, including semantic, syntactic and lexical organisation and output, will include both cerebral hemispheres in order to specify and target the exact level of difficulty that the patient is experiencing.

Motor speech programming is the next stage in the process and oral and speech dyspraxias will be assessed as appropriate. Speech functions such as fluency and articulation will all be rated. In cases of severe speech impairment, as, for example, the dysarthia of Parkinson's disease or Huntington's Chorea, the patients may be assessed for their suitability for an augmentative or alternative communication system such as Makaton (Walker 1979), which is most commonly used for clients with learning difficulties. On occasions, there may be value in pursuing the issue of a computerised communication aid (Enderby 1987).

Eating and swallowing problems may be a feature that will often coincide with the dysarthrias, particularly in the older patients and those with superimposed neurological problems or drug-induced side effects. Skill in the management of dysphagia (Logemann 1983) needs specialised training.

Finally, a significant contribution can be made in describing, assessing and managing specific features of functional communication. The study of pragmatics is often undertaken in three discrete areas: communicative intent, pre-supposition and discourse (Roth and Spekman 1984). This is discussed in greater depth in Chapter 11. This approach aids building the verbal and non-verbal skills of interpretation and use of the message contained within a conversation – it also aids the ability to take another person's perspective in an interaction and the actual flow and change of what takes place when people communicate and meanings are negotiated in therapy. As a means of assessment, we should not underestimate the value of dialogue between the therapist and patient – even the shortest interview will produce a wealth of information as well as help establish the therapeutic relationship.

Traditional Therapy Approaches

The following highlights the major input to therapy:

- individual and group therapy in traditional formats
- cognitive behavioural therapy
- support and counselling
- aspects of dynamic psychotherapy
- care of the elderly interventions
- packages of advice and information
- delivery of a range of education and training.

Therapy may be given individually to meet specific assessment of management requirements or in groups (Muir 1992). Traditional speech and language therapy techniques for the management of the aphasic syndromes are based on cognitive neuropsychological principles (Lesser 1987). Exercise regimes for voice (Martin 1987) or stutter (Rustin, Purser and Rowely 1987) and for dysarthria (Robertson and Thomson 1982) will also be akin to those of traditional practice. With the elderly and long-stay client group there is likely to be a need for dysphagia advice and management, augmentative and/or alternative communication strategies may be implemented for some people, as previously mentioned.

Therapy and Schizophrenia

Recent developments in the treatment of schizophrenia have integrated educational methods, skills training, family-based stress management and specific cognitive/behavioural strategies with optimal pharmacotherapy (Falloon 1992). These approaches have demonstrated considerable promise in alleviating the impairment, disability and handicaps associated with schizophrenia. It is known that no one profession has all the skills necessary for the assessment, treatment and rehabilitation of mentally ill people (Hume and Pullen 1986), just as no one treatment had been found to be fully effective in all cases.

Literature concerning schizophrenic patients continues to inform us that they frequently present with incoherent and bizarre speech which leads to difficulty in communicating with other people. Newby (1995) states that speech does not necessarily precisely mirror thought and that the relations between these two areas need to be explored. Anand *et al.* (1994) write that a variety of linguistic deficits have been described in psychotic speech (deficits in semantics, syntax, cohesion and discourse planning) and goes on to state that the presence of a distinct language disorder in psychosis has implications for the investigation of this aetiology.

Barch and Berenbaum (1994) inform us that the majority of the research on the aetiology of language disturbance in schizophrenia has focused on the role of information processing and that the schizophrenic individual exhibits a variety of information processing deficits including, but not limited to, selected attention, short term memory and speed of information processing. When the speech of a psychotic person confuses rather than communicates, psychiatrists label it 'thought disorder'. However, Hoffman (1994) states that it is not always apparent *how* such utterances confuse or derail the listener. Language disorder has been described as including deficits such as reduced syntactic complexity and reduced number of ideas of the number of words spoken, therefore direct work on the semantic pragmatic elements of communication, even along the lines more usually undertaken for those with aphasia (Carlomagno 1994), is central – particularly with people whose main diagnosis is one of psychosis or personality disorder.

All aspects of communication will be experienced in social and communication skills sessions and practised in a structured way, which will help draw out and expand specific details related to pragmatic aspects of communication. The social skills training will focus on the importance of non-verbal skills as well as the development of verbal skills of conversational initiation and maintenance (Trower, Bryant and Argyle 1978). It will also likely involve some vocal skills training with attention to pitch, volume and rate.

Therapy Approaches

The aim of therapy will be to increase insight (David 1990) not only into the patient's mental illness but also the view of their future. Sessions will need to be flexible but there should be some continuity in both duration and location and therapists will need the unconditional positive regard of a Rogerian approach (Rogers 1951) and will call upon the techniques from both relaxation training and assertion training. We understand, therefore, the need for speech and language therapy involvement in psychotherapy to range from using cognitive and behavioural approaches to dramatherapy and psychodrama techniques and supportive and psychodynamic psychotherapy. All these methods can be employed to stimulate communication competence and improve vocal quality and expressive and receptive language development, with particular emphasis upon increasing lexical store and enhancing fluency of utterance (France 1995).

Cognitive/behavioural psychotherapy is a structured form of treatment that can focus on particular topics or areas of functioning and work through programmes over periods of several months – with an ending, but not a fixed finishing time, in advance to allow groups, in particular, to spend a shorter or longer time on topics according to the needs of the patients (Quayle, France and Wilkinson 1995). Structured treatment can include such things as social skills (previously mentioned), assertiveness training and anger management (Novaco 1975). Work on interpersonal relationships – including sex education and other sexual topics – self and sensory awareness, family issues, moral dilemmas and, in a forensic setting, victim empathy. (These latter subjects are both complex and demanding).

Cognitive behavioural principles based on the work of Beck *et al.* (1979) are of proven value (Meichenbaum 1985; Birchwood and Tarrier 1992) and can be used in individual settings to build insight and ensure a measure of carry-over towards success in groups (Alladin 1988). These methods can also help functional analysis of communication and behavioural problem-solving and can break down tasks and set goal stages with the use of modelling, shaping and re-enforcement techniques aided by role play and homework assignments.

Other psychotherapeutic techniques of proven value are counselling and Personal Construct Psychology, as described by Hayes in detail in Chapter 12, and Neurolinguistics Programming, described in Chapter 13. Also, Transactional Analysis (Berne 1961; Lapworth, Sills and Fish 1994) because of its theory of social interaction and its systematic analysis of interpersonal communication which allows for matching of communication and clear planning to attempt to avoid communicative breakdown. These techniques offer structure to both patient and therapist and are both experiential and reconstructivist.

Supportive Psychotherapies

Supportive psychotherapy can be practised in a number of settings and on an individual or group basis with patients or with their families and friends. Speech and language therapists are most likely to work in this way in a formal group setting in a psychiatric unit, ward or day centre. Brumfitt (1986) supports the speech and language therapist as having the listening and reflective skills required in counselling and they need not be afraid to take this step. Many chronically mentally ill people can only survive with constant support in order to prevent social isolation. Psychotherapy in these cases is not always aimed at psychological change but at the maintenance of emotional stability, as many of these people lack the capacity for understanding their psychological difficulties: 'It's no use you coming to see me I can't talk properly…' After an action-packed 35 minutes filled with past history and his present predicament, the patient announced that he had done well, enjoyed the exchange and requested further appointment to help his 'speaking confidence'. The group setting offers a chance for patients to learn to redefine their own means of communication so that they can adapt to changing situations and learn to inter-communicate, in particular to establish social skills between each other. Groups for severely disturbed patients provide evidence that they have a marked effect on adjustment. The primary goal of this type of psychotherapy is to increase the patient's ability to handle his own problems and take responsibility for his own actions.

Some of the results observed in these groups have been that chronic schizophrenics are more likely to be transferred to less disturbed wards and maintain improved behaviour, and that, together with medication, delusional thinking lessens – which helps toward discharge. Many patients remember these groups with pleasure and reminisce about past sessions and are able to recall quite sophisticated interactions, develop links between each other and, to their surprise, share similar details of their mental illness and past difficulties – this is often a revelation and a comfort to them. Support groups can also avert the need for more direct psychotherapeutic intervention (Gordon 1976) and can be particularly effective during the resettlement period – dealing with issues of how communication changes affect both receptive and expressive speech, particularly when accompanied by anxiety or depression. Groups can be organised to deal with specific situations or issues and they are better dealt with in more informal ways than might be possible in the more structured social and communications skills groups.

Counselling is an integral part of the overall treatment plan for the patient. For example, a speech and language therapist working on a communications problem might also provide counselling in order to help adjustment to the difficulties and feelings arising from the patient's disability. Dalton (1994) states that counselling has different aims with differing speech pathology, but all with the emphasis on helping the person not only to maintain or restore communication as far as possible but also to maintain or restore some sense of personhood and self-worth.

Translating and/or clarifying information shared with the patient by other professionals is often necessary. It would appear that the speech and language therapist is adept at identifying when confusion or apparent misunderstandings occur and this provides the opportunity to interject to ensure that the exact message has been given, received and understood by all parties!

Care of the Elderly

Reality orientation (Holden and Woods 1982), reminisance therapy (Norris 1986) and validation and resolution therapies (Goudie and Stokes 1989) will feature as part of the methodology and underpinning of the management of the dementias and may have some relevance for long-stay elderly clients. Reality orientation will encourage the use of time, place and person reminders in order to bring some structure and clarity into a confusional state. Reminiscence therapy reduces depression and promotes communicative attentiveness and output and has been shown to improve short-term cognitive functioning (Hughston and Merriam 1982). Validation therapy (Feil 1982) encourages the therapist to try and establish an interaction in response to the client's own communicative statements and behaviour rather than set an agenda for what is 'normal or acceptable'. Resolution therapy allows the therapist to give credence to the underlying feelings and cognitive processes which may be triggering seemingly anomolous or meaningless communicative output and and behaviours.

Advice and Information

Support will take the form of information, both written and verbal, and can offer opportunities to re-state previous information and further develop insight and coping strategies. As the speech and language therapy service in mental health is still geographically thinly spread, possibly due to financial constraints, and a long-established system is slow to implement change and encompass other clinical aspects and competences, exchanging information within the team is of paramount importance. Speech and language therapists will need to inform fellow professionals on their role as well as on specific management techniques. Advice will be needed regarding the place of linguistic and communicative needs in care planning and consultation will be needed on the optimum level of input required by an individual patient – which will, in turn, maximise his or her understanding and input. Relatives and carers can also benefit from having a clear written and verbal explanation of the complexities of communication, a skill which few fully understand and most take for granted, which helps avoid misunderstandings and can also avert an intensification of any relationship breakdown between the family, the patient and the therapist and ensure that all have the same information and the same understanding of that information.

Education and Training

All professionals who work in mental health have a responsibility for improving communication but the processes are often incompletely understood and seldom directly taught (Koury and Lubinski 1991). Training, which needs to be versatile, is an effective use of the speech and language therapist's time and access should be made for undergraduate and postgraduate students and members of other clinical specialisms as well as the carers. Therefore, training sessions may need to be organised to suit the appropriate groups and accommodate their specific needs. Multi-disciplinary planning and facilitation of training sessions can be a powerful team-building exercise. Improved knowledge and skills for staff will most certainly have a direct benefit for patients.

Conclusion

The aim of speech and language therapy is to maximise communication potential within a patient's and carer's environment. Linguistic and communicative breakdown is central to mental illness, both in terms of diagnosis and pathology. For carers, it is often the difficulties in communication and interaction which both sadden and create problems. Mental illness states are vastly complex and the whole microcosm of speech and language disorder can be found in mental health settings. It therefore seems logical that the speech and language therapist has a part to play in contributing towards diagnosis and management, both with the clients and with the carers.

The currently small voice of speech and language therapy in psychiatry is now becoming audible and, due to the profession's willingness to undertake audit procedures (Royal College of Speech and Language Therapists 1993), is providing quality outcome measures and the specialism is gradually being validated.

CHAPTER 10

Conversational Skills and Schizophrenia
An Exploration

Irene Walsh

This chapter presents preliminary findings resulting from an exploration of the conversational skills of people with schizophrenia. The chapter is presented in two parts, with the first part focusing on the conversational skills of pre-schizophrenic children, while the second part outlines some observations made while implementing a conversational skills programme for people with chronic schizophrenia.

Part 1 Conversational Skills of Pre-Schizophrenic Children

Introduction

Schizophrenia is a devastating and puzzling form of mental illness. To date there is no 'cure' but the illness can be controlled and the symptoms treated. The cause of this disorder remains elusive despite clearly delineated conditions associated with it.

Thornton and Seeman (1991) describe schizophrenia as a 'medical illness which interferes with a person's ability to think, to feel and to interpret sensory information; behaviour can also be disturbed' (p.3). In addition, the communication skills of some people with schizophrenia can differ markedly from normal spoken interaction and can be characterised by, for example, irrelevancies, perseverative statements, tangentiality, incoherence and the overuse of questions (Andreasen 1979; Rochester and Martin 1979; Rutter 1985; Frith 1992; 1994). It is often the unusual style of language usage in people with schizophrenia that is most noticeable in the presenting disorder.

Thomas (1994) has drawn parallels between features of Andreasen's (1979) Thought, Language and Communication Scale (a widely used clinical tool for the assessment of thought disorder in schizophrenia) and areas within linguistics. Such a comparison has led Thomas to conclude that many of the features of thought disorder could be described in linguistic terms, for example incoherence (syntax) or neologisms (phonemic or word level). In addition, many of the terms could be described in terms of pragmatic (poverty of speech and poverty of content of speech) or discourse deficits (derailment and loss of goal). Thus a greater understanding of the language problems of some people with schizophrenia, coupled with increased awareness in psychiatric circles of the subject area of linguistics (particularly discourse analysis), has led to the consideration that schizophrenia may be increasingly regarded as a disorder of language (Murray 1994). This in itself has major implications for the speech and language therapist working in adult psychiatry.

PRE-MORBID POINTERS TO VULNERABILITY IN THE PRE-SCHIZOPHRENIC CHILD

Based on evidence indicating that schizophrenia tends to be familial, possibly genetic, and may have a neurodevelopmental component, studies of children of schizophrenic parent(s) are frequently reported in the literature (e.g. Watt *et al.* 1984; Walker 1991). Such studies attempt to find possible pre-morbid pointers to vulnerability, given that such children may be at risk for developing the disorder. The following areas of development have been looked at:

○ Attention skills: Harvey (1991) cites data from the New York High-Risk Project (Erlenmeyer Kimling and Cornblatt 1987; Erlenmeyer-Kimling, Golden and Cornblatt 1989) that suggests that global attentional failures mark vulnerability to schizophrenia in children of parents with schizophrenia.

○ Social adjustment: Done *et al.* (1994) have shown that abnormalities of social adjustment are detectable in childhood in some people who go on to develop psychotic illness.

○ Language Skills: There is a paucity of research into the linguistic functioning of children or adolescents at risk for developing the disorder. However, Harvey, Weintraub and Neale (1982) examined speech abnormalities in terms of the frequencies of several reference performance variables. Reference performance is the process by which spoken text is organised into a coherent framework and thus easy for the listener to interpret (Halliday and Hasan 1976). Harvey, Weintraub and Neale found that children of schizophrenic parents made significantly more reference failures than normal speakers and characterised the speech of high risk subjects as having lower information content and being more vague than that of controls.

SCHIZOPHRENIA: A DISORDER OF LANGUAGE?

As schizophrenia is increasingly regarded as a disorder of language (Murray 1994) the question arises as to the presence or absence of poor pre-morbid

...nctioning in the pre-schizophrenic child. Hollis (as reported by ...994) studied 61 schizophrenic individuals and 61 non-psychotic ...ric controls. Looking back to their language development in childhood, ...found that, together with evidence of pre-morbid motor impairment, 23 ...cent of the schizophrenics had pre-morbid language impairment compared to only 6.6 per cent of the controls. Jones *et al.* (1994) showed that pre-schizophrenic children, presenting with delayed attainment of gross motor milestones, also had delayed attainment of speech and language milestones and presented with greater speech problems in childhood and adolescence. This points to the fact that in some adults with schizophrenia there may have been particular difficulty with the development of language in childhood, which may persist as a feature of later schizophrenia.

Harvey (1991) discusses Meehl's (1962) hypothesis that 'vulnerability (to schizophrenia) is genetically transmitted and marked by certain identifiable language behaviours' (p.141). Therefore, if there is evidence of poor speech and language functioning pre-morbidly, what is the nature of these 'identifiable language behaviours' in the child who may go on to develop schizophrenia in later life?

Method

A FOLLOW-BACK APPROACH

Focusing on the children of people with schizophrenia has the advantages and disadvantages of any prospective high-risk approach to research. A follow-back approach, however, begins by identifying a sample based on adult psychiatric outcome. Precursors are then examined by using medical or academic records.

This short study attempts such a follow-back approach to research into the pre-morbid precursors of schizophrenia with regard to speech and language functioning in the pre-schizophrenic child. A disadvantage to a follow-back approach is the possibility of poorly documented case notes; this study was severely hampered by such a disadvantage.

Five files of children who went on to develop schizophrenia in adulthood were identified and examined. These children, who had been referred to a child psychiatric service for assessment, had parents who were schizophrenic or who had some history of mental illness. On examination, only two files had *any* reference to the communication abilities of the children and these notes were usually made by psychiatrists; though lacking in detail, these two case descriptions are presented. (It is important to note here that no speech and language therapy service was available at the centre at the time these children were referred. Therefore, no detailed assessments of speech and language functioning were available in these files and the author had to rely on notes made by other professionals.)

Results

CASE DESCRIPTION: CHILD A

On referral, Child A (male) was described as a very dependent, nervous, fidgety, agitated child with a short attention span. Parents were separated and mother worked in the home. This child was the second of four children. There was a strong family history of psychiatric illness: father was described as a paranoid schizophrenic who was violent in the home and mother also had some history of psychiatric disturbance, the nature of which was unclear. Child A's sister also had schizophrenia and had anorexia nervosa. A brother was referred to the child guidance service with difficulties in school (poor concentration) and relationship difficulties with his mother.

Child A's birth history was reportedly normal and the parents were unsure about attainment of developmental milestones but presumed that they were within the normal range. A clinical report on child A at chronological age (CA) six years described him as being emotionally immature and exhibiting restlessness, poor concentration and anxiety symptoms. He was disorganised and noisy during play and reportedly enjoyed long and complex games with toy soldiers but could easily lose the theme when he became over-excited. A further report at CA 11 years described him as being very disturbed emotionally, restless, agitated with bizarre thinking and occasional aggressive outbursts. Reference was again made to his limited concentration span. Intellectual assessment at CA 10 years 4 months put child A in the high mild mental handicap range of ability on the Wechsler Intelligence Scale for Children-Revised (WISC-R).

Table 10.1 Recorded case notes of speech and language features of child A

At CA 6 years: Comprehension of language reasonably good when he attended but problems with expressive speech. If asked any direct questions, would rarely answer or would say 'and that's the why' or 'yes' inappropriately. He may later spontaneously give the correct answer as though he had heard the question earlier in the conversation but wasn't going to bother answering until later (i.e. a few turns later when it would be irrelevant). Stammers and talks in whispers.

At CA 10 years (report from school): Obsessional questioning but never happy with answers. Talks in muted low tone.

At CA 11 years: Asks a great number of hypothetical questions: 'What would happen if?'

The case notes also described child A's brother as being very 'careful and precise' with his speech, displaying 'a veneer of intelligence and poise'. Child A's mother was described (when mentally well) as being witty and entertaining and a very interesting conversationalist conversing on a wide range of topics. Table 10.1 shows an account of references made to child A's communication abilities as recorded in the case notes:

CASE DESCRIPTION: CHILD B

Child B's case notes gave even less detail than in child A's case. Reportedly, there was a strong family history of psychiatric illness as both parents had been given a tentative diagnosis of schizophrenia. A clinical report at CA six years described child B as being very disturbed but with above average intelligence. He was also reportedly 'very fond of general knowledge' and preferred to play alone as he had difficulty getting on with his peers. Table 10.2 outlines the references made to child B's communication abilities:

Table 10.2 Recorded case notes of speech and language features of child B

Disturbing element of concrete thinking in the interpretation of proverbs, e.g. 'A rolling stone gathers no moss' interpreted as 'Something that goes so fast it can't gather anything'.

Poor eye contact during conversation – covered face and turned away as he spoke.

Child said of his father's physical abuse towards the family: 'If you have any evil thought, you act on that thought, he was protecting us, if you didn't act on it you wouldn't think of it'.

Child said to have incorporated father's delusional thinking.

Discussion

From the brief references to child A's communication skills, it is evident that he had some difficulty in using language appropriately for social interaction (i.e. pragmatics). In conversational interactions, he had difficulties in responding to questions asked of him, giving inappropriate or delayed responses. Such features would pose difficulties for the conversational partner and would possibly lead to conversational breakdown. In addition, he also spoke in whispers or muted low tones, again making it difficult for a conversational partner to continue with the conversation. Another inappropriate conversational feature was his overuse of questions. Finally, there was reference made to the speech and language styles of both mother and brother, which may suggest an unusual style of conversational interaction in the family. Keeping Grice's (1975) Co-operative Priniciple/Conversational Maxims in mind (i.e. Be truthful; Be brief; Be relevant; Be clear), one can see how child A could break many of the rules of conversational interaction, leading to conversational breakdown.

In Child B's case, again working from very limited and incomplete case notes, it is apparent that he presented with poor eye contact during conversational interactions. He also had difficulty with the figurative use of language and reportedly interpreted proverbs in a concrete way, being unable to express the underlying abstract meaning. Because the age of the child was not given when the particular proverb cited was presented to the child for interpretation, we cannot say that this necessarily posed a problem, as his interpretation may be one that would be in keeping with his developmental level. Most studies of proverb comprehension have found that children have difficulty understanding the figurative form of language before adolescence (Nippold 1985; Lund and Duchan 1988). Child B also displayed an incidence of poor use of reference markers for his listener, thus resulting in vague statements (as illustrated in the last example quoted above) which may lead to conversational breakdown. Finally, the reference to child B being 'very fond of general knowledge' might suggest an element of verbosity or irrelevancy apparent in day-to-day conversation (again compare Grice's (1975) Maxims).

Concluding comments

It is clear that this study was severely hampered by poorly-documented case notes, particularly pertaining to the speech and language functioning of these children. Though one cannot make generalisations from such a brief study, the following points are worth making:

- The study supports findings relating to vulnerability markers in the pre-schizophrenic child, for example evidence of attention and linguistic difficulties pre-morbidly.

- The comments made about these children's communication abilities, though lacking in detail, would largely fall into the area of language usage, that is pragmatics, and could be termed a conversational disability. Appropriate use of language for communicative purposes seemed to be an obvious area of difficulty for these children. No specific comments were made in the case notes about difficulties in vocabulary, grammar or phonology.

- Though only briefly referred to in the case notes, it is obvious that one cannot ignore the influence of cognitive factors on the communication skills of the children presented.

- It is also important to note that these children had been referred to a child and family psychiatric service in the early 1970s, prior to a speech and language therapy service being set up at the centre. Thus no file had detailed records of assessment of the child's speech and language functioning.

Despite its limitations, this short follow-back study highlights the need for routine screening of speech and language skills in children who are referred to a child psychiatric service and detailed history-taking and an in-depth assessment of those children who may be at risk for developing a mental illness such as schizophrenia (e.g. congenital-type schizophrenia with insidious onset). Such assessments would not only enhance our overall understanding of schizophrenia but may enable some preventative measures to be put in place.

Finally, we cannot ignore the fact that, in some adults with schizophrenia, there may have been particular difficulties with the development and use of language in childhood – difficulties which may persist as a feature of later schizophrenia.

Part 2 Implemention of an Informal Conversational Skills Programme for People with Schizophrenia: Some Observations

Part two of this chapter takes a closer look at the conversational abilities of adults with schizophrenia – as observed while implementing an informal conversational skills group.

Introduction

We have seen how the language difficulties apparent in the pre-schizophrenic child may be described as a pragmatic or conversational disability. The following questions arise: Could it be that these conversational difficulties persist into adulthood and become exacerbated by the illness? Or could the conversational difficulties be considered as part of the insidious development of the disorder we call schizophrenia? Having posed these questions, I make no attempt to answer them, but consideration of such possibilities may help us to explain the nature of the conversational difficulties in schizophrenia.

Frith (1992) proposes three principal abnormalities in cognitive processing that may account for the major signs and symptoms in schizophrenia. Applied to communication they can be described as follows:

1. Disorders of action (inability to generate spontaneous (willed) acts):

    (a) poverty of action (e.g. poverty of speech),

    (b) perseveration of action (e.g. poverty of content)

    (c) inappropriate actions (e.g. incoherent speech and use of neologisms).

2.   Abnormalities of self-monitoring

3.   Abnormalities in the awareness of others (i.e. patient fails to take account of the knowledge of the listener when constructing utterances).

All three categories, when applied to the discourse of schizophrenics, adequately describe what is going on and why the listener is often 'left in the dark' in a conversational interaction with a person with schizophrenia.

As already referred to in Part 1 of this chapter, many of the features of the communication difficulties of people with schizophrenia can be described in terms of *pragmatic* or *discourse* deficits (Thomas 1994 and this volume). Frith (1994) translates these difficulties into problems with a *theory of mind* – in terms of not being able to take account of the listener's needs in communicative interactions: why tell somebody something you think they already know? (For further discussion of a *theory of mind*, as applied to communication problems in schizophrenia, see Frith 1992; 1994 and this volume). Thus, the individual may either refrain from engaging in conversation or converse in an inappropriate and incoherent way, often leaving the listener confused and unable to follow the line of conversation, leading to conversational breakdown. As one of Mc Ghie and Chapman's patients reportedly said, 'people listening to me get more lost than I do'. Frith goes on to state that 'the abnormalities of schizophrenic language lie at the level not of language competence but of language use. The problems arise when the patient has to use language to communicate with others' (1992, p.98).

Using language to communicate with others through conversational interactions is the concern of the proposed programme which is outlined in this part of the chapter.

Background to the study

From recent observations, it is apparent that *some* people with schizophrenia display an apparent degree of metacommunicative awareness, that is they are aware of their difficulties in communicating and behaving as a conversational partner in any spoken interaction. Their metacommunicative awareness enables them, as normal speakers do, to 'talk about talk' and make comments like the following: 'Am I talking too fast for you?'; 'Do you understand what I'm saying?'; 'Sometimes I find it hard to know what to say to people'; 'Some days I'm able to talk better than this', etc. The ability to monitor one's own discourse is essential if one is to communicate effectively and meaningfully. The person with schizophrenia who has an apparent degree of metacommunicative awareness may be enabled to monitor his or her own output and, in so doing, 'correct' or make more meaningful his or her utterances, thus taking the listener's needs into account (c.f. points (2) and (3) above, Frith 1992). Thus, in doing so, the person with schizophrenia may improve his or her conversational skills, leading to improved social relationships.

However, it is interesting to note that the conversational skills of people with schizophrenia have received little *specific* attention from the therapeutic point of view, aside from being included in general social skills approaches (e.g. Rustin and Kuhr 1989; Mueser and Sayers 1992). Some studies that have focused on conversational skills *per se* include Urey, Laughlin and Kelly (1979), Holmes, Hansen and St. Lawrence (1984) and Wong and Woosley (1989).

Urey, Laughlin and Kelly (1979) and Holmes, Hansen and St. Lawrence (1984) showed that teaching conversational skills to higher functioning clients in after-care or partial hospitalisation programmes resulted in marked or immediate improvements in conversational behaviour. However, Wong and Woosley's (1989) attempt to re-establish conversational skills in overtly psychotic chronic schizophrenics met with variable success.

The observation that some people with schizophrenia have an awareness of their difficulties in conversing, and become frustrated by same, led to the idea that a programme targeted at increasing awareness of and promoting appropriate conversational skills may lead to improved conversational abilities and improved social relationships. This may in turn serve to reduce the frustration resulting from poor communication in some schizophrenic speakers. Implementing such a programme would also give the author a forum for exploring this apparent metacommunicative ability, while at the same time observing the conversational skills of this population in a group situation. The following is a brief outline of the implementation of a conversational skills programme in a day centre for people with a mental illness.

Method

PARTICIPANTS

A group of seven clients, who were already involved in group work in a day socialisation programme, were invited to participate in a conversational skills group to be run once a week for seven weeks. The group consisted of three females and four males. Of the seven participants, five lived in supervised hostel accommodation with the remaining two living independently in flats. All but one of the clients had a diagnosis of chronic schizophrenia, mostly presenting with negative symptoms (i.e. in terms of communication, displayed poverty of speech, poverty of content of speech, increased latency of response, etc). The age range of the clients was 43–65 years, with a mean age of 50 years.

PROGRAMME STRUCTURE

The length of the weekly sessions depended on the group members' attention span but usually lasted for approximately one hour with a short break included.

The author, a careworker and a student nurse led the group. An outline of the programme follows:

Session 1: Introduction to conversational skills.

Session 2: Co-operation in conversation.

Session 3: Listening skills.

Session 4: Initiating conversations; answering and responding.

Session 5: Turn-taking and conversational breakdown and repair.

Session 6: Maintaining, changing and terminating topic.

Session 7: Summary and evaluation.

SESSION PLAN

Each session began with an introductory discussion on one of the above themes, for example turn-taking. The introductory discussion was then followed by group activities that focused on that theme – enabling the participants to practise skills, for example repairing conversation or coping with interruptions. Each session concluded with a summary of the main points covered and further group discussion. An outline of a sample session is included in Appendix 1 (p.112). Thus the general thrust of the group was to talk about what is involved in conversational interactions, using activities to reinforce ideas being presented.

FRAMEWORK FOR INTERPRETATION OF FINDINGS

Interesting outcomes of the programme can be presented within the organisational framework put forward by Roth and Spekman (1984), as discussed in the previous chapter. This was originally designed for the assessment of pragmatic abilities in children and is a useful framework for looking at conversational abilities in particular or pragmatic abilities in general. The framework encompasses: Social Organisation of Discourse, Preupposition and Communicative Intent. Before discussing preliminary findings within this framework, a brief description of each level is given along with examples of group activities/tasks that were used as probes:

SOCIAL ORGANISATION OF DISCOURSE

This aspect of conversation involves the ability to engage in dyadic or multi-party talk. Such skills include the ability to turn-take, initiate, maintain and terminate topics, and to repair conversational breakdowns when they occur. Conversational interactions thus require the participant to function both as speaker and listener, assuming the responsibilities of both roles. Roth and Spekman describe this area as focusing on the 'dynamics and reciprocal nature of an ongoing social interaction'.

People with schizophrenia have difficulties with most of the areas included under this heading. As can be seen from the course outline, this area formed an integral part of the conversational skills programme. Activities included those that focused on turn-taking, conversational initiations, roles of speaker and listener and coping with interruptions. Requesting clarification of ambiguous utterances spoken out of context (e.g.'There's nothing in it' or 'She said she had to go now') was also included as a task. Examples of target items are given in Appendix 2 (pp.113–114).

PRESUPPOSITION

Included in this area of conversational interaction is the the ability to take the listener's needs into account in the conversational interaction. The ability to presuppose entails the ability to infer and make predictions about the listener's information needs in the interaction (i.e. what information is already shared and what is new). Making a message accurate and adequate requires consideration of the following: How much does the listener need to know? How much does the listener know already?

A person with schizophrenia may say to a stranger 'Jack's back today', expecting the listener to understand the message. Unless there is shared knowledge between the speaker and listener, this message will lead to a conversational breakdown because of the speaker's inability to presuppose and make appropriate inferences regarding shared knowledge and partner's needs (e.g. Who is Jack? and Where was he?). In other words, the speaker would not have given enough or adequate information for the message to be fully understood by the listener unless the context was previously known to both speaker *and* listener.

This aspect of conversational interaction was explored within the group programme through role-taking and problem-solving tasks which involved the ability to make appropriate inferences in differing contexts. Referential communication tasks were also undertaken to investigate the participants' ability to give enough, and adequate, information to their listener in a dyadic interaction. Referential communication has been described by Bowman (1984 cited in Bunce 1989) as 'the ability to select and verbally code the characteristics or attributes of a given referent(object or action) in a manner that will enable a listener to accurately identify that referent' (p.93).

The tasks involved a speaker describing simple and complex designs to a listener who had to replicate the design relying only on the verbal directions of the speaker. Giving directions from a map was another format used for this task (See Appendix 3, p.115).

COMMUNICATIVE INTENTION

Communicative intent involves the intention a speaker wishes to convey and would include, for example, the ability to request, protest, state, promise, greet or direct the behaviour of others (Roth and Spekman 1984). Conveying intent means being able 'to do things with words', in terms of the speaker's ability to convey his or her message meaningfully in what is known as direct or indirect speech acts (Austin 1962; Searle 1969).

Group activities, which focused on the above abilities, included tasks which involved the recognition of the intent of others, in terms of responding to indirect speech acts in appropriate and inappropriate ways. For example, the participants were required to respond appropriately and inappropriately to utterances such as: 'I'm really fed up today' or 'Oh dear it's raining and I have no umbrella'. Other tasks involved responding to 'good' versus 'bad' news, for example 'I've just won the lotto' or 'My flat was broken into last night' (See Appendix 4, p.116).

Results

The following is not a session-by-session evaluation of the programme. Rather, it is an overview of the responses of the group members to different tasks presented during the course. Of particular note was the variability of performance, both within individuals and across group members, throughout the sessions. Before outlining some preliminary findings within the above framework, the presence of an apparent degree of metacommunicative awareness among group members is worth commenting upon.

Members displayed a degree of metacommunicative awareness, for example in expressing their conversational difficulties and in coming up with solutions to questions about conversation which were posed to them. It is interesting to note the group's responses to the following questions (which were posed as part of the introduction to the course): Do you have difficulties in trying to make conversation with people? If so, what are these difficulties?

The following conversational difficulties were reported by the group:

- a difficulty in putting points across in conversation, leading to anger and frustration

- a difficulty knowing what to say or what to start talking about

- a tendency to 'dry up' in conversation, with difficulties in keeping the conversation going

- easily losing track of conversation

- people turning away or ignoring you when attempting to initiate a conversation

- problems in using the telephone as a means of communication.

The above responses provided interesting discussion material and thus served as an appropriate starting point for the programme.

PRELIMINARY FINDINGS
SOCIAL ORGANISATION OF DISCOURSE

The turn-taking skills of the group members improved during activities as they began to show some understanding of the roles of speaker and listener following discussions of same. The author is aware that turn-taking in a planned group situation is very different from that of a dyadic, spontaneous conversation but group activities and discussion proved useful to highlight what was involved in the turn-taking process, as applied to conversational interactions. Group members also had ideas on how to initiate a conversation (e.g. in a coffee shop) – examples of conversational initiations included: 'I was dying for that cup of coffee' or 'How's it going?' Group members also recognised the importance of greeting people in an appropriate manner because 'it breaks a barrier'. Using the listener's name while conversing was also seen as important because, according to one member, it 'may sound aggressive if you don't but sounds friendly if you do'. Attempting to repair conversations through requests for clarification proved a difficult task for the group members. For example, requesting clarification of the ambiguous utterance 'There's nothing in it' rendered the following response 'I know'. Many of the responses given to each stimulus item were inappropriate and didn't serve as a request for clarification. For further examples of responses see Appendix 2 (pp.113–114).

PRESUPPOSITION

Group members had no difficulty drawing inferences from pictures of hypothetical problem situations and were able to predict appropriately what the people might be saying or thinking in the situation presented in the picture (See examples in Appendix 3, p.115). A simple referential communication task (e.g. describing a simple design to another) posed no difficulties for members, but when the task increased in complexity, their skills broke down – they had difficulty in providing accurate and adequate information for the listener. Giving directions on a map to another posed some difficulties and showed inconsistencies in marking referents and use of cohesive ties, though self-monitoring of a message was apparent in one example: 'Start at the bottom. I want you to go up this road, the straight road, the Link road; go straight through; go up all the way; turn left, no right you'll find a fish and chip shop there'.

COMMUNICATIVE INTENT

Recognising the communicative intent of others, in terms of responding to indirect speech acts, was not a problem for the group members – in fact they were able to give responses that they considered would be appropriate and inappropriate in certain situations. For example, in response to the utterance

'Oh dear it's raining and I have no umbrella', the appropriate responses were given as 'Share mine' or 'Put up your hood' while the inappropriate ones were 'Tough!' or 'Buy one!' Likewise, they had little difficulty in responding appropriately to 'good' and 'bad' news (see Appendix 4, p.116).

Discussion

This informal conversational skills group enabled the author to explore the apparent metacommunicative awareness present in some people with schizophrenia and observe conversational skills of this client group in general. A notable feature of the group members was the extreme variability in performance both across group members and within individual's performance from session to session.

The group were able to talk about conversation in general, displaying a level of metacommunicative awareness. They had little difficulty in coping with many of the activities involving conversational role-taking, for example turn-taking, initiating conversations, coping with interruptions and interpreting communicative intent. Difficulties were noted in requesting clarification of ambiguous utterances to avoid conversational breakdown and performing more complex referential communication tasks (i.e. being unable to provide adequate and accurate information for the listener, thus failing to take listener's needs into account). The possibility that this latter difficulty could be attributed to a lack of a *theory of mind* in schizophrenic speakers may be considered (see Frith 1994 and this volume). However, further exploration of these apparent difficulties in requesting clarification, and in referential communication, might enhance our understanding of the causes of conversational breakdowns in schizophrenic communication.

An obvious limitation of the study is the fact that although members of the group participated well and seem to gain from being involved in the conversational skills group, the prognosis for carry-over of such skills, worked on in group activities, may be poor. As Frith predicts: 'patients with negative signs should perform well with tasks in which responses are largely specified by the experimenter. They should perform badly when there is no such specification even if the actual responses required are the same' (1992, p.43). Another limitation was the fact that participants were chosen solely on the basis of being involved in other group programmes together and thus were not required to meet any selection criteria for this conversational skills group. A group of clients who show an obvious level of awareness of their difficulties may be targeted specifically in a future study.

Conclusions

Some people with schizophrenia seem to display a level of awareness of their conversational difficulties. This apparent metacommunicative awareness can be used as a starting point to explore the conversational difficulties of people with schizophrenia.

Despite its limitations, an informal group situation is a more natural way of carrying out such exploration in terms of facilitating discussion around conversational difficulties and practising conversational skills through group activities. Thus, a programme targeted at increasing awareness of, and promoting, appropriate conversational skills may lead to improved conversational interactions. More specifically, working on the ability to self-monitor, coupled with working on increasing the awareness of listener's needs in conversation, may enable the person with schizophrenia to engage in more successful conversational interactions.

Finally, a group situation enables the therapist to gain greater insight into the complex nature of the conversational difficulties of this population and, in so doing, define a role for the speech and language therapist in rehabilitation. Such involvement also enables the therapist to witness the extreme variability of performances not only across individuals in the group but also within individuals across time, for, as Lieberman (1982) quoted in Wong and Woolsey (1989) states, 'The only reliable characteristic of schizophrenia is its variability'.

APPENDIX 1

Sample Session

Session 5: Turn-taking and Conversational Breakdown and Repair

Introductory discussion: What is involved in conversational turn-taking? Speaker and listener roles in turn-taking; simultaneous talk; eye gaze in turn-taking; conversational breakdown; conversational repair; responding to interruptions.

Group Activities to promote turn-taking skills and awareness of factors leading to conversational breakdown; practise of strategies to repair breakdowns.

Points for further discussion:

Why is it necessary to turn-take in conversational interaction?

What happens when speakers speak at the same time?

How do we indicate that we would like to contribute to the conversation?

How do we repair a conversation once it has broken down because of a misunderstanding for example?

Why should we attempt to repair conversational breakdowns?

How do we cope with interruptions?

What does it feel like like to be interrupted (a) once or twice (b) repeatedly?

APPENDIX 2

Organisation of Discourse

Roles of speaker and listener:

Task:

'What do we do as a listener?'

'What do we do as a speaker?'

Responses:

As listener: talk back to speaker, look at speaker, use facial expression to show interest/disinterest, sigh, fidget if disinterested, show 'sparkling eyes' if interested.

As speaker: ask about other person, show interest in them.

Use of person's name in conversation:

Task:

eliciting responses to the question 'Why it was important to use a person's name during a conversation?'

Responses:

'Gives person an identity'

'A sign of friendship'

'May sound aggressive if you don't but sounds friendly if you do'

'A sign of courtesy'.

Conversational Initiation:

Task:

Eliciting initiations from group in response to the question 'How might you start up a conversation with someone, for example in a coffee shop?'

Responses:

'Nice day'   'Are you doing a bit?'

'How's it going?'   'Do you mind if I smoke?'

'I was dying for that cup of coffee'

'What did you think of the match?'

Importance of greeting:

Task:

Eliciting ideas from the group in response to the question 'Why is it important to greet people?'

Responses:

'Breaks a barrier'

'Helps you get to know the person or to find out about them'

Conversational Repair:

Task:

Following a greeting, each member was given an ambiguous/confusing utterance, out of context, that could lead to conversational breakdown. The members were encouraged to respond with request for clarification. One model was given.

Stimulus: 'I just didn't know what to do'
Responses: 'Neither did I'; 'Explain yourself'

Stimulus: 'That one over there is nice'.
Responses: 'What's nice?'; 'So are you'. Others: 'Don't know.'

Stimulus: 'There's nothing in it'
Responses: 'Nothing in what?'; 'I know'

Stimulus: 'She didn't give a damn'
Responses: 'How do you spell damn?'; '...about me not feeling very well'

Stimulus: 'I just gave up!'
Responses: 'Gave up on what?'; 'Hope. Gave up hope on the clients'

Stimulus: 'She said she had to go now.'
Responses: 'Bye!'

Role play tasks were also carried out which focused on interrupting and responding to interruptions.

APPENDIX 3

Presupposition

Problem solving – making inferences, role taking:

Tasks:

Pictures of problem situations; What might the person be saying or thinking?

Stimulus:	Woman who has no umbrella standing beside a woman who has an umbrella and it starts to rain.
Response:	'I think it's raining'; 'I forgot my umbrella'; 'Can I stand under it?'

Stimulus:	Woman waiting in a queue to use a telephone
Response:	'Oh I wish she'd hurry up!'

Stimulus:	Woman in a flower shop holding up two bunches of flowers and trying to make a choice.
Response:	'Oh my God which one will I pick'.

Stimulus:	Customer in a drycleaners passing garment to assistant; customer has a broken arm
Response:	'Oh god help you I'll clean that for you.'

Referential Communication: i.e.

Tasks:

(a) describing simple designs (simple shapes using three primary colours)

(b) describing more complex designs

(c) giving directions from simple street map to another who has to rely on verbal directions *only*.

Responses:

e.g. 'Start at the bottom. I want to go up this road, the straight road, the Link Road; go straight through; go up all the way; turn left, no right you'll find a fish and chip shop there'

e.g. 'Go up to the Link road then you go up to the pedestrian walkway; go up to the top and turn right; turn right.'

APPENDIX 4

Communicative Intent

(i) Activity focused on recognising the intent of others; responding to indirect speech acts (a) appropriately and (b) inappropriately.

Stimulus: 'I'm really fed up to day'

Responses: OK (appropriate): 'Are you in bad form?'; 'What has you fed up?'; Not OK (inappropriate): 'Pull yourself together'; 'Tough!'; 'Cop on!'

Stimulus: 'I'd love to go for a walk'

Responses: OK: 'Wear my summer clothes'; 'Go to the park' Not OK: 'Take a hike'; 'Suit yourself'

Stimulus: 'Oh dear it's raining and I have no umbrella'

Responses: OK: 'Put up your hood'; 'Share mine'; Not OK: 'Tough!' 'Buy one!'

Stimulus: 'I'm lost'

Responses: OK: 'Look at your map'; 'Ask a policeman' Not OK: 'Softie!' 'Tough!'

(ii) Another activity focused on the ability to respond appropriately to GOOD vs BAD news.

e.g. 'I won the lotto'; 'My flat was broken into last night'

Responses: e.g. 'That's great'; 'Oh you poor thing'

CHAPTER 11

Semantic Pragmatic Disorder and the Role of the Speech and Language Therapist in Psychiatry

Niki Muir

Introduction

The role of the speech and language therapist working in psychiatry is a comparatively recent one. A major difficulty experienced by small professions, such as speech and language therapy, is that of being very thinly spread across generalist as well as specialist fields in both paediatric and adult services. This is particularly the case for a small professional group which takes as its brief the broadest of all human cognitive and behavioural skills – namely, communication – meaning that the areas into which the profession could justifiably spread are endless. For those speech and language therapists who have worked in psychiatric settings for some time, the role seems to be indisputable but, as yet, this specialism within the profession is only at the very early stages of producing the academic and research-based proof to substantiate this claim.

In order to reach a diagnosis of mental state, communication is observed and assessed. Yet once that diagnosis has been arrived at it is still common practice to concentrate on pharmacological and activity-based models of care. The author would suggest that input specifically aimed at management of communication can add a significant other dimension (Muir, Tanner and France 1991). Another problem with being a small specialism within a small profession is that it falls to those therapists who have chosen to work in psychiatric settings to publicise the role, carry out research and publishing, undertake the vital inter-disciplinary networking and develop the skills of others against a background of other people's beliefs that the main function of a mental health speech and language therapist is either to help people talk 'properly' or to stop clients swearing! Speech and language therapists undeniably have a helpful role to play in psychiatry based on the strength and breadth of the four-year degree course – of which, central to the training are the three core studies of psychology, neurology and linguistics – and it could thus be argued that this makes the profession well placed to offer an input to diagnosis and management, as well as to research and education. Mental illness states are still like a jigsaw puzzle, as many theories abound and the behaviours of clients are, unsurprisingly, as varied as the human personality itself. Speech and language therapists can contribute vital pieces to the puzzle and our experiences can, perhaps, extend the theories. Although the case-loads of most therapists working in psychiatry will include clients from all the current major classifications (DSM IV), as well as those with mixed diagnoses and co-existing pathologies, this chapter will confine itself mainly to looking at the specific role of the speech and language therapist in one mental illness state: schizophrenia.

The Role of the Speech and Language Therapist

Speech and language therapists are trained to listen and to de-code and reconstruct deteriorated language and degraded speech. These skills have been demonstrated clearly in the study carried out by Faber, Abrams and Taylor (1983), which compared schizophrenics with formal thought disorder with neurologically impaired patients with Aphasia – as has an MSc dissertation by a speech and language therapist working in psychiatry (Tanner 1987). In this, the reconstructive skills for schizophrenic discourse of general nurses, psychiatric nurses, generalist speech and language therapists and speech and language therapists working in psychiatry were tested and compared. Both groups of speech and language therapists came out significantly higher, with the group having experience of working with psychiatric clients, unsurprisingly, at the top. Speech and language therapists are also going to be involved with studying receptive language skills, which could be very helpful in correctly targeting the level of understanding and evaluating output behaviours in the mentally ill patient. This role in itself will redress the over-weighting of emphasis generally placed on output. The following table may give some indication of the way in which most speech and language therapists might break down communication into component parts which would be assessed separately and treated both separately and in combination.

Semantic Pragmatic Disorder

In all areas of the speech and language therapy profession there has been recent emphasis on the aetiology and management of semantic pragmatic disorder (Shields 1991; Lesser and Milroy 1993). We have been mooted in assisting people to acquire, or to regain, the various elements of the wide-ranging instrument of communication and are now increasingly aware that semantic

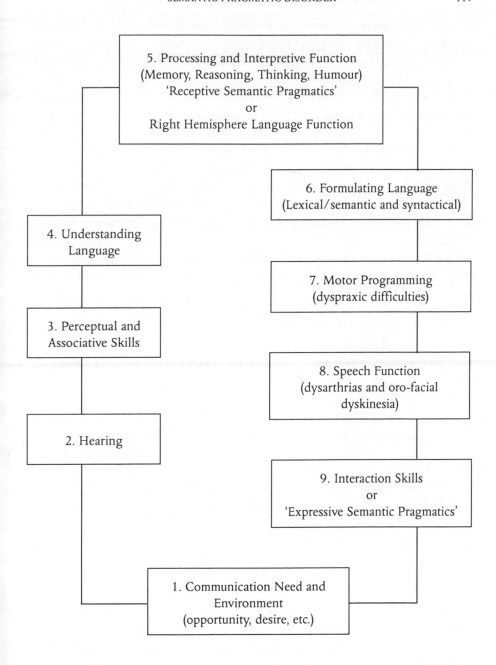

Source: Niki Muir 1995

Figure 11.1 Communication chain

pragmatics are what give our communication colour, depth and truly interactive properties (Leach 1983). Eugen Bleuler (1911) discussed the presence of early character anomalies, many of which could be said to relate to communicative isolation. This might point to what a speech and language therapist would now describe as being on the continuum of semantic pragmatic disorder. Also, some of Laing and Esterson's theories (1970), particularly in relation to parent–child interaction and the presence of impaired cognitive functioning, could also be seen as neurolinguistic or pragmatic functioning. The Medical Research Council (MRC) follow-up studies by Dr Peter Jones *et al.* (1994) and other longitudinal studies, such as the National Child Development Survey (Done *et al.* 1994), are providing clear evidence that behavioural disturbances, detectable at an early age, are likely antecedents of schizophrenia in significant numbers. Amongst the antecedent behaviours of interest to speech and language therapists must be those that we would describe as delayed milestones in speech and language development, for example slowness in talking, solitary and uncommunicative play, over-communicating and even voice and fluency problems. Irene Walsh endorses this view in Chapter 10. The subjective experience of many speech and language therapists practising in psychiatry and working with people with schizophrenia would bear out her findings. The question this information would seem to pose might be: is unresolved semantic pragmatic disorder a possible precursor to, or marker for, some psychotic illnesses?

At a recent symposium in Nottingham, Chadwick and Trower (1994) presented some of their new theories of schizophrenia – derived to some extent from a further look at R.D. Laing's work. One theory related to a model of 'the self' in people with schizophrenia resulting from lowered self-esteem. There is reason to contest that a contributory factor in the development of lowered self-esteem is the addition of a long history of communicative failure, constantly reinforced by family and peers, as well as, most importantly, from within the self. If people are missing the subtleties of communication due to inadequately developed skills and are feeling distanced in interactions, both external and internal, feedback regarding self-worth may become increasingly negative and even punitive.

Understandable interest is being shown in the results of all the imaging work done over the last few years and in the theories put forward by, amongst others, Frith (1992) and Crow (1993), particularly with regard to auditory association anomalies and deviance of inner thought processes as well as to the involvement of the right hemisphere (Cutting 1990). It could perhaps be argued, from an eclectic point of view, that much is linking the evidence and the ideas and the theories of schizophrenia and one link – or perhaps one predisposing factor for a number of sufferers of this complex illness – is that of unresolved developmental communication delay, compounded by personal psychosocial circumstance.

The following represents one way in which speech and language therapists view semantic pragmatic disorder in relation to schizophrenia. Roth and Spekman (1984) indicate that a Pragmatic approach offers a way of making informed judgements on the social and contextual use of communication skills, that is the functional aspects of an individual's linguistic and interpersonal skills. The three main areas for consideration are those of Communicative intent, Presupposition and Discourse.

Communicative Intent

Communicative intent may be described as the message contained *within* a given part of a conversation and not just the message conveyed by the linguistic / semantic form of the sentence. There are both range and forms of communicative intent; these will be verbal as well as non-verbal and some aspects to consider are set out in Table 11.1.

Table 11.1 Range of communicative intentions

- ° Attention seeking – for self or for an object
- ° Protesting, Denying, Rejecting
- ° Requesting Action
- ° Requesting Information
- ° Responding to Requests
- ° Stating or Commenting
- ° Conversational Devices
- ° Greeting

Forms of Communicative Intention

- ° Tone of voice
- ° Gesture
- ° Facial Expression
- ° Body Posture
- ° Proximity
- ° Prosody

Source: Niki Muir 1995

Presupposition

Presupposition can be said to be the ability to take the other person's perspective in a conversation and to make judgements based on their reasoning and belief systems and not on one's own. This enables us to deal with the level of meaning which is only implied or metaphorical and could, therefore, be seen as a function of the right hemisphere (Cutting 1990). Presupposition relies on shared knowledge of a person and of the world and our environment, shared experiences, awareness of physical context and awareness of differing social contexts, for example those dictated by age, status, familiarity, social setting, etc. Good presupposition skills allow for the prevention of ambiguity – when intent belies content. They also allow for the explicit use of implicit information and thus for relationship building and moving a conversation along comfortably.

Discourse

Discourse, in the context of analysis of the communication of people with schizophrenia, is focusing on what actually takes place when the person attempts to communicate. It could be said to be viewing communication within imaginary or real life contexts in which meanings are negotiated between the participants and would look at the flow and change of roles between speaker and listener. The major areas of discourse which would require analysis in schizophrenia are laid out in Table 11.2.

Table 11.2 Discourse analysis

- Attention
- Listening
- Monitoring (in particular, self-monitoring)
- Turn-taking
- Initiating and Responding
- Topic Maintenance
- Recognition of Conversational Breakdown
- Ability to activate Conversational Repair strategies.

Source: Niki Muir 1995

Assessment

Assessment of the semantic pragmatic elements of the communication of clients could be based on looking at communicative intent, presupposition and discourse in some detail. In order to obtain information, use would be made of observation, structured questioning and interaction, questionnaires, checklists and audio and video recording as well as sub-tests of some formal language assessments. The value in encouraging the client to undertake a little self-rating should be mentioned, particularly since this may help them set goals and, later, measure change. For *Communicative Intent,* one would wish to know first the range and appropriateness of the intents, how frequently they are demonstrated and how different and marked they are and second how appropriate are the client's responses to the range of communicative intents directed at them and does social context affect the range and/or the form of the intent that the client is using. Finally, some judgements need to be made on the general effectiveness of the client's ability to communicate intent – does it fluctuate? Is it situation or even person dependant?

In the case of *Presuppositions* the speech and language therapist would look at what might be called 'Right Hemisphere' language functions (Bryan 1988), for example inferential thinking skills (both verbal and non-verbal), ability to refer to abstract concepts rather than demonstrating concrete thinking and the use and processing of metaphor, humour and logical reasoning. Also, in this area of making judgements on presupposition skills, the therapist would need to consider the effect of differing social contexts on the client – can they adjust communicative styles of interaction and can they regulate appropriateness? If so, how is the client able to imply information across a range of social contexts? When undertaking observations, the clinician should also consider whether the client can take into account the experiences of the listener and whether they are retaining information from past encounters with that person or constantly going over old ground. Finally, assessment of presupposition should, in the author's view, elicit whether the client is using personal knowledge of the world, and past experiences, to gain full understanding of an incomplete message; is the client getting distracted by irrelevancies and sub-themes, rather than being able to extract the key information from an utterance? and can the client carry their side of a communicative interchange and their responsibility in a social situation?

Discourse analysis is naturally going to be an expanded science if undertaken by a linguist but, in the main, speech and language therapists will look at whether there is initiation of conversation and if it is appropriate in form and content, if there is an ability to introduce new topics and to cope with such introductions of new subject matter if others do it, are cohesive ties present between the elements of the conversation? Is there recognition of communicative breakdown on the part of the client? When it occurs, is there any use of repair strategies and, if so, of what type? Is there use of verbal and non-verbal turn-taking and interruption techniques and, if any are present, what type are being employed and how appropriately are they being used and responded to if used by others? A measure of the client's ability to respond to, follow and extend topics introduced by others in an appropriate way is required – as is a measure of their ability to close a conversation and respond to signals from other participants that an interaction should be closed and a monologue brought to an end. Finally, in all areas of discourse analysis, evaluation is needed as to whether the client is actually failing to produce these behaviours because they choose not to, have insufficient opportunity to do so, are moving towards an acute psychotic phase or have co-existing perceptual or comprehension deficits prompting investigation via formal assessment measures.

Findings

Several years of exposure to the unique communication of people with schizophrenia have led the author to offer Table 11.3 as a possible description of some of the main features, consistently revealed by assessment practices, of what might be described as the semantic pragmatic disorder that can be found in schizophrenia.

Table 11.3 Disordered pragmatic features of schizophrenic speech

- Confuses object/action/event and may have delayed or failed acquisition of such words
- Fails in verbal and sometimes non-verbal expressive behaviours
- Comprehension problems at a variety of levels
- Misinterprets situational cues
- Remarks are not semantically contingent upon previous utterances by self or partner/s but are tangential
- Preposition and/or pronoun problems
- Uses better language in test or teaching situations than socially
- Word finding difficulties
- Neologisms other than for fun
- Difficulties in initiating, maintaining, changing or closing topics
- Insensitivity to the listener
- Perseveration
- Echolalia
- Lack of repair strategies
- Poor turn-taking ability
- Problems with being category specific – both given and new
- Attention to unimportant aspects of communication

Source: Niki Muir 1995

Therapeutic Management

Speech and language therapists in this specialised area are likely to offer therapy within a cognitive behavioural framework (Alladin 1988) since this is rewarding for the client, provides encouragement and seems to assure reasonable compliance and comprehension. By increasing the client's grasp of a problem in verbal terms, this approach seems to improve insight and allow new and changing patterns of communicative behaviour to generalise and be carried over to situations outside those discussed and practised in therapy. Therapeutic management will often involve counselling and, for those therapists who have dual training, there may be aspects of dynamic psychotherapy. There will also be significant use of traditional speech and language therapy techniques for attention setting, initiating conversational repair and maximising receptive language. Therapy is likely to break down the complex skills of social interaction and then plan to re-integrate them. Major target areas for a rehabilitation client group, for example, would be along the lines of Table 11.4.

Table 11.4 Target Areas for Speech and Language Therapy Intervention

- attentiveness
- gaining attention
- sharing perceptions of an interaction
- turn-taking
- interpreting
- guessing
- timing contributions
- integrating non-verbal components
- constructing sentences
- task analysis
- problem solving
- coping strategies
- reference to past interactions
- planning for future interactions
- goal setting
- vocal skills practice

Source: Niki Muir 1995

Each of these target areas would likely be taught by direct instruction and also by providing experience of high-quality interaction and by role play (particularly observing the role play of the therapist). The aim of therapy would be to facilitate clients in becoming more effective communicators in a general sense, rather than people who are skilled in producing drilled components of communicative ability, with the emphasis on listening and self-monitoring. Therapeutic aims might not always be wholly achievable but a limited, but generalised use with insight on the client's part, will be preferable to extensive forced production. It could be said that increased insight, increased confidence and communicative assertiveness, coupled with improved self-monitoring and self-esteem, are the key issues for the majority of clients. As one said (when hearing himself on tape): 'who's that bloke? I can't understand a word he's saying' followed, after a period of therapy, by: 'he's speaking too fast, too loud and he keeps repeating what he's saying. I can tell him to slow down and to calm down now, he's doing much better and likes talking a bit better now'. That statement seems to be a validation of the role of speech and language therapy in psychiatry and one which can hopefully be borne out objectively as the profession finds opportunities for the research needed in this area to support the growing body of anecdotal and empirical evidence.

CHAPTER 12

Applying Personal Construct Psychology
Communication Skills Groups for People with Mental Health Problems

Carmel Hayes

Introduction

The aim of this chapter is to describe how Personal Construct Psychology (PCP) can contribute to group therapy aimed at developing the communicative potential of clients with mental health problems. This approach is chosen because, as Dalton (1987) reminds us: 'PCP is an approach to people and as such can help us in our work with any client. Our wish to understand our client's views and something of the ways in which they set about construing what is happening to them remains the same, whatever their problem' (p.59). This chapter is based on the experience of a team of speech and language therapists working originally in a psychiatric institution and now with clients with mental health problems in the community. In addition, it owes much to the writing of those using PCP in the fields of stuttering therapy (e.g. Fransella and Dalton) and social skills work (e.g. Winter and Bannister).

Communicative competence is often the yardstick for measuring the quality of interpersonal relationships and is necessary to fulfil three human needs:

1. identity: a sense of belonging to a group and having a feeling of involvement and acknowledgement.

2. control: ability to initiate action and respond to others and to determine to whom we speak and what we say.

3. acceptance: the desire to make friends and be liked, to fit in and be accepted. (Schutz 1988).

However, it has been suggested that seven per cent of the 'normal' population have fairly serious difficulties with social behaviour and, therefore, skill in

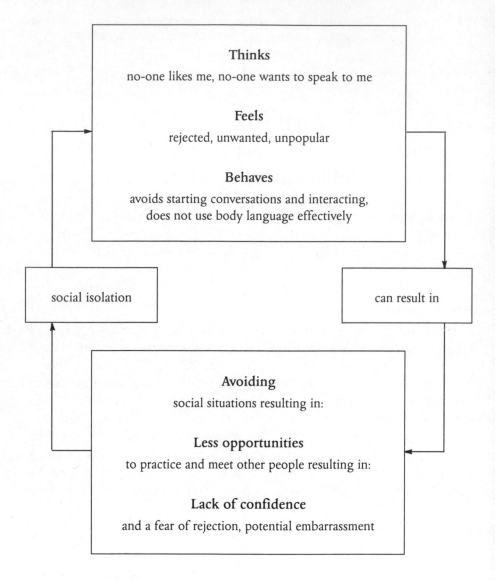

Source: Hutchings *et al.* 1991

Figure 12.1 The social isolation cycle

communicating is not something that should be taken for granted (Argyle 1981).

The effects of mental illness on communication can be of an infinite variety. Reusch (1987) states that 'almost all phenomena included under the traditional heading of psychopathology are disturbances of communication.' All aspects of speech and language, non-verbal communication and pragmatics can be effected. Institutionalisation can also have profound effects on clients: they can become passive, withdrawn and dependent – all of which can be reflected in a person's communication or lack of it. Typical communication difficulties presented by clients include a limited repertoire of verbal and non-verbal communication skills, stereotyped responses, negative images of themselves as effective communicators, reduced number of social contacts and settings, lack of regular, positive feedback from significant others, lack of confidence in their ability to communicate and reduced awareness of how to present themselves to others, anxiety in social situations and a lack of insight into others' communicative intent. Clients therefore find it very difficult to relate to others, often failing to establish friendships or form lasting interpersonal relationships. Many people with mental health problems have had many unproductive communication experiences and have become caught up in the 'social isolation cycle.' Once inside this cycle, it is very difficult for them to break out and seek social and personal development. This is illustrated in Figure 12.1.

It would seem to follow that the most suitable format of treatment for these clients is within a group setting, so that social and communication skills can be developed (Muir 1992).

Winter (1985) describes the what he terms the Skills Deficit Model – an approach to treatment which involves teaching clients social skills as one would teach any motor skill. In this model, 'shy' or 'socially inadequate' behaviour is seen as a behavioural deficit. The client is viewed as either having failed to learn appropriate social behaviours and rules or as having had his learning disrupted in some way, that is he has learned inappropriate behaviours. The aim of therapy then becomes one of training the client in the lacking skills and reinforcing and rewarding improved performance, hopefully resulting in the client gaining competence and, from this, confidence.

Such social skills training can be very useful. However, for many clients its benefits have often proved limited and/or short-lived. While there are some clients who lack a range of communication skills and, therefore, *need* to develop basic skills, there are also many clients for whom the problem lies more in putting their already competent skills into practice. For them, the difficulty appears to lie more in their perceptions of themselves as communicators and the options available to them, that is the meaning that confidence, competence or opportunity holds for them. Clearly, for these clients, something more than the acquisition of behavioural skills is required. This 'something' needs to be a framework which acknowledges the importance of understanding the person as a whole before attempting to modify one aspect of their behaviour, in this case communication.

The Theory

This is not intended to be a comprehensive account of the theory of PCP as it is covered excellently in many texts, among them Burr and Butt (1992) and Fransella and Dalton (1990).

PCP is essentially a theory of personality. For Kelly (1955), human beings are complete and are not divided up into emotions, thoughts, motives, desires and perceptions. According to the theory, an understanding of how people interpret events is essential to understanding why they experience things in the ways that they do. Central to the process of interpretation is the process of construing, which in turn leads to the formation of constructs. Constructs are how we make distinctions between events based on similarities and differences. A construct is a discrimination of things as being alike and yet different from others. We apply our constructs to new situations in order to help us structure our perceptions and plan how to behave. In other words, what people construe is the replication of events, that is we are looking for recurrent themes. In this way, we are constantly attempting to make sense of ourselves, other people, situations and events. Importantly for Kelly, there are always alternative ways of construing events: 'no one needs to paint himself into a corner; no one needs to be completely hemmed in by circumstances; no one needs to be the victim of his biography'. So, although there is a 'reality', no one has direct access to it. Construing is something we do and, therefore, something which we could do differently. Because the rules of our construct systems are personally created, they can be altered by personal choice also.

This leads to Kelly's second basic idea: that of Man The Scientist. He views people 'as if' we are scientists. By this he means that our behaviour is guided by the theories we hold about ourselves and others. These theories are put to the test by behaving and the facts either confirm or invalidate the theory. Theories, therefore, are open to constant revision based on the facts. Equally, the theories we hold direct attention to some facts rather than others. Thus, in this model, our behaviour becomes the experiment with which we test our theory. Behaviour is part of the process, rather than the end result. Of fundamental importance is the idea that theories or constructs are neither true nor untrue, some are simply more useful than others. 'Good' theories provide us with information we can use to help us act in relation to situations or people, 'bad' theories yield unhelpful or unsuitable information and can lead to us becoming stuck using unproductive responses or behaviours. Problems are seen as being the result of poor experiments. Therefore, the answers to questions like 'why did he do/not do this/that?' come from understanding that person's theories, how they were developed, the experiments he is prepared to test them with and what he is prepared to accept as evidence (Burr and Butt 1992).

A third important concept for Kelly is that of Anticipation. The way we construe our relationships is manifested in the way we live our relationships.

How we construe others is manifested through the way we anticipate what they will say and do, so that anticipation can encourage or even coerce people into roles that are provided for them – for example once a person is identified as aggressive, they are thought of as nothing but aggressive. It may become the main thing about them, cancelling out other qualities they may have and prescribing the way they are to be treated (Burr and Butt 1992).

PCP does not deny that a person's experiences can have a powerful impact upon their lives, but Kelly insisted that it is not the event itself but the meaning that the person extracts from their experiences that is the important ingredient. 'There is nothing either good or bad, but thinking makes it so' (Shakespeare, *Hamlet* II.2).

Implications for Personal Change

The person with a problem is seen as being 'stuck.' The way they construe life and the world around them is found to be inadequate in some way and they cannot, therefore, continue developing. 'From the standpoint of the psychology of personal constructs we may define a disorder as any personal construction which is used repeatedly in spite of consistent invalidation' (Kelly 1955, p.831). Long-standing problems are viewed as having become part of a person's construing of himself. For Kelly, the aim of therapy is to open up the personal world of experience in which the person feels stuck, so that they may find alternative ways of coping with the world of events which confronts them. The starting point is the present personally-construed world of the client (Fransella and Jones 1995). PCP is, therefore, an attractive approach when working with clients with mental health problems because of its focus on what people do rather than on what they are, which leaves open the possibility of them acting differently at another time.

Winter (1987) states that, from the PCP viewpoint, interpersonal difficulties are seen as stemming directly from a person's particular construction of their social world. It assumes that these constructions are the best available means of anticipating events and that they, and the consequent 'social skill deficit', represent the client's 'way of life.' As well as helping the client make himself more explicit and test out his existing constructions, the therapist encourages the client to explore whether alternative constructions might provide a firmer basis for anticipation. Rather than being trained in specific social skills, either behavioural or cognitive, the client will be helped to adopt a broad strategy of approaching social situations with a propositional style of construing and a concern with understanding the construction processes of others. A primary intention of such an approach is that the client will develop a more elaborated construction of the self as a socially competent person and one that carries fewer negative implications. This last point is particularly important as Winter found that, in 80 per cent of clients, social competence carried some negative implications in terms of their own constructs, that is confident, assertive extraverts were construed as likely to be selfish, uncaring, unsympathetic, hard, aggressive and dishonest. Therefore, what clients need is to develop new theories about themselves and others which would entail new ways of relating to others, not the piecemeal acquisition of behavioural skills. The therapist invites the client to consider alternative constructions rather than providing prescriptions for correct social behaviour. The PCP therapist recognises the importance of understanding that people are naturally reluctant to make any leap into the unknown, however attractive the idea may seem to them. They must first have some understanding of the implications of new roles. Using a PCP model of personal development, they can be encouraged to experiment and try on new roles, without commitment, in the hope that they may glimpse new possibilities of themselves (Butt and Bannister 1992). This contrasts with the social skills training approach, which takes at face value the client's request for change. It sees the skill as the alternative to the nothing they are doing now and does not question what clients really want to do.

The PCP therapist encourages the client to develop new and more productive theories and questions. Similarly, with a skills training approach there is an emphasis on action and experiment, but within a new theoretical framework. Problems are seen as highly rational and meaningful from the clients viewpoint and it is this viewpoint that is the focus of therapy. The client relates how things are from his or her point of view. The therapist can tell the client how he or she sees things, can raise questions and can encourage enquiry and experiment. Construct theory is essentially an educational exercise in that it encourages the asking of new questions. It recognises that people choose their courses of action, but choices are appreciated as having implications – some far reaching and threatening. Therefore, the focus is seldom, or never, simply on the training of isolated skills or the modification of isolated cognitions.

PCP and Groups

Given such an emphasis on the personal construing of individuals, what might PCP contribute to groups for the rehabilitation of communication skills?

Kelly himself suggests some advantages to working with groups: the group acts as a base for each client to develop a new, more comprehensive role (Experimentation); members can discover which of their constructs can be applied to several persons and which are applicable to only a few (Discrimination); snap judgements about people or situations can be challenged in the group situation (Pre-emptive construing); in the same way, stereotyping can be questioned when there are people present who do not fit into some pattern

(Constellatory construing) and the group provides validation and feedback, both positive and negative (Validational evidence) (Dalton and Dunnett 1990).

Fransella, as discussed by Dalton (1987) outlined a number of principles of group work in relation to the treatment of stammering. These principles are equally valid when considering communication groups for mentally ill clients. In such groups the *aim* of the group is to help clients build new concepts of themselves as competent communicators. The *emphasis* is on changing perceptions as well as behaviour in order to free the person from the constrictions of his or her old role as not being a confident or effective communicator. The *focus* of the group is on communication. Therapy is aimed at changing peoples' personal philosophy about themselves as communicators, rather than treating isolated skills, since how people see the world determines how they behave towards it. In groups, activities encourage people to elaborate many aspects of themselves, get a variety of reactions and gradually through feedback, initially from the therapist and later from peers, build this into their construing of themselves.

Groups can help clients make changes in the following areas of functioning:

Reconstruing situations: Many people with mental health problems, whose communication is ineffective or poor, approach social situations with extreme caution or anxiety. The focus is entirely on their speech performance. For such clients the difficulties are highlighted and the feelings involved are vividly experienced. They give themselves little opportunity to construe others and only focus on their own performance, that is to say the context of conversation becomes secondary. Thus social events become narrowed down to the issue of their ability to cope with their side of the interaction. They are afraid that if they have been silent or lacking in confidence many times before, they will be so again because it is the only way they know how to make the outcome predictable.

For clients who already have a basic repertoire of communication skills, therapy may be concerned with learning the rules of communication, that is asking them to actively construe communication events which they would normally not notice or ignore and in terms wider than their own performance (Dalton 1983). Such clients need to begin to consider situations more broadly and in all their aspects, for example the physical surroundings and other people and their intentions. Clients with a more limited range of skills need to first experience communication as enjoyable, so simply taking part with others and receiving positive feedback for so doing is the main aim of therapy in the initial stages.

While Kelly regarded the ability to make appropriate predictions about social situations as central to constructive personal relationships, he also emphasised anticipation of the *construing of others*. Kelly's sociality corollary basically states that relating to others involves construing how they construe things. We come to 'know' people by listening, looking and sensing how they view their worlds. If we are only concerned with our own processes we cannot get to know others or form relationships. Many people have difficulty relating in this way and, as Frith proposes in Chapter 2, all the abnormalities of communication experienced by those suffering from schizophrenia may arise because they have difficulty making inferences about the mental states of others. Van den Bergh, De Boeck and Claeys (1985) suggest that schizophrenics construe in a less precise way because only one or a few aspects are considered or others are left out of consideration in order to avoid inconsistencies. Similarly, Neimeyer (1985) proposes that people suffering from depression record, store and encode negative information about themselves and others, and that they view themselves as essentially different from others. Assumptions may therefore be made about what they believe to be others' reactions towards them, and these are often seen as only criticising or rejecting. Consequently, they restrict their view of people to self-related constructs, for example inadequacy, inferiority or lack of worth. In the same way, 'normal' people are construed as full of unshakeable confidence and able to deal with any situation, in contrast to their own perceived inability to cope, for example, with rudeness, refusals, etc. Much discussion is needed before they begin to see that there are problems of interpersonal interaction quite independent of the question of mental health problems. Part of therapy is therefore aimed at helping clients construe others more fully, rather than simply making assumptions. This process may take a long time as clients are learning to understand that others may have different points of view and concerns other than those that are of importance to the client him or herself.

Elaboration of the self involves clients in elaborating roles other than that, for example, of 'schizophrenic', 'depressive' or 'poor communicator'. This frequently involves placing the 'problem' in a more peripheral position in order to allow other aspects of the person to assume more significance in their dealings with the world and others, for example their interests, skills or values. Clients suffer from low self-esteem and experience 'failure' in all areas of their lives. They need to elaborate areas of their selves other than the problems or the deficits before they can begin to contemplate making conscious changes in their communication. Group activities encourage the elaboration of roles and the application of different constructs in a non-threatening way and in an environment where communication is highly facilitated and always fun. The activities used in groups give us detailed knowledge of how clients construe themselves and others, that is to say their personal philosophies. We use this to provide feedback and help clients to reconstrue and elaborate themselves. This is true of all groups, regardless of the level of communicative competence of members.

Reconstruing situations, construing others and elaboration of the self do not necessarily happen simultaneously. Groups tend to have a 'life' and two stages can be identified in this life. In the initial stages the focus is the formation of initial relationships. Little attempt is made to elaborate clients' construct systems, the focus being on facilitating basic communication between members. This results in the development of group cohesion and personal or social support between members. Many clients, particularly those with chronic mental health problems or the long-term institutionalised, need a prolonged period in this stage to gain confidence in being with others and to use and practise the foundation skills of communication. At this stage the facilitator is also encouraging the expression of feelings, opinions and ideas. Reinforcement is given for what people are already doing and gradually, through shaping and encouragement, change is achieved. As therapists we need to be realistic and recognise that, for this client group, many may need to remain at this stage indefinitely – perhaps simply in order to maintain their current level of skill.

Following this stage, group members may move on to clarify and discuss differences which enable the elaboration of their construct systems and understanding of others. As relationships within the group develop, each person is encouraged to contribute to the provision of feedback to others. It is important to remember that the group process may be hindered if validation is provided exclusively for an extended period. A balance between validation and feedback is essential to the personal development of members.

Thus PCP can be applied to groups with basic, intermediate or higher levels of communication skill, regardless of psychiatric diagnosis. An important consideration of groupwork is that emphasised by Dalton and Dunnett (1990) who say that 'there is a need for the emphasis to be taken off the problem shared by the members, once the reassurance and support gained through sharing has been established' (p.115). The focus widens naturally, or is never placed on the central issue or narrows and widens, depending on the issues discussed. This is reiterated by Blowers and Acinar (1995): 'in placing problems within a personal construct context it is important to focus not just on the problem but on what is not a problem' (pp.1–16). Focusing on behavioural skills or deficits alone may help maintain clients' preoccupation with themselves as speakers rather than as whole people with many other priorities and aspirations. This must be avoided if people are to develop their potential for effective communication.

Specific group activities are therefore selected according to the needs and existing communication skill of the participants. The aim is to foster elaboration of the self, reconstruing of social situations, construing others more fully and the development and use of the foundation and complex skills of communication. Clients learn to see things from each others' point of view and to clarify their views of themselves, as distinct from those of others. This may be achieved using a variety of means including: giving news and opinions, sharing memories, group discussion, problem solving, role play, pairs activities, etc. Activities are presented in a structured format, as in Figure 12.2, in order to encourage the development of cohesiveness and safety. Within this structure it is possible to create an infinite variety of activities which facilitate communication and can be adapted and varied according to the needs of participants. The range of methods or activities which can be used is infinite and will be limited only by the imagination of the therapist. Using a PCP framework within which to approach communication skills work allows the therapist to be eclectic in the choice of methods used to achieve group goals.

Group Structure

Introduction: Safe, undemanding. Facilitates cohesiveness, minimal self-disclosure and interaction.

How Feeling: Opportunity to express feelings and needs. Facilitates sharing and promotes support.

Warm-up: Simple game involving everyone. Encourages eye-contact, observation, upright posture, fun relaxation.

Core Activity: Selection of activity based on skill levels. Aim is to elicit and reinforce behaviour. Careful structure of activity important to avoid failure. Could include modelling, role-play, discussion, brainstorms, problem-solving. Feedback and evaluation by participants should be encouraged.

Fun Activity: Similar in function to warm-up but winding down. Should be fun and non-demanding.

Ending: Safe, undemanding, supportive and positive. Sets tone for next meeting.

Source: Brown and Saunders 1988
Figure 12.2 The group structure

The question remains as to whether this approach is effective. In common with therapists in other areas, we are concerned with effectiveness and measure outcomes objectively by comparing rating scales of communicative competence across a range of skills. Clients are also involved in this process and are asked to assess their own progress, that is to say their viewpoint is sought as this should, after all, be the starting point of therapy. The following represents a sample of clients' own evaluation of themselves and the groups in which they participate: 'the group helps us in rebuilding our lives by talking about and *sharing our experiences*'; 'we can *communicate more* than otherwise, that is we express our feelings in the group'; 'its *safe* to say what you think'; 'through talking with each other *we can build our confidence*'; 'we get to know each other better and *discover the things we have in common*'; 'we talk about ourselves – *the focus is on us, not on an activity or topic*'; 'in the beginning I was withdrawn and tried to hide from others, now *I feel more confident with people and can talk more*'; 'people listen to each other and so I feel that *others know me better and understand me more now*'.

It can be seen that this experiential modality can have a powerful effect in helping people explore, state and make change.

Summary

It could be said that PCP is another construction with no more right to the label of 'truth' than any other (Burr and Butt 1992). Speech and Language Therapists working in psychiatry believe it often has more usefulness. PCP gives the therapist a clear, consistent and useful framework applicable to the difficulties in communication and with change encountered by clients. This approach is essentially empowering: the client is seen as capable of taking responsibility for himself rather than as someone needing to be 'cured.' PCP is essentially a humanising and holistic approach in that the focus is the clients' view of the world rather than the teaching of new skills. The therapist attempts to try and understand the client by entering into his world and taking him seriously, thus allowing for communication on more common ground. The client is seen as trying to make sense of his experiences and the therapist as helping him to achieve some understanding of himself and others. It enables the therapist to see refusal to co-operate not as resistance or bloody-mindedness but rather to look at what important constructions of the client are being threatened. The PCP framework allows for eclecticism as regards which therapy techniques can be used and allows for the use of techniques from other approaches. PCP is also a reflexive theory, therefore we can use it to look at ourselves as therapists and the theories we hold about clients and change. Finally, PCP can be a non-confrontational alternative to other 'talking' therapeutic interventions.

The concern of some, that PCP can only be used with 'intellectual' clients, can be answered by pointing out that exploration and reconstruction can proceed without a mention of a construct or a single reference to roles or processes. Likewise, the suggestion that we are dabbling in areas that not the province of the Speech and Language Therapist is answered by the belief that the person is our province. If we are to help someone make communicative change, then the more we understand of the way in which his or her world is construed the more likely we are to be able to suit the therapy we offer to individual needs and less likely to impose our own beliefs and models of improvement.

CHAPTER 13

Neuro Linguistic Programming as an Experiential Constructivist Therapy for Semantic Pragmatic Disorder

Laurie Macdonald

Psychotherapy has been used as a form of rehabilitation with patients who have a schizophrenic type of illness for many years with varying degrees of success (Birchwood, Hallet and Preston 1988). The variations in impact from psycho therapy require careful analysis as it is important to determine the causes of its success or failure. This has become increasingly important over the last 20 to 30 years as psychotherapies involving different processes, compared to the more traditional analytic therapies, have become more widely used. It may prove to be that those patients with a schizophrenic-type illness find therapies that take a more focused approach than the traditional types are more accessible and useful for them. One such therapy is Neuro Linguistic Programming (NLP).

NLP is an experiential constructivist therapy because the emphasis of the therapy is towards understanding the process by which a person understands his world, rather than the content of his understanding. NLP tends to ask the question 'How?' rather than 'Why?', 'How do you generate that behaviour?' rather than 'Why do you behave like that?' or 'How did you arrive at that belief' rather than 'Why do you believe that?'. There are both cognitive and particularly linguistic theories behind this methodology, some of which will be explored later in this chapter.

The strong linguistic emphasis of NLP is one of the reasons why this methodology compliments the psycholinguistic framework that speech and language therapists are already using in their work with schizophrenic patients.

As the communication difficulties of schizophrenia become more clearly understood, there seems to be a natural logic towards using a form of therapy that works with their communication difficulties on as many different levels as possible and in an infinitely flexible manner. At the same time, NLP offers the patient who is finding communication difficult a structured framework that can be simple and concrete in nature when needed. It is also a form of therapy in which the therapist can take a more active role if need be and, therefore, does not require as high a level of verbal communicative competence on the part of the patient.

The skill of the therapist, when taking a more active role, is to ensure that a deeper rapport is maintained at all times and that they are clear about working from the patient's 'model of the world' rather than their own. The schizophrenic patient's model of the world may be very different to our own due to his/her disorder in perception, interpretation and understanding of social interaction.

Nevertheless, an NLP approach to psychotherapy allows the therapist to acknowledge the patient's model of the world in such a way that he can 'feel understood', often for the first time, without reinforcing the patient's beliefs. This is one of the vital preliminary steps towards developing a trusting, therapeutic relationship with a patient who may have had minimal experience of supported relationships in the past. From this position, the patient can be guided in exploring new and more flexible ways of understanding the world and, particularly, social situations which will, in turn, lead to new behaviour. When the patient experiences the value of his new behaviour to himself and his quality of life, it is more likely to become self-perpetuating.

NLP was developed in the early 1970s at the University of Santa Cruz by the computer scientist Richard Bandler and linguist David Grinder. Their influences were derived from Fritz Pearlis, known in gestalt therapy, Virginia Satir, a family and systemic therapist, Milton Erikson, a psychiatrist and hypnotherapist and Gregory Batson, anthropologist and philosopher, amongst others. Since then, NLP has used these founding influences to grow into an episystemology in its own right and it is at the forefront of shedding light on how we cognitively process subjective experiences, how experience construes our understanding of the world and how this may lead to restrictive or unuseful ways of behaving.

One aspect of NLP is that it has a more outcome-oriented approach than other therapies. This can be illustrated by looking first at the 'problem-oriented approach'. NLP is an experiential form of therapy and uses the learning experience extensively. With the following simple exercise you have an opportunity to experience some NLP:

First think of something that has been causing you to perceive it as a problem, for example 'Why is it taking me so long to get started on this chapter?', then run through the following set of questions giving your answers to them:

1.   What is your problem?

2.   Why do you have this problem?

3. What caused this problem?

4. Who or what is at fault?

5. Why have you not resolved this problem?

Having asked yourself these questions, are you more confident about a resolution or are you experiencing the same or increased levels of frustration, etc.?

If you are a therapist yourself, you may be thinking that your therapy sessions would not follow this sort of approach, and yet these questions were taken from observations of qualified psychotherapists, counsellors, psychologists and psychiatric interviews/therapy sessions.

Now, thinking of the same problem as used with the last set of questions, ask yourself the following:

1. What do you want? In what way do you want yourself or 'things' to be different in the future?

2. What do you need in order to get 'it' (the changes that you want)?

3. What resources (these may be abilities, skills, commodities, e.g. time, money, etc.) do you currently have that will help you to get 'it'?

4. Where are you now in your progress towards 'it'?

5. What do you need to do to take the next step towards gaining 'it'?

6. How will you know when you have achieved 'it'?

7. What is most important (or what do you value) about achieving 'it'?

8. What will it be like when you have already achieved 'it' or if you choose not to achieve it?

For many people this second style of asking questions leads to a more useful outcome with a specific plan of action. This demonstrates, in a simple manner, an approach that NLP may take towards problem solving and is something that many schizophrenic patients find useful. When using NLP as a more 'in depth' form of psychotherapy, facilitating the patient towards answering any one of those questions may become his outcome for several sessions. During their work together, both patient and therapist may become aware of the neurological processes which the patient employed, that both lead him to be 'stuck' somewhere in the process and the different changes in neurological processing that lead him towards 'freeing-up the cognitive log jam'.

An example may be that he can identify what he wants, but is unable to break the process of achieving it down into 'manageable' and 'achievable' steps. This may indicate that he habitually sees 'the larger picture' but is unable to focus on detail and so needs guidance, e.g. someone who recognises that they are lonely and needs to develop a social network, but thinks that he is unable to do this because he does not recognise the skills he already has or those he needs to gain. If he is unable to see 'the larger picture' and, therefore, is unaware of what he may personally gain from the situation, he is unlikely to be motivated towards making any changes at all. The NLP therapist would aim to enable the patient to make these perspective shifts of cognition.

This knowledge may be used by client and therapist in other situations, as the neurological pattern or programme may also be occurring again and limiting the patient's neurological or cognitive processing options.

Motivation is a common therapeutic challenge when working with this client group. NLP may offer a model of working with motivation that is more concrete in manner. An over-simplified approach to the Meta Programme Model would enable the identification of a client's 'motivational direction', for example if the client is motivated by anticipated pleasure, he will go out and get something that is desirable and valued by himself or if he is motivated to move away from unpleasant, uncomfortable situations, he will take avoiding action – an example of this might be asking someone out on a date(two of the social skills groups facilitated by the author are predominately made up of young males whose stated outcome was to feel socially confident with young women and 'to develop a relationship'). When faced with a similar situation, do you think of the pleasure and excitement of a developing relationship? Do you enter into the relationship hoping that this will be 'the one'? Do you see yourself 'growing old together'? If so, then your motivational direction is taking you towards your desired outcome. If you needed some additional prompting, your therapist might remind you of how it feels to have your invitation accepted, how interesting it is to find out about the likes and dislikes of another person, what it is like when you find out that they like the same things that you do, the comfort of knowing that someone cares for you and you can care for them and so on. If, on the other hand, you find yourself thinking of the loneliness you are experiencing because you do not have a partner, that you do not have someone to confide in or share your successes with, and that you dislike the feeling that no one would miss you if you had an accident and were kept in hospital for a week and if it is these thoughts that motivate you to ask someone out, then your motivational direction is away from the undesired outcome. For additional prompting, your therapist might remind you of what it is like to come home to an empty house, how difficult it is to carry alone the burden of everyday stress, that it was very annoying to have to pay the single supplement on the last package holiday you took, and so on. All of this would help to move you away from the undesirable outcome of remaining single. From this position of feeling, understood by the therapist because he has used the same perspective of thinking about your problem, he may well encourage you to 'see the other side of the same coin' and think positively about your problem, that is rather than stating what you *don't* want (moving away from an undesired outcome), state what you *do want* (move towards the desired outcome). This is an important concept because of the way we both consciously and subconsciously find the processing of negative concepts more difficult (De Villiers and De Villiers 1978). The fact that the motivational direction was already part of the neurological approach taken by the patient means that 'enhancing' or 'emphasising' what already exists for the client makes it effective and potentially more self generative.

There are many other aspects to the Meta Programme (Bailey 1991) such as motivational levels, motivational sources, attention directions, working styles, working in organisations (with other people), response to stress, convincer strategies and so on. There is no judgement involved in identifying your own or patient's neurological processes; it is not the case that one process is better than another, it depends upon the situation or context in which decisions about behaviour is being made. NLP aims to promote cognitive flexibility for the patient so that he can change his habitual response patterns, that have proved limiting in the past, to something more useful. If the neurological or cognitive process is achieving your outcome in an efficient and effective manner, it is probably the right one for that situation. If not, then you need to adopt a more flexible approach and try a different process.

NLP, as the name implies, has an intrinsic linguistic component. As Bandler and Grinder (1975; 1976) explored other forms of therapy, as used by therapists of proven excellence, they noted that the precise form of language used by the therapist was significant. They also observed that clients would often give clear linguistic 'signs' about the ways in which they, neurologically or cognitively, processed events and experiences and which, when recognised by the therapist, could be worked with in the following therapeutic ways:

Pacing and Leading

This is perhaps the most important stage of any therapeutic intervention. It is part of rapport building and the foundation of any therapeutic relationship (Macdonald 1994). Pacing someone at the level of using the same or similar language patterns as they do, for example predicate systems or meta model violations (see below), can be profound. The patient will experience a sensation of being 'understood' and that the therapist is like himself and must, therefore, like him as well. This may not be strictly the case as it is not necessary to fully 'understand' the content of what the client says, but the therapist will understand his processing.

The 'Leading' element begins as the therapist encourages the client to process things differently. If the client is not 'following' the therapist into new processes, more Pacing is required. When the client finds himself processing the world in a way he finds more useful and valuable, this will be observable in the language used as well as his behaviour.

One way of leading a patient towards new cognitive or neurological processing may be the use of psycholinguistics – known in NLP as the Meta Model (Lewis and Pucelik 1982).

The Meta Model

A linguistic approach to understanding cognitive or neurological processing and facilitating change.

In the following brief description of the meta model, an attempt has been made to give examples from the author's own work with patients. It is important to remember that all comments or quotes taken out of context and unconnected to previous events, history environments and so on can become meaningless or misrepresentations. This made it difficult to find examples that would 'stand alone' and represent meta model violations, as they often come in more subtle forms.

The aims of the meta model are threefold:

1. Gathering Information: as with all forms of therapeutic interventions whether psychotherapeutic, social or medical, this is the most important, and too often undervalued element, of the therapeutic intervention process.

2. Expanding Limits: looks at how often beliefs both prevent us from achieving our goals and yet how often they can also take us forward to exceptional goals. It is important to realise that we all have a choice about the limitations we set on our own beliefs, or as Henry Ford said: 'Whether you think you can, or whether you think you can't – you're right'.

3. Changing Meaning: changing the meaning of a past event or series of events, or reinterpreting the encoded message within an event, is invariably an element of psychotherapy that enables a person to accept the past, leave it in the past and take forward into the future that which is useful from the past. It enables the client to take the weight of the past off his shoulders, to throw light onto his brighter future and hear the calling of a new life.

The following transcripts from some of the author's work with patients are an attempt to expand on these meta model aims:

Gathering Information
Lost referential index
Referential index provides clarity or 'ownership' of statements:

Patient:	Therapist:
'I need help'	'*What* do you need help with?'
	'*What* kind of help?'
	(Italic indicates vocal emphasis)
'I'm being forced into it'	'*Who* is forcing you into *What?*'
'This isn't working'	'*How* is it not working?'
'People are so inconsiderate'	'*Which* people?'
	or
	'*Who* says people are?'

Nominalisation
This occurs when a verb is turned into a noun and has the effect of turning an active process into a static non-changing or changeable event. If you need more examples of nominalisation, listen to politicians.

Patient:	Therapist:
'The relationship isn't working'	'Tell me more about the way in which you are *relating* and how it is not working?'
'He did it because of an argument'	'Something occurred as you were *arguing* that caused him to do it?'
Psychotherapy grounded in respect is the epitome of rapport. In this example, 'respect' and 'rapport' are nominalisations. An attempt to de-nominalise this statement is opposite.	Psychotherapy, when practised in a deeply respectful manner, will demonstrate a high degree of mutual understanding, trust, similarity, sympathy, empathy…

Nominalisations may be used as a form of verbal shorthand, which can be useful.

Unspecified verbs
Clarification is needed:

Patient:	*Therapist:*
'He always hurts me'	'*How* does he hurt you?'
'He could show some concern'	'*In what way* could he show concern?'
'She doesn't love me'	'*What kind of love* doesn't she have?'

Expanding Limitations

Model operators

Also known as the model operators of possibility, necessity, and often 'mark' a belief. The main ones are 'can', 'could', 'shall', 'should', 'may', 'might' and 'must' but there are others.

Patient:	*Therapist:*
'I must have eight hours sleep a night'	'What would happen if you had seven or nine?'
'She said I had to'	'What will happen if you don't?'
'I must be back by 12 o'clock'	(Said with humour) 'Will you turn back into a pumpkin at 12.05?'

A short piece of conversation:

Patient:	*Therapist:*
'She said I mustn't do it'	(said with humour) 'Well then, you absolutely mustn't do it'.
'But I want to'	'What's that got to do with it?'
'I can do it if I want to'	'I guess so, but will you?'
'I could…'	'What would it be like?'
'Exciting, fun'	'Oh well, you shouldn't have any fun in your life should you?'
'Yes I should'	'So what are you going to *do* about it?'
'I will do it!'	

This conversation was with a young lady who had an over-protective carer, about a weekend in Blackpool with her boyfriend. They had a great time.

Universal qualifier

Again, this indicates a belief about which the therapist may only need to encourage the patient to have some doubt about as a precursor to change.

Patient:	Therapist:
'It always rains in Manchester'	'*Every* day?'
'I've always been like this'	'What, even when you were a child?'
'Everyone hates me'	'I like you'
'He never helps me'	'I thought he drove you here today?'
'Life was great before I lost the job'	'I seem to remember you telling me about mountains of paperwork…'

Changing Meanings

Mind reading

In semantic pragmatics (see other chapters) this might be called presupposition, a necessary element of communication, but you need to know when you are doing it and be open to the fact that you may be mistaken.

Patient:	Therapist:
'I know what that look means'	'How do you know?'
'He hates me'	'Has he said so?'
'I know exactly how she will take that!'	'Is she so predictable? If so, it must be very easy to manipulate her in the way that you want, which seems strange as she so often takes you by surprise'.
'I know what you're going to say'	(Said with humour) 'That's clever of you, because at the moment I haven't any idea myself'.

Comparisons

These only prove useful when the comparative reference is also stated.

Patient:	Therapist:
'I want to be better'	'Better than what?'
'I'm just awful'	'At what and compared to whom?'
'The Oprah Winfrey show is the best'	'Is that a statement of fact or a personal preference?'

Judgements

It is important to know who 'owns' or has made the judgement.

Patient:	Therapist:
'I'm useless at it'	'Says who?'
'It's obvious he must go'	'Is it obvious? It's not to me!'
'They all think it's a great idea'	'Who is they? How have they been able to make such a judgement? Do They know all the facts?'

Cause and effect

Identifying cause and effect, when accurate, is very empowering but when unrelated events are linked, it can be equally limiting.

Patient:	Therapist:
'You make me feel angry'	'Are you sure that it is what I do that makes you angry? Could it be anything else?'
'He does it deliberately to make me upset'	(Said with humour) 'He set off on his bike, thinking I'm going to make Mum upset then threw himself off and broke his arm'

Complex equivalents

When X = Y, which sometimes is true, but when it isn't, the belief can prevent the patient from looking for alternative explanations.

Patient:	*Therapist:*
'I know they hate me, I never get to watch the TV programmes I like'	'You like football and snooker don't you? What do the ladies like to watch? If one day you all watched football, does it mean that you didn't like the ladies that day?'
'I know he's having an affair. He's coming home later and later from work'	'What's happening at work for him? I seem to remember you telling me that his Company was struggling – could this be a reason for him working late?'
'If I change I will not be the same person'	'In some ways that's true, but deciding to change one aspect of your life doesn't mean the same as changing your whole personality. What if you decide to keep some things that are important to you exactly the same?'

Presuppositions

Within the meta model, this term is used to mean something slightly different to the semantic pragmatic model as discussed in chapter 11. Here it means 'The Truth behind The Truth' or an implied message.

Patient:	*Therapist:*
'You can't help me' (Help is possible but not from you)	'Who can help you?'
	'What would you like to talk to me about?' (you want to talk and you know the topic).
'It didn't work this time'	'It worked in the past. What's changed to prevent it working this time?'

Two of the most useful NLP presuppositions are: 'Communication is the response that you get' and 'Doing what you have always done will get you what you have always got'.

Another way of classifying the meta model would be under the following headings:

Deletions:

>   Lost Referential Index
>
>   Unspecified Verbs
>
>   Comparison
>
>   Judgements

Distortions:

>   Nominalisations
>
>   Mind Reading
>
>   Cause and Effect
>
>   Complex Equivalents

Generalisations

Model operators and universal quantifiers

When the language of a patient is analysed in this way, it becomes clearer how language may reflect some of the basic neurological or cognitive processing that is taking place. All of us make deletions, distortions or over-generalise in our cognitive processing – it is a necessary measure for preventing mental 'over-load', as is the ability to exercise selective attention. However, the degree to which these linguistic and, therefore, cognitive violations are made seems to the author to be more prevalent in schizophrenic patients than normal people (Macdonald 1994).

When using a technique such as the meta model in therapy, it is important to recognise that it is one small piece of a complex process and can, if used inappropriately, do more harm than good. This is why it is so important to emphasise again the need for maintaining rapport at all times, or ensuring that the loss of rapport was done deliberately for therapeutic purposes. When used unsympathetically, the meta model can become reminiscent of the Spanish Inquisition. The therapist needs to bear in mind that the gathering and clarification of information from the content of the patient's beliefs is not necessarily about the therapist coming to an understanding of the patient, but to understanding the limiting neurological or cognitive processes that he/she is using and enable him/her to be more flexible.

There are times when clients will tell you that you have been really helpful and given them new insight into a problem, while you are left realising that you did not know what the problem was but had recognised that the patient was using a large number of model operators of necessity, for example, and pointing this out to the patient had been enough to start the process of change. In this way, it may be seen that it is not always necessary to understand the 'content' of a patient's beliefs, which can be very complex and inexplicable, but understanding the neurological processes that are used to build the beliefs and then enabling there to be a choice within these processes may be helpful towards functional behaviour that is more appropriate.

NLP has been considered by some to be doing psychotherapy by the recipe book, as it uses some simple and clearly explained techniques. Unfortunately, there are some people who call themselves psychotherapists, and who use it in such a manner, but this devalues both psychotherapy and the potential of NLP.

To take the food metaphor further, the effective NLP psychotherapist needs not only to know the different recipes but be able to anticipate their client's taste, and how to substitute ingredients if they are out of season, and even how to make a satisfying meal that is tasty and nourishing when the only ingredients in the store cupboard are a tin of spam, a packet of lentils and half an oxo cube!

As an experiential constructivist therapy, NLP complements the psycholinguistic work of the speech and language therapist working in rehabilitation with patients who have schizophrenia. The psycholinguistic approach to semantic pragmatic disorder is, in the author's opinion, the construction or reconstruction of a person's ability to perceive and respond to social situations. Many therapists will recognise the dilemma of generalisation of therapeutic work from the therapy room to 'real life' and so psychotherapy can offer patients the opportunity to put skills learnt in therapy into context within their lives.

Dilts unified field theory demonstrates the spectrum of areas for therapy and the need for a holistic approach (O'Connor and Seymour 1993). This model for understanding an individual's problems from different perspectives needs to read as if each field is running in parallel, rather than a hierarchy of levels – either 'top down' or 'bottom up' – as it is only when all levels have been addressed that the patient can feel that he/she can adopt a congruent approach to life. Figure 13.1 shows an adaption of Dilt's unified field theory and how it may relate to the holistic work of a speech and language therapist who also uses psychotherapeutic approaches.

Lieberman et al. (1986) in their research have found that the multi-disciplinary approach to the rehabilitation of people with schizophrenia is necessary. In particular, they advocate psychosocial rehabilitation in conjunction with traditional medical approaches. When used in this way, both approaches

The fields	Areas of exploration	Therapeutic approach
Spiritual	Who or what else? Mission in life?	Psychotherapy
Identity	Who am I?	Psychotherapy
Beliefs	Why?	Psychotherapy
Capabilities	How?	Speech and Language Therapy
Behaviour	What?	Speech and Language Therapy
Environment	With whom? Where?	Speech and Language Therapy

Source: Laurie Macdonald 1996
Figure 13.1 Adaptation from Dilts – Unified Field Theory

become more effective than when either is used alone. Experiential constructivism, as a form of psychotherapy, lends itself well to working alongside other
models or approaches to rehabilitation. It operates from the basic premise that
there are many models for explaining reality, and that no one model is correct.
All models have validity and, providing the feedback following experimentation is fully observed and responded to, the evolving model will effectively
provide the desirable outcome. Experiential constructivism is accessible to a
wide range of clients as it does not require high levels of insight, the ability to
be articulate, or to put oneself in stressful situations before you can cope with
them. NLP also has the advantage of being linguistically based and can,
therefore, compliment the emerging psycholinguistic approach to rehabilitation.

NLP can be used as a brief form of focused psychotherapy in many situations.
In working with schizophrenic patients, the author works in a flexible manner
– some patients staying in therapy for a few years, others for a few months and
some coming back into therapy briefly at times of relapse. The flexible nature
of this form of therapy fits well with the demands of the new NHS in this
country.

CHAPTER 14

Social Networks and their Development in the Community

David Abrahamson

Introduction

It might be expected that the fields of social networks and community care would have developed vigorous interactions, since they have much in common. The former can be clearly defined as the connections amongst a set of individuals. The concept of 'community' is notoriously more difficult to define; nonetheless, common to the many different definitions of the word is, as Scherer (1972) has pointed out, the idea of people together rather than alone. Unfortunately, the opposite is the case. Contrary to any expectation that the massive move from mental hospital to community care would have involved extensive work on the social networks of the patients concerned, most of it has taken place without any studies, or even consideration, of this aspect. The reasons for this omission are complex but at least some of its roots lie in stereotypes of long-stay patients formed during the institutional era.

Ghostly Figures

The most extreme view of such patients has been that schizophrenic illnesses destroy their ability to make social links to such an extent that they form aggregations of isolated individuals rather than networks or communities.

Sommer and Hoffer (1962) argued this view very strongly in a paper entitled *The Schizophrenic No Society*, suggesting that: 'Like the crew of the Flying Dutchman, long-stay patients are ghostly figures, who can walk through one another without leaving a trace' (p.252). They drew on the assertion of Sir Francis Galton, published more than fifty years earlier, that solitariness was an almost universal characteristic of mentally ill people. He based this opinion on glimpses of patients, walking in 'gloomy isolation' in the exercise yard of the then Hanwell Asylum, from trains of the Great Western Railway on which he travelled to London. More surprisingly, Russell Barton (1959), in his classic work opposing institutional practices, made only passing reference to relationships between patients. Indeed, a picture of patients walking in isolation from one another, reminiscent of Galton's observations, appears on its cover. He considered it 'surprisingly rare' for friendships or confiding relationships to develop amongst long-stay patients, despite expecting that this would be easy given the environment (although he later became one of the pioneers of patients' clubs). Similarly, Goffman (1968), in his well-known counterculture critique 'Asylums' – which had considerable influence in promoting the public mood for deinstitutionalisation – suggested that patients in a large American mental hospital had mainly hostile relationships with one another.

Wing and Brown's (1970) seminal study of three mental hospitals makes no reference to relationships amongst the patients. They defined institutionalism, in individual psychological terms, as representing a gradual loss of interest in the outside world with increasing time spent in hospital. This influential definition left the stereotype of isolated individuals unchallenged, as little account was taken of other factors that might have been operating – including the possibility that they had made friends they did not want to leave.

In a series of studies at Goodmayes Hospital (Abrahamson and Brenner 1982; Abrahamson, Swatton and Wills 1989), it was found that long-stay patients did indeed often have very understandable reasons for not wanting to leave hospital and needed information about community living and an opportunity to acquire the skills to cope before they could be expected to consider the possibility positively. Amongst other aspects, it was clearly important that they should know if they would be able to maintain relationships which they might have built up over many years. In confirmation of this, it also became clear at this time that, in practice, patients who had left hospital to live in small group homes in the community, though generally satisfied with the move, often regretted losing the larger and more varied social networks which they had in hospital. The title of a study of patients who had left Claybury Hospital (Goldie 1988) summed up the results as: 'I hated it there, but I miss the people'. The second part of this title, though not the first, typifies our findings then and subsequently.

Preparation Houses

In 1976 the first of a series of preparation for discharge houses had been established on the Goodmayes' campus; patients resident in them undertake realistic rehabilitation programmes for several months to a year before moving on to group homes or other community accommodation.

Patients' ideas about future accommodation become clarified during this process as they learn more about alternatives, their coping skills improve and the social networks they want to preserve or develop become clearer. In turn, we have come to appreciate how important for success and satisfaction are their own choices of future living situations and companions. Not unexpectedly, it has also become clear that, however valuable, group homes are not suitable for everyone. The physical and emotional closeness in these small environments is too intense for some patients who want more independence yet had become socially isolated when living in single flats prior to hospitalisation.

Fortunately, an opportunity to widen the range of choices open to them arose in the early 1980s when a former nurses' hostel became available in Newham, which is part of Goodmayes Hospital's catchment area. Springboard Housing Association was able to convert the main building into three flats and seven bedsits with two communal lounges and a kitchen/dining room. An additional seven flats were built at the end of a long garden. Three staff were appointed to be on site during office hours on weekdays and available for emergencies at other times. The project provides a combination of privacy and readily available social contacts, in whatever degree of intensity is preferred, of the kind preparation house residents often request. The project has become very popular in the twelve years it has been in operation and, as well as preparation house residents, several of our clients with their own flats in the community have sought places there after getting to know it through visits to friends or by word of mouth on the local 'grapevine'.

Social Networks

We examined, in detail, the social networks of a group of patients in the, by then, two preparation houses, again after they had spent three or four months in the new project (known as '209') and, finally, after another six months living there (Abrahamson and Ezekiel 1984). This was, in fact, the first social network study of the transition from hospital to community.

In terms of network size, that is the number of people with whom each person had contact, the averages in the preparation houses and on both the assessments after moving to '209' were around thirty. It must be stressed, however, that averages provide a very incomplete picture as there was a wide range of from 3 to 53 people. This compares to averages of 10 to 12 in several studies of the Goodmayes Hospital long-stay wards (range 0–55) and similar averages in two other mental hospitals (Abrahamson 1991; Leff et al. 1990) and of 4 and 14 in two community studies (Pattison et al. 1975; Dozier, Harris and Bergman 1987). The striking feature of the networks' composition was that in the first assessment they were made up largely of hospital-based and, in the second and third, community-based patients, ex-patients and staff, with an additional 10–17 per cent of family members. There were very few (3–4%) contacts within the supposed general community.

'The Community' and Normalisation

In considering these results, we came to realise how unsatisfactory is the conventional, inclusive concept of 'The Community' – as in 'Care in the Community' (Acheson 1985). The reality is rather that of overlapping sub-communities formed around shared backgrounds, ethnicity, work, or leisure activities, etc. This point is underlined by experience in the USA where, prior to the Second World War, immigrant groups were expected to be absorbed in the 'melting pot' of the wider community. Since then, however, it has become clear that links are retained with those of similar background and experiences, so that the final result has been described as more like a salad than a melting pot.

The late 1980s and 1990s have seen further drives to move long-stay patients into 'The Community' with the aim of closing the large mental hospitals. Unfortunately, lessons learned from the earlier era of resettlement have tended to be ignored. One widely propagated view has been that the only legitimate form of provision is 'the ordinary house in the ordinary street' and that any form of special building format is stigmatising (Heginbotham 1985). This reflects the concept of normalisation (Wolfensberger 1972), which has been beneficial in many respects. However, both in its original formulation and the later mutation to social role valorisation, the reference group is a putative 'normal' community with shared values. The lifestyles at which disabled or handicapped people are expected to aim tend to be based on this hypothetical construct rather than these reflecting more thoroughly the preferences and experiences of those who live them.

One of the most disturbing results of this has been that contacts and relationships among handicapped or disabled people are less welcomed than those within the 'normal' community. In some cases, individuals have been discouraged from retaining contacts with hospital patients they have known for many years and expected instead to make relationships with virtual strangers. It is also reflected in the pressure for individuals to live alone or in small groups, and for the groups themselves to be distanced from one another, mentioned above. This not only may lead to a very limited range of relationships but is also an extreme form of stigmatisation – in the name of destigmatisation – which would not be tolerated for other minority groups. Clearly, it is vital that realistic opportunities for mentally ill persons to make contacts as widely as possible are vigorously developed, but this does not require depreciation of mutually-supportive relationships with those to whom they may feel closest.

Registered Care Homes

We have gone against this trend by developing housing projects for larger groups of mainly ex-hospital patients. These resemble '209' but are fully staffed, around the clock, seven days per week. Each tenant has a flat rather than a room

– to provide space and privacy – and can choose the extent of mixing which they prefer in the communal lounges and dining rooms – which are also designed to provide ample space. There are, at present, 63 places in four such projects – which vary in size, with the largest catering for twenty-two tenants and the smallest ten. They also vary in structure, both between one and another and within the same project – that is, a central building and other flats nearby, a set of flats with two linked houses and varied size and formats of flats. The central concern is to offer as much individual choice as possible.

Experience over more than five years suggests that these projects provide a very satisfying quality of life for their residents with relatively large social networks, and can cater for the more ill, disturbed or restless patients who are potentially disruptive within a single house. It is also easier for new residents to be introduced, which is notoriously difficult in small group homes. Comparing their milieus, and that of '209', with those of single houses, there is a loose analogy with the differences between nuclear and extended families – which may be particularly significant for schizophrenic patients.

None of this is to suggest that single houses and flats are not also important as part of the range of choices which needs to be available; we have in Newham, at present, ten staffed houses as well as a variable number of supported flats. Some of the houses are paired, which has been shown to expand social networks and reduce the danger of isolation (Meltzer, Kemp and Smith 1994).

Combined Group and Individual Out-Patient Clinics

The above developments relate mainly to resettlement of patients from hospital, although some community patients spend periods in the preparation houses before returning to their own homes or going to group homes, '209' or other projects.

Provision is also needed for improving the social networks of long-term psychiatric patients who have not spent long periods in hospital, especially the so called 'revolving door' patients who rotate between short admissions and often poor-quality lives in the community.

Our approach to this was much influenced by an experience in 1980 during an out-patient clinic of the old style with waiting patients sitting on benches outside the consulting room door. On opening the door to find one lady, rather than the usual small crowd, I remarked that she must be pleased that for once she had not had to wait to be seen. On the contrary, she was upset by the unusual situation on the grounds that the best part of her out-patient appointments was the period spent talking with other patients and the clinic nurse prior to seeing me – as she forcefully pointed out, she generally spent only a short time with me and I usually asked the same questions!

As a result of this experience, together with information about the attractively named 'Coffee and...' psychotherapy with severely ill patients (Masnik *et al.* 1971) and successful results from a group-based out-patient clinic in Ireland (Ward 1975), two out-patient clinics for long-term patients were set up in 1984 and 1985 – both held weekly on the premises of day hospitals (Abrahamson and Fellow Smith 1991). Ten to fifteen patients usually attend the one-hour group components of each, which are also attended by myself or my clinical assistant, one or two community psychiatric nurses and a psychologist or speech and language therapist. These sessions are followed by individual medical appointments, often attended also by the patient's CPN or another member of the rehabilitation team whom they know well. Tea separates the two components of the clinic. One of the advantages of these arrangements is that professionals and patients see each other in a more human light – the importance of which cannot be over-estimated. It also became evident that links were being made between patients which extended outside the clinics so that, for example, CPN's on home visits found them meeting sociably together. This led to the creation of a club, which has also been very successful. As well as meetings each Thursday – when activities such as bingo, scrabble, trivial pursuit, table tennis and snooker take place – as well as talking, listening to music, tea drinking and just sitting, a meal is prepared. There are also outings and weekends away. Two rehabilitation team members help each week and I often mix in, as much as possible as an ordinary club member. We feel that this involvement is important as, in all our social network studies, staff have emerged as significant components. Furthermore, this bridging between social and professional relationships reduces any sense of illness as something separate and shameful. Club members recognise the boundaries between the club's social purpose and clinical concerns and only seek advice when essential; similarly professionals preserve this distinction, although situations occasionally arise when it is very useful to be able to offer immediate advice or treatment in the rehabilitation team's office nearby.

It would seem that ventures of this sort will become increasingly important in the future, especially in view of growing official and media emphasis on patients as dangers to themselves or others and the negative focus this entails. Only by working side-by-side with our patients can we avoid the pendulum swinging back to aspects of the institutional era that seemed to have been left behind.

CHAPTER 15

Conclusion
The Way Forward

Jenny France and Niki Muir

The success of the symposium *Communication and the Mentally Ill Patient* was to be evaluated on the number of fulfilled expectations which arose out of the planning and its eventual presentation. Publishing the papers in the form of a book was ambitious in prospect but proved to be successful. Contact with all those who agreed so generously to give of their time and professional expertise to help make the symposium a prestigious and worthwhile event was one of the major objectives. Putting speech and language therapy on the map by way of introducing ourselves to other mental health professionals, for example psychiatrists, psychiatric nurses, clinical psychologists and others – including speech and language therapists as yet uninitiated into the challenging and rewarding work in mental health – was another achieved objective.

At the latter end of 1995, The Royal College of Psychiatrists invited representatives from The College of Occupational Therapy, The Chartered Society of Physiotherapy, The British Association of Arts Therapists, The British Association of Social Workers, The Association of Directors of Social Services, The British Psychological Society, The Royal College of Nursing and The Royal College of Speech and Language Therapists to attend a meeting to consider establishing a Joint National Forum. As a result of this positive meeting, members will, on invitation, gather to work on a needs-based arrangement. The most important aspect of that meeting was the forgeing of communication links between the professions allied to medicine and others within the Royal College of Psychiatrists, thus allowing the dialogue to begin. Without doubt, this was a serendipitous piece of good fortune and inadvertent clever timing.

Many topics raised at the symposium were echoed through the National Forum meeting, leading us to suppose that, across the professions in mental health, many are struggling with similar problems and frustrations – for example working towards improved standards of service, particularly for those patients in the community – whilst others are involved in diverse research projects. Themes recurred throughout the symposium and they sprang from the opportunity to focus exclusively on language and communication and to dissect and discuss their complexities.

Language is known as a highly developed and revealing ability and consists of the linguistic elements of recognition, interpretation, planning, speech, writing and reading. These require learnt usage of the rules of semantics, syntax, pragmatics, morphology and phonology, as well as of voice, articulation and fluency. Added to this are the paralinguistc elements of intonation, pitch, stress, rate and pause, the metalinguistic elements which allow for accurate perception and for monitoring acceptability and the non-linguistic elements encompassing the non-verbal skills of gesture, posture, facial expression, proximity, use of space and body movement. Thought and language cannot be seen as isolated phenomena and exploring language offers a way of uncovering belief systems and delusional ideation, it gives a window to 'the self'.

During the symposium, we learnt, on investigation, that the case histories of many clients revealed delayed milestones linked to linguistic, social and communicative behaviours and many others pointed to pervasive developmental disorders. As Walsh, in Chapter 10, reminds us, we should not ignore the fact that for some adults with schizophrenia there may have been a particular difficulty with the development and use of language in childhood – difficulties which may persist as a feature of later schizophrenia if unresolved semantic pragmatic disorder is found to be an underlying or predisposing factor in schizophrenia across the life span. Implications would be significant in terms of education, health and social requirements and would demand a mixed economy of resources to adequately meet needs and a more diverse care programme approach. Investigation into the pattern and type of the semantic pragmatic disorder that seems to be present in those with schizophrenia, and recognition of links between this and general and specific mental health problems, could lead to active management of these linguistic and communication disorders at an earlier age. This is already being undertaken for children and young people whose behavioural traits show marked similarities to those of psychosis and whose difficulties are placed on the Autistic/Aspergers continuum or who are described as having a specific learning disorder or a developmental dysphasia.

In the abstract introducing their paper *Language and Speech Disorders in Children Attending a Psychiatric Day Programme*, Kotsopoulos and Boodoosingh (1987) found that of 46 children referred consecutively to a day psychiatric programme and assessed for speech and language deficits, 33 (71.7%) presented with speech and/or language impairment requiring therapy. Large samples of children with speech/language impairment show psychiatric symptomatology and there is an association between language and/or speech disorders and psychiatric disorders, suggesting that children with linguistic impairment are at risk for psychiatric pathology (Cantwell and Baker 1985). Their study confirmed that the prevalence of speech and language impairment is high amongst children with psychiatric disorders. This knowledge links with Crow and Done's chapter (Chapter 7), in which they discussed the childhood precursors of adult psychosis by use of retrospective studies of the childhoods of individuals who later develop schizophrenia. They found that intelligence scores in the children who became schizophrenic were significantly reduced compared to their siblings and that the deficit in IQ and the poor school performance, relative to siblings, applied particularly to males. Individuals who later develop psychosis are distinguished from those who do not by impaired academic performance and difficulties in establishing inter-personal relationships.

Elaine Chaika, in Chapter 3, shared with us her thoughts on language as being the aforementioned set of intricately interrelated skills and knowledge that is fashioned to be infinitely creative. She is of the opinion that schizophrenic speech is a lack of pathway control, but she asks the question 'what is the cause?' In the language of schizophrenia, the literature reports impairment of executive function and working memory and a range of cognitive as well as pragmatic impairments. Disturbances have been noted of both receptive and expressive functions, semantically and syntactically compromised by attentional and volitional deficits and changes and characterised by fluctuating self-monitoring abilities. New methods of technology will also allow Professor Chaika to continue and extend these areas of her research.

Professor Frith, in Chapter 2, informs us that the abnormalities of schizophrenic language appear to lie at the level of language *use* rather than competence and that they may stem from inadequate development of a 'Theory of Mind', which he supports by showing that the problems arise when the patient has to use language to communicate with others. In support of Professor Frith's statement, we observe, during therapy, that these problems apply not just to speech but to all the non-verbal modes of communication and that speech disturbances vary and are are inconsistant. Patients say this could be as a result of their distress associated with their developing insight into their mental illness. As the medication for mental illness, and in particular for schizophrenia, improves, the patient's own descriptions and memories play an important part in our understanding of their communication difficulties and should play an integral part in our research into the origins of communication and language disturbanaces in schizophrenia. A young man, for example, remembers his communication difficulties during the development of his illness when a young child as:

> I just couldn't talk, I couldn't get any words out, there were no words to get out, words were just not appearing. I thought that all I had to do was to say a sentence and that would clear me forever, but I just couldn't say that sentence. I wasn't in the spotlight enough as a kid. The new medicine (Rispiridone) has helped me to get out of myself and it is all gradually becoming easier. Looking back on it now I knew I needed to communicate at the time and not being able to do so was torture.

So it can be seen that, perhaps for many patients such as this young man, pain through insight may, in turn, result in disruptive language behaviour for self-protection.

Professor Pamela Taylor, Forensic Psychiatrist at Broadmoor Hospital and The Institute of Psychiatry, commented on the need for therapeutic intervention with these patients and went on to say, during her opening of the second session of the symposium, that a psycholinguistic model is well suited to this work. This nicely supports both Chaika and Frith's chapters and might well have implications towards therapy.

In Chapter 4, Philip Thomas informed us that communication disorders can be used to describe a group of phenomena which are generally subsumed under the category of thought disorder. He thinks that assessments using proverbs and word association tests provide limited information about the nature of language or speech in real situations. This statement may prove helpful in finding new directions for research into assessments. In another recent study, Barch and Berenbaum (1996) examined the relationship between language production (LP) processes and thought disorder. The implications for the results of their study helps in the understanding of the multi-faceted nature and aetiology of thought disorder.

McGuire, Shah and Murray (1993) show, with single positron emission tomography, that the production of auditory hallucinations is associated with increased activity in a network of cortical areas specialised for language. There are known concomitant mechanical difficulties resultant from medication and, although traditional antipsychotic drugs are said to relieve symptoms in 75 per cent of patients, in many cases speech, attention and volition can be compromised by extrapyramidal side effects and, in most cases, social function remains poor (Drug Ther. Bull. 1995). The reference to social function could be seen in terms of communicative function, which medication alone does not appear to ameliorate. Perhaps the reason for this inability to fully lift the symptomatology of social and communicative functioning could be sought in further exploration of the neurodevelopmental perspective. Looking at communication, both developmentally and neuropsychologically, would seem to be immensely revealing and towards this end, speech and language therapists can benefit the multi-disciplinary team.

In the quarterly newsletter of the Ontario Friends of Schizophrenics (November 1995), Dr Daniel Weinberger discussed new drugs, stating that they are cleaner and more beneficial but, despite their improved effectiveness for many, do not cure schizophrenia. Sometimes, there are miraculous experiences but people are not 'brought back to base line'. Therefore, one of the most pressing research questions is to determine what disability lingers, even after the hallucinations and delusions have been brought under control, and what methods can be identified to remedy those deficits. He endorses the fact that good neuropsychological work has led to greater clarity about what cognitive deficits or disabilities characterise schizophrenia, but this is an area for further research and one in which speech and language therapists, with their unique skills in the neuropsychology of language, may have an input. Weinberger further states that none of the available anti-psychotic medicines improve cognitive disability, yet greater clarity about the disabilities that characterise schizophrenia sharpens the challenge, for all mental health professionals, to find methods to ameliorate them.

As Chapter 11 intimates, active listening, the ability to reconstruct and reflect back degraded language and distorted speech, and the grasp of both social and neuropsychological models of communication, are at the heart of the speech and language therapist's clinical ability – another area for research which might lead to improved assessments and new therapy approaches.

The psychiatric profession has research expertise and access to research opportunities which could be enriched by input from the speech and language therapy profession (see Fraser et al. in Chapter 6). We are aware also that many psychiatrists are ready to accept that some training in linguistics could add a significant depth to their interviewing techniques and to their interpretation of meaning (McGuire et al. 1989 and Thomas in Chapter 4).

Research is already yielding further studies on the language of schizophrenia and other mental illnesses and in some studies investigations into the use and types of therapy to improve the quality of language use is under way. In their latest paper Thomas et al. (1996) found that studies have revealed linguistic differences between diagnostic groups. Their study investigated the extent to which these difficulties are accounted for by factors such as chronicity or disturbances in cognition associated with acute psychosis. Equally, research continues within the area of overall communication difficulties and the treatment of semantic pragmatic disorder.

Atkinson et al. (1996) have recently published that, whilst there is widespread interest in psychoeducation programmes for relatives, there has been little investigation of the effects of their illness on the people actually suffering from schizophrenia. They set out to investigate whether giving people with schizophrenia information about their condition would have an effect on their quality of life – specifically, social functioning. They found that the clinical implications were that education groups for people with schizophrenia would have a positive effect on social functioning, social networks and quality of life, that the intervention involved no specific skills training and that the groups were more acceptable to patients with a high compliance with medication. There were of course limitations: only a minority of patients were interested in groups. The role of increased social contact in groups is a compounding variable and the groups required comparisons with other types of patient education which need to be developed. This is a very interesting paper and has further implications for therapy with schizophrenic patients. Many speech and language therapy groups have the core aim of information giving, which is seen as empowerment.

Woolis (1995) lists 19 essential skills and attitudes for care givers which have been shown to decrease the relapse rate for people with schizophrenia, some of which are: learn about your relative's experience, diagnosis and symptoms; accept the person is ill; attribute the symptoms to the illness; learn about the medications and available services, etc. She went on to give five useful recommendations for the family on the 'treatment team' – number 3 is 'collaborate with and support providers. There is need for good communication!' There are interesting links with treatment here for both sufferers and their families – an area in which those speech and language therapists working in the community could be jointly involved.

The way forward for speech and language therapy in psychiatry is a fascinating challenge. Speech and language therapy is a small profession, the role of which is often misunderstood. All opportunities should be taken for explanation and core skills should be clearly defined in order to gain credibility. The profession has responded to the current demands for quality services with clear guidelines on its professional standards (Royal College of Speech and Language Therapists 1996) and all branches of the profession are looking to the use of clear and varied audit procedures and measurement of outcome (Royal College of Speech and Language Therapists 1993).

The specialism of speech and language therapy in psychiatry is still in its early stages and it will be important to look at realistic ways of developing this branch of the profession. It takes time to make change for clients with enduring mental health problems and also to change public perception regarding this client group. It follows that it takes time to make professional and service developments. The ideal view of the contribution which can be made by speech and language therapists has been described in Chapter 9. However, many services are without any designated provision, are unable to access any level of service and are largely unaware that such provision may have value. It is certainly true that transfer to, and maintenance in, the community will be significantly improved by addressing the comprehension abilities and communication skills of service users. Inadequate skills will mark them as 'different' and fuel suspicion and confusion amongst the general public, whereas improved skills will empower them to put their own case.

In the current situation, and given the current constraints, it may be that the profession will have to look to a different model of care delivery in order to make the best use of limited resources, one that is perhaps based on a consultative and educative role within a variety of mental health teams. This may initially mean a move away from a workload of predominantly face-to-face contacts with patients and necessitate assessment and advice which will enrich the ongoing care planning, as well as general and specific packages of training for staff and carers on aspects of language and communication and direct management strategies. It will fall to speech and language therapists currently working in psychiatric settings to find logical and long-term strategies for development and the continued implementation of change. Given that the speech and language therapy service in mental health is very thinly spread, due to financial constraints and the slowness of a long-established system to implement change and encompass other clinical aspects and competencies, those therapists are having to find flexible and more far-reaching ways of delivering care and developing the specialism. Thus, information within the team, and on a much wider scale, is of paramount importance.

For services without any access to speech and language therapists, training may be a way of acquiring some level of input. Most speech and language therapists working in the NHS are usually willing to undertake training sessions on the nature of speech, language and communication and members of the Psychiatry Special Interest Group offer specific training packages on all aspects of communication and mental health. This is seen by the group as having potential for developing the specialism and as an effective way for unprovided units to use limited resources.

A further way of flexible working in the current financial climate might be for the instigation of short-term contracts, enabling speech and language therapists to be seconded to undertake needs surveys, prioritisation ratings and efficacy measures which could lead to informed discussions as to providing a level of dedicated service. Therapists working single-handed or part-time could offer a rotational service between the various localities, determined on the unique profile of priorities that the unit yields both in regard to client and staff need. Specialist therapists could be enlisted to offer *ad hoc* support, supervision and development for others who may have an interest in mental health, or find themselves treating a person with a psychiatric illness.

For those speech and language therapists presently working in psychiatry, networking within the multi-disciplinary team will be a prime objective. The national group can expand this principle in the wider sense by actively seeking opportunities to talk and write about the role and also by regular updating of the data base of references and resources which can be made available to members and to others. One vital short-term aim would be to establish a forum for post-graduate training, given that, with the full realisation of care in the community, the speech and language therapy profession will need to provide training opportunities for its members through expanded undergraduate and, more specifically, post-graduate courses in mental health. Non-specialist speech and language therapists will need to feel informed as to the nature and potential of the role and, with training, feel empowered to undertake interventions with people with speech, language or communication needs resultant from mental health problems and to stress that working in any aspect of mental health will not be necessarily dilute their skills but enrich them and build on those existing skills and help them to acquire others. This will diversify into most major areas of clinical practice (Muir 1996).

Speech and language therapists working in psychiatric settings have, over the last two years, experienced a sense of timeliness which crystalised throughout the symposium *Communication and the Mentally Ill Patient*. The fact that contributors to the symposium, whose ideas are expressed in this book, come from both the psychiatric and speech and language therapy professions is certainly a welcomed and natural development allowing the interchange of ideas and the acknowledgement of similar avenues of investigation, thought, research and practice.

References

Abrahamson, D. (1991) 'The social networks of long-stay patients.' *British Journal of Psychiatry 158*, 718–719.

Abrahamson, D. and Brenner, D. (1982) 'Do long-stay psychiatric patients want to leave hospital?' *Health Trends 14*, 95–97.

Abrahamson, D. and Ezekiel, A. (1984) 'The social networks of patients moving from hospital to the community.' *Paper presented at the conference: social networks in Hospital and in the Community*. London: Kings Fund Centre.

Abrahamson, D., Swatton, J. and Willis, W. (1989) 'Do long-stay psychiatric patients want to leave hospital?' *Health Trends 21*, 16–21.

Abrahamson, D. and Fellow-Smith, E. (1991) 'A combined group and individual long-term out-patient clinic.' *Psychiatric Bulletin, The Journal of Trends in Psychiatric Practice 15*, 486–487.

Acheson, D. (1985) 'That overused word community.' *Health Trends 17*, 3.

Alladin, W. (1988) 'Cognitive behavioural group therapy.' In M. Aveline and W. Dryden (eds) *Group Therapy in Britain*. Milton Keynes: Open University Press.

Allen, H.A. (1983) 'Do positive and negative language symptom subtypes of schizophrenia show qualitative differences in language production?' *The Journal of Psychological Medicine 13*, 787–797.

Allen, H.A. and Frith, C.D. (1983) 'Selective retrieval and free emission of category exemplars in schizophrenia.' *British Journal of Psychology 74*, 481–490.

Allen, H.A., Liddle, P.F. and Frith, C.D. (1993) 'Negative features, retrieval processes and verbal fluency in schizophrenia.' *British Journal of Psychiatry 163*, 769–775.

Alpern, G.D., Boll, T.J. and Shearer, M.S. (1980) *The Developmental Profile II*. Aspen, Colorado: Psychological Development Publications.

Alverson, H. and Rosenberg, S. (1990) 'Discourse analysis of schizophrenic speech: A critique and a proposal.' *Applied Psycholinguistics 11*, 2, 167–184.

Anand, A., Wales, R.G., Jackson, H.J. and Copolov, D.L. (1994) 'Linguistic impairment in early psychosis.' *Journal of Nervous and Mental Diseases 189*, 9, 488–493.

Andreason, N.C. (1979a) 'Thought, language and communication disorders: 1. clinical assessment, definition of terms and evaluation of their reliability.' *Archives of General Psychiatry 35*, 1315–1321.

Andreason, N.C. (1979b) 'Thought, language and communication disorders: 2. diagnostic significance.' *Archives of General Psychiatry 36*, 1325–1330.

Andreason, N.C. (1980) *Scale for the Assessment of Thought, Language and Communication Disorders*. Iowa City: University of Iowa.

Annett, M. (1985) *Left, Right, Hand and Brain*. London: Lawrence Erlbaum.

Anthony, A., Bogle, D., Ingram, T.T. and McIssac, M.W. (1971) *The Edinburgh Articulation Test*. Edinburgh: Churchill Livingstone.

Aram, D. and Nation, J. (1980) 'Pre-school language disorders and subsequent Language and academic difficulties.' *Journal of Communication Disorders 13*, 159–170.

Argyle, M. (1981) 'The contribution of social interaction research to social skills training.' In J. Wine and M. Symes (eds) *Social Competence.* New York: Guildford Press.

Astington, J.W. and Gopnik, M. (1991) 'Theoretical explanations of children's understanding of mind.' *British Journal of Developmental Psychology 9,* 7–31.

Atkinson, J.H., Cuia, D.A., Gilmout, W.H. and Harper, P.J. (1996) 'The impact of education groups for people with schizophrenia or social conditioning and quality of life.' *British Journal of Psychiatry 68,* 199–205.

Austin, J.L.J. (1962) *How to do Things With Words.* Oxford: Clarendon Press.

Baars, B.J. (ed) (1992) *Experimental Slips and Human Error: Exploring the Architecture of Volition.* New York: Plenum Press.

Bailey, R.C. (1991) *Language and Behaviour Institute.* West Park, New York. Training Materials: unpublished.

Baker, L. and Cantwell, D.P. (1982) 'Psychiatric disorder in children with different types of communication disorder.' *Journal of Communication Disorders 15,* 113–126.

Baker, L. and Cantwell, D.P. (1987) 'Comparison of well, emotionally disordered and behaviourally disordered children with linguistic problems.' *Journal of the American Academy of Child and Adolescent Psychiatry 26,* 193–196.

Bandler, R. and Grinder, J. (1975) *The Structure of Magic. Vol I.* Palo Alto, CA: Science and Behaviour Books.

Bandler, R. and Grinder, J. (1976) *The Structure of Magic. Vol II.* Palo Alto, CA: Science and Behaviour Books.

Barch, D. and Berenbaum, H. (1994) 'The relationship between information processing and language production.' *Journal of Abnormal Psychology 103,* 2, 241–250.

Barch, D.M.D and Berenbaum, H. (1996) 'Language production and thought disorder in schizophrenia.' *Journal of Abnormal Psychology 105,* 1, 81–88.

Baron-Cohen, S., Leslie, A.M. and Frith, U. (1985) 'Does the autistic child have a "theory of mind"?' *Cognition 21,* 37–46.

Barta, P.E., Pearlson, G.D., Powers, R.E. (1990) 'Auditory hallucinations and superior temporal gyrus volume in schizophrenia.' *American Journal of Psychiatry 147,* 1457–62.

Barton, R. (1959) *Institutional Neurosis.* Bristol: John Wright and Sons.

Beaumont, J.G. and Dimond, S.J. (1973) 'Brain disconnection and schizophrenia.' *British Journal of Psychiatry 123,* 661–2.

Beck, A.T., Shaw, A.J., Rush, B.F. and Emery, G. (1979) *Cognitive Therapy of Depression.* Chichester: Wiley.

Beitchman, J., Nair, R., Clegg, M., Ferguson, F. and Patel, P. (1986) 'Prevalence of speech and language disorders in 5-year-old kindergarten children in the Ottowa-Carleton region.' *Journal of Speech and Hearing Disorders 51,* 98–109.

Beitchman, J., Hood, J., Rochon, J., Peterson, M., Mantini, T. and Majumder, S. (1989a) 'Empirical classification of Speech/language impairment in children: I. identification of speech/language categories.' *Journal of the American Academy of Child and Adolescent Psychiatry 28,* 112–117.

Beitchman, J., Hood, J., Rochon, J. and Peterson, M. (1989b) 'Empirical classification of Speech/language impairment in children: II. behavioural characteristics.' *Journal of the American Academy of Child and Adolescent Psychiatry 28,* 118–123.

Benasich, A.A., Curtiss, S. and Tallal, P. (1993) 'Language, learning and behavioural disturbances in childhood: a longitudinal perspective.' *Journal of the American Academy of Child Psychiatry 32,* 3, 585–594.

Berne, E. (1961) *Transactional Analysis in Psychotherapy.* New York: Grove Press.

Berrios, G.E. (1992) 'History of mental symptoms, diseases and mechanisms.' *Current Opinion in Psychiatry 5*, 705–709.

Bilder, R.M., Wu, H., Degreef, G., Ashtari, M., Mayerhoff, D.I., Loebel, A. and Lieberman, J.A. (1994) 'Yakovlevian torque is absent in first episode schizophrenia.' *American Journal of Psychiatry 151*, 1437–47.

Birchwood, M., Hallet, S. and Preston, M. (1988) *Schizophrenia: An Integrated Approach to Research and Treatment.* London: Longman.

Birchwood, M. and Tarrier, N. (1992) *Innovations in the Psychological Management of Schizophrenia.* Chichester: Wiley.

Bishop, D.V.M. (1983) *Test for the Reception of Grammar.* Manchester: University of Manchester.

Bishop, D.V.M. (1994) 'Developmental disorders in speech and language.' In M. Rutter, E. Taylor and L. Hersov (eds) *Child and Adolescent Psychiatry: Modern Approaches,* third edition. Oxford: Blackwell Scientific Publications.

Bishop, D.V.M. and Adams, C. (1990) 'A prospective study of the relationship between specific language impairment, phonological disorders and reading retardation.' *Journal of Child Psychology and Psychiatry 31*, 1027–1050.

Blakemore, C. (1988) *Madness (Programme 6): The Mind Machine.* UK: BBC 2 Publications.

Bleuler, E. (1911) 'Dementia praecox or the group of schizophrenia.' (1987 Trans.) In J. Cutting and M. Shepherd (eds) *The Clinical Routes of the Schizophrenia Concept.* Cambridge: Cambridge University Press.

Blowers, G. and Acinar, K. (1995) 'Construing contexts: problems and prospects of George Kelly's personal construct psychology.' *British Journal of Clinical Psychology 34.* 1–16.

Bogerts, B., Ashtari, M., Degreef, G., Alvir, J.M.J., Bilder, R.M. and Lieberman, J. (1990) 'Reduced temporal limbic structure volumes on magnetic resonance images in first episode schizophrenia.' *Psychiatry Research and Neuroimaging 35*, 1–13.

Brown, I., and Saunders, T. (1988) 'The Group Structure.' Speech and Language Therapy Department (Mental Health), Camden and Islington Community Services NHS Trust. Unpublished.

Brumfitt, S. (1986) *Your Patient may Need Counselling.* Oxford: Winslow.

Bryan, K. (1988) 'Assessment of language disorders after right hemisphere damage.' *British Journal of Disorders of Communication 23*, 111–123.

Bryan, K. (1989) *The Right Hemisphere Language Battery.* London: Whurr.

Bunce, B. (1989) 'Using a barrier game format to improve children's referential communication skills.' *Journal of Speech and Hearing Disorders 54*, 33–43.

Burd, L. and Fischer, W. (1986) 'Central auditory processing disorder or attention deficit disorder?' *Journal of Developmental and Behavioural Paediatrics 1*, 215–216.

Burden, V., Stott, C.M., Forge, J. and Goodyer, I.M. (1996) 'The Cambridge language and speech project (CLASP): i) detection of language difficulties at 36–39 months.' *Journal of Developmental Medicine and Child Neurology.* (In Press)

Butt, T. and Bannister, D. (1987) 'Better the devil you know.' In W. Dryden (ed) *Key Cases in Psychotherapy.* London: Croom Helm.

Burr, V. and Butt, T. (1992) *Invitation to Personal Construct Psychology.* London: Whurr.

Cantwell, D.P., Baker, L. and Mattison, R.E. (1980) 'Factors associated with the development of psychiatric disorder in children with speech and language retardation.' *Archives of General Psychiatry 37*, 423–426.

Cantwell, D.P. and Baker, L. (1985) 'Speech and language: development and disorders.' In M. Rutter and L. Hersov (eds) *Child and Adolescent Psychiatry*. Oxford: Blackwell.

Carlomagno, S. (1994) *Pragmatic Approaches to Aphasia Therapy*. London: Whurr.

Caulfield, M.B., Fischel, J.E., DeBaryshe, B. and Whitehurst, G.J. (1989) 'Behavioural correlates of developmental expressive language disorder.' *Journal of Abnormal Child Psychology 17*, 187–201.

Chadwick, P. and Trower, P. (1994) 'Psychological approaches to schizophrenia: problems and opportunities.' *Paper given at the National Forum for Mental Health Conference 'Schizophrenia – Current developments in psychosocial treatments'*. September 1994: Nottingham.

Chaika, E. (1974) 'A linguist looks at "schizophrenic" language.' *Brain and Language 1*, 257–276.

Chaika, E. (1977) 'Schizophrenic speech, slips of the tongue and jargonaphasia: A reply to Fromkin and to Lecours and Vaniers-Clement.' *Brain and Language 4*, 464–475.

Chaika, E. (1982a) 'A unified explanation for the diverse structural deviations reported for adult schizophrenics with disrupted speech.' *Journal of Communication Disorders 15*, 167–189.

Chaika, E. (1982b) 'Thought disorder or speech disorder in schizophrenia?' *Schizophrenia Bulletin 8*, 587–591.

Chaika, E. and Lambe, R. (1985) 'The locus of dysfunction of schizophrenic speech.' *Schizophrenia Bulletin 11*, 8–14.

Chaika, E. and Alexander, P. (1986) 'The ice cream stories: A study in normal and psychotic narrations.' *Discourse Processes 9*, 305–328.

Chaika, E. (1990) *Understanding Psychotic Speech: Beyond Freud and Chomsky*. Springfield Illinois: Charles C. Thomas.

Chapman, S.B., Culhane, K.A., Levin, H.S., Harward, H., Mendelsohn, D., Ewing-Cobbs, L., Fletcher, J.M. and Bruce, D. (1992) 'Narrative discourse after closed head injury in children and adolescents.' *Brain and Language 43*, 42–65.

Chomsky, A.N. (1957) *Syntactic Structures*. The Hague: Mouton.

Clare, A. (1992) 'The Jansson Memorial Lecture: Communication in medicine.' *European Journal of Disorders of Communication 28(1)*; 1–12.

Clementz, B.A., Iacono, W.G. and Beiser, M. (1994) 'Handedness in first-episode psychotic patients and their first-degree biological relatives.' *Journal of Abnormal Psychology 103*, 400–403.

Cohen, B. (1978) 'Referent communication disturbances in schizophrenia.' In S. Schwartz (ed) *Language and Cognition in Schizophrenia*. Hillsdale, NJ: Lawrence Erlbaum.

Cohen, N.J., Davine, M. and Meloche-Kelly, M. (1989) 'Prevalence of unsuspected language disorders in a child psychiatric population.' *Journal of the American Academy of Child and Adolescent Psychiatry 28*, 107–111.

Cohen, N.J., Davine, M., Hordezky, M.A., Lipsett, L. and Isaacson, B.A. (1993) 'Unsuspected language impairment in psychiatrically disturbed children: prevalence, language and behavioural characteristics.' *Journal of the American Academy of Child and Adolescent Psychiatry 32*, 595–603.

Crichton-Browne, J. (1879) 'On the weight of the brain and its componant parts in the insane.' *Brain 2*, 42–67.

Crow, T.J., Colter, N., Frith, C.D., Johnstone, E.C. and Owens, D.G.C. (1989) 'Developmental arrest of cerebral asymmetries in early onset schizophrenia.' *Psychiatry Research 29*, 247–53.

Crow, T.J. and Done, D.J. (1992) 'Prenatal exposure to influenza does not cause schizophrenia.' *British Journal of Psychiatry 161*, 390–3.

Crow, T.J., Brown, R., Bruton, C.J., Frith, C.D. and Gray, V. (1992) 'Loss of Sylvian fissure asymmetry in schizophrenia: findings in the Runwell 2 series of brains.' *Schizophrenia Research 6*, 152–3.

Crow, T.J. (1993) 'Origins of psychosis and the evolution of human language and communication.' *International Academy for Biomedical and Drug Research 4*, 39–61.

Crow, T.J. (1995a) 'Constraints on concepts of pathogenesis.' *Archives of General Psychiatry 52*, 1011–4.

Crow, T.J. (1995b) 'A Darwinian approach to the origins of psychosis.' *British Journal of Psychiatry 167*, 12–25.

Crow, T.J., Dose, D.J., and Sucker, A. (1996) 'Cerebral lateralisation is delayed in children who will later develop schizophrenia.' *Schizophrenia Research* (in press).

Crystal, D. (1991) *A Dictionary of Linguistics and Phonetics*, third edition. Oxford: Blackwell.

Cunningham, D.J. (1892) *Contribution to the Surface Anatomy of the Cerebral Hemispheres*. Dublin: Academy House.

Cutting, J. (1990) *The Right Cerebral Hemisphere and Psychiatric Diagnosis*. Oxford: University Press.

Cutting, J. (1991) *The Right Cerebral Hemisphere and Psychiatric Diagnosis*. Oxford: University Press.

Dalton, P. (ed) (1983) *Approaches to the Treatment of Stuttering*. London: Croom Helm.

Dalton, P. (1987) 'Some developments in Personal Construct Therapy with adults who stutter.' In C. Levy (ed) *Stuttering Therapies: Practical Approaches*. London: Croom Helm.

Dalton, P. (1994) *Counselling People with Communication Problems*. London: sage Publications.

Dalton, P. and Dunnett, G. (1990) *A Psychology for Living: Personal Construct Theory for Professionals and Clients*. London: John Wiley and sons.

Daniel, D.G., Myslobodsky, M.S., Ingraham, L.J., Coppola, R. and Weinberger, D.R. (1989) 'The relationship of occipital skull asymmetry to brain parenchymal measures in schizophrenia.' *Schizophrenia Research 2*, 465–72.

David, A.S. (1990) 'Insight and psychosis.' *British Journal of Psychiatry 156*, 798–808.

De Bonis, M., Epelbaum, C., Feline, A., Grize, J.B., Hardy, P. and Somogyi, M. (1990) 'Pensee formelle, operations logico-discursive et schizophrenie: Estude experimentale d'un case clinique.' *Canadian Journal of Psychiatry 35*, 64–70.

De Villiers, J.G. and De Villiers, P.A. (1978) *Language Acquisition*. Harvard: University Press.

Dixon, J., Cott, A. and Law, J. (1988) 'Early language screening in City and Hackney: Work in progress.' *Child Care, Health and Development 14*, 213–229.

Dozier, M., Harris, M. and Bergman, H. (1987) 'Social network density and rehospitalisation among young adult patients.' *Hospital and Community Psychiatry 38*, 61–65.

Drug Ther. Bull. (1995) 'The drug treatment of patients with schizophrenia.' *Drug and Therapeutics Bulletin 33*, 11, 81.

D.S.M IIIR (1987) *Diagnostic and Statistical Manual of Mental Disorders*, third edition. Washington DC: American Psychiatric Association.

D.S.M. 1V (1994) *Diagnostic and Statistical Manual of Mental Disorders,* fourth edition. Washington DC: American Psychiatric Association.

Done, D.J., Johnstone, E.C., Frith, C.D., Golding, J., Shepherd, P.M. and Crow, T.J. (1991) 'Complications of pregnancy and delivery in relation to psychosis in adult life: data from the British perinatal mortality survey sample.' *British Medical Journal 302,* 1576–80.

Done, D.J., Crow, T.J., Johnstone, E.C. and Sacker, A. (1994a) 'Childhood antecedents of schizophrenia and affective illness: Social adjustment at ages 7 and 11.' *British Medical Journal 309,* 699–703.

Done, D.J., Crow, T.J., Johnstone, E.C. and Sacker, A. (1994b) 'Childhood antecedents of schizophrenia and affective illness: intellectual performance at ages 7 and 11.' *unpublished.*

Dunn, L.M., Whetton, C. and Pintilie, D. (1982) *British Picture Vocabulary Scale: Manual for Long and Short Forms.* Windsor: NFER Nelson.

Eastwood, M.R., Corbin, S.L., Reed, M. (1986) 'Acquired hearing Loss and Psychiatric illness: an estimate of prevalence and psychomorbidity in a geriatric setting.' *British Journal of Psychiatry 147,* 552–6.

Ebert, D. (1991) 'Formale Denkstorungen und Sprachstorungen bei Schizophrenien: Neue Erkenntnisse aus empirischen Untersuchungen?' *Fortschrift für Neurologie und Psychiatrie 59,* 397–403.

Eberstaller, O. (1884) 'Zur oberflächenanatomie des grosshirnhemisphären.' *Weiner Medizinische Blätter 7,* 479–82.

Edwards, G. (1972) 'Diagnosis of schizophrenia: an Anglo-American comparison.' *British Journal of Psychiatry 120,* 385–90.

Ellis, A.W. and Young, A.W. (1988) *Human Cognitive Neuropsychology.* Hove: Lawrence Erlbaum.

Emerson, J. and Enderby, P. *Prevalence of Speech and Language Disorders in a Mental Illness Unit.* Bristol: (in print).

Enderby, P. (1987) *Assistive Communication Aids for the Speech Impaired.* Edinburgh: Churchill Livingstone.

Enderby, P. (1988) *The Frenchay Dysarthria Assessment.* Windsor: NFER Nelson.

Erlenmeyer–Kimling, L. and Cornblatt, B. (1987) 'The New York High Rise Project: A follow up report.' *Schizophrenia Bulletin 13,* 451–461.

Erlenmyer–Kimling, L., Golden, R., and Cornblatt, B., (1989) 'A taxometric analysis of cognitive and neuromotor variables in children at risk for schizophrenia.' *Journal of Abnormal Psychology 98,* 203–208.

Evans, B.J., Stanley, R.D. and Burrows, G. (1993) 'Measuring medical students' empathy skills.' *British Journal of Medical Psychology 66,* 121–133.

Faber, R., Abrams, R. and Taylor, M. (1983) 'Comparison of schizophrenic patients with formal thought disorder and neurologically impaired patients with aphasia.' *American Journal of Psychiatry 139,* 1348–51.

Falkai, P., Bogerts, B., Greve, B. Pfeiffer, U., Machus, B., Folsch–Reetz, B., Majtenyi, C., and Overy, I. (1992) 'Loss of Sylvian fissure asymmetry in schizophrenia. A quantitative post-mortem study.' *Schizophrenia Research 7,* 23–32.

Falloon, R.H. (1992) 'Psychotherapy of schizophrenia.' *British Journal of Hospital Medicine 48,* 3/4, 164–169.

Feil, N. (1982) *Validation: The Feil Method.* Cleveland Ohio: Edward Feil Productions.

Flor-Henry, P. (1983) *Cerebral Basis of Psychopathology.* Boston: John Wright.

Forrest D. (1976) 'Nonsense and sense in schizophrenic language.' *Schizophrenia Bulletin* 2, 286–298.

Forrest, A.D., Hay, A.J. and Kushner, A.W. (1969) 'Studies in speech disorder in schizophrenia.' *British Journal of Psychiatry 115*, 833–41.

France, J. (1991) 'Psychoses.' In R. Gravell and J. France (eds) *Speech and Communication Problems in Psychiatry.* London: Chapman and Hall.

France, J. (1993) 'Assessment in psychiatry.' In J.R. Beech, L. Harding and D. Hilton-Jones (eds) *Assessments of Speech Therapy.* Routledge, NFER Assessment Library.

France, J. (1995) 'Communication, speech and language.' In C. Cordess and M. Cox (eds) *Forensic Psychotherapy: Crime, Psychodynamics and the Offender Patient.* London: Jessica Kingsley Publishers.

Fransella, F. and Dalton, P. (1990) *Personal Construct Counselling in Action.* London: Sage Publications.

Fransella, F. and Jones, H. (1995) 'Personal construct counselling.' *Counselling 6*, 41. 299–301.

Fraser, W.I., King, K.M. and Thomas, P. (1986) 'The diagnosis of schizophrenia by language analysis.' *British Journal of Psychiatry 148*, 275–278.

Frederikson, C.H., Bracewell, R.J., Breuleux, A. and Renaud, A. (1990) 'The cognitive representation and processing of discourse: function and dysfunction.' In Y. Joanette and H.H. Brownell (eds) *Discourse Ability and Brain Damage – Theoretical and Empirical Perspectives.* New York: Springer-Verlag.

Frith, U. (1989) *Autism: Explaining the Enigma.* Oxford: Blackwell.

Frith, C.D. (1992) *The Cognitive Neuropsychology of Schizophrenia.* Hove: Lawrence Erlbaum.

Frith, C.D. (1994) 'The theory of mind and language.' Paper presented at the Annual Meeting of the Royal College of Psychiatrists (July 1994) Cork, Ireland.

Frith, C.D., Friston, K.J., Herold, S., Silbersweig, D., Fletcher, P., Cohill, C., Dolan, R.J., Frackowiak, R.S.J. and Liddle, P.F. (1995) 'Regional brain activity in chronic schizophrenic patients during a verbal fluency task.' *British Journal of Psychiatry 167*, 343–349.

Fromkin, V.A. (1975) 'A linguist look at schizophrenic language.' *Brain and Language 2*, 498–503.

Gascon, C.G., Johnson, R. and Burd, L. (1986) 'Central auditory processing disorder and attention deficit disorders.' *Journal of Child Neurology 1*, 27–33.

Geschwind, N. and Levitsky, W. (1968) 'Left – right asymmetry in temporal speech region.' *Science 161*, 186–7.

Gittelman-Klein, R. and Klein, D.F. (1969) 'Premorbid asocial adjustment and prognosis in schizophrenia.' *Journal of Psychiatric Research 7*, 35–53.

Goffman, E. (1968) *Asylums: Essays on the Social Situations of Mental Patients and Other Inmates.* London: Penguin Books.

Goldie, N. (1988) '"I hated it there but I miss the people": A study of what happened to a group of ex-long stay patients from Claybury Hospital.' *Research paper 1. Health and Social Services Research Unit, Dept. of Social Services.* London: South Bank University.

Goodman, R., Simonoff, E. and Stevenson, J. (1995) 'The impact of child IQ, parent IQ and sibling IQ on child behavioural deviance scores.' *Journal of Child Psychology and Psychiatry 36*, 3, 409–425.

Gordon, E. (1976) *A Bi-disciplinary Approach to Group Therapy for Wives of Aphasics*. A paper presented at the American Speech and Hearing Association Convention. Houston.

Gordon, R., Silverstein, M.L. and Harrow, M. (1982) 'Associative thinking in schizophrenia: a contextualist approach.' *Journal of Clinical Psychology 38*, 684–696.

Gorham, D.R. (1956) 'The use of the proverbs test for differentiating schizophrenics from normals.' *Journal of Consulting Psychology 420*, 535.

Goudie, F. and Stokes, G. (1989) 'Understanding confusion.' *Nursing Times 85*, 35–37.

Gould, L.N. (1949) 'Auditory hallucinations and subvocal speech.' *Journal of Nervous and Mental Disease 109*, 418–427.

Green, H. (1964) *I Never Promised you a Rose Garden*. London: Victor Collanex.

Green, M.F., Satz, P., Smith, C. and Nelson, L.D. (1989) 'Is there atypical handedness in schizophrenia?' *Journal of Abnormal Psychology 98*, 57–61.

Grice, H.P. (1975) 'Logic and conversation.' In P. Cole and J. Morgan (eds) *Syntax and Semantics 3: Speech Acts*. London: Academic Press.

Griffiths, R. (1970) *The Abilities of Young Children*. Bucks: The Test Agency Ltd.

Griffiths, R. (1984) *The Abilities of Young Children. Revised Edition*. Bucks: The Test Agency Ltd.

Grinell, S., Scott-Hartnet, D. and Glasier, J.L. (1983) 'Language disorders.' *Journal of the American Academy of Child and Adolescent Psychiatry 22*, 580–581.

Gualtieri, T., Koriath, U., Van Bourgondien, M. and Saleeby, N. (1983) 'Language disorders in children referred for psychiatric services.' *Journal of the American Academy of Child and Adolescent Psychiatry 22*, 165–171.

Halliday, M.A.K. and Hasan, R. (1976) *Cohesion in English*. London: Longman.

Hallowell, E.M. and Smith, H.F. (1983) 'Communication through poetry in the therapy of a schizophrenic patient.' *Journal of the American Academy of Psychoanalysis 11*, 133–158.

Harrison, P.J. (1992) 'Conceptual analysis of psychiatric languages.' *Phenomenology, Physiology and Classification, Current Opinion in Psychiatry 5*, 727–731.

Harrow, M., Grossman, L.S., Silverstein, M.L. and Meltzer, H.Y. (1982) 'Thought pathology in manic and schizophrenic patients: its occurrence at hospital and 7 weeks later.' *Archives of General Psychiatry 39*, 665–671.

Harrow, M. and Prosen, M. (1978) 'Intermingling and disordered logic as influences on schizophrenic "thought disorders".' *Archives of General Psychiatry 35*, 1213–1218.

Harvey, P.D., Weintraub, S. and Neale, J.M. (1982) 'Speech competence of children vulnerable to psychopathology.' *Journal of Abnormal Child Psychology 10*, 373–388.

Harvey, P.D. (1991) 'Cognitive and linguistic functions of adolescent children at risk for schizophrenia.' In E.F. Walker (ed) *Schizophrenia: A Life-course Developmental Perspective*. California: Academic Press.

Heginbotham, C. (1985) *Good Practices in Housing for People with Long-term Mental Illnesses*. London: Good Practices in Mental Health.

Herbert, R.K. and Waltensperger, K.Z. (1982) 'Linguistics, psychology and psychopathology: The case of schizophrenic language.' In L. Obler and L. Menne (eds) *Exceptional Language and Linguistics*. New York: Academic Press.

Heyhow, R. and Levy, C. (1989) *Working with Stuttering: A Personal Construct Approach*, Oxford: Winslow.

Hoff, A.L., Riordan, H.. O'Donnell, D., Stritzke, P., Neale, C., Boccio, A., Anand, A.K., and Delisi, L.E.(1992) 'Anomalous lateral sulcus asymmetry and cognitive function in first-episode schizophrenia.' *Schizophrenia Bulletin 18*, 257–70.

Hoffman, R.E. (1986) 'Verbal hallucinations and language production processes in schizophrenia.' *Behaviuoral and Brain Sciences 9*, 503–548.

Hoffman, R.E. (1994) 'Dissecting psychotic speech.' *Journal of Nervous and Mental Diseases 182*, 4, 212–215.

Hoffman, R.E. and Satel, S. (1993) 'Language therapy for schizophrenic patients with persistent "voices".' *British Journal of Psychiatry 162*, 755–758.

Holden, U.P. and Woods, R. (1982) *Reality Orientation: Psychological Approaches to the Confused Elderly.* Edinburgh: Churchill Livingstone.

Holmes, M.R., Hansen, D.J. and St. Lawrence, J.S. (1984) 'Conversational skills training with aftercare patients in the community: Social validation and generalisation.' *Behaviour Therapy 15*, 84–100.

Hughston, G.A. and Merriam, S.B. (1982) 'Reminiscence: A non-formal technique for improving cognitive functioning in the aged.' *International Journal of Ageing and Human Development 15*, 139–149.

Hume, C. and Pullen, I. (1986) *Rehabilitation in Psychiatry: An Introductory Handbook.* Edinburgh: Churchill Livingstone.

Hurt, S., Holzman, P.S. and Davis, J.M. (1983) 'Thought disorder: the measurement of its changes.' *Archives of General Psychiatry 40*, 1281–85.

Hutchings, S., Comins, J. and Offlier, J. (1991) *The Social Skills Handbook.* Oxford: Winslow Press.

Hymes, D. (1962) 'The ethmography of speaking.' In T. Gladwin and E.E. Stuntevant (eds) *Human Behaviour.* Washington: Anthropological Society of Washington.

Jablensky, A., Sartorius, N., Ernberg, G., Anker, M., Korten, A., Cooper, J.E., Day, R. and Bertelsen, A. (1992) 'Schizophrenia: manifestatations, incidence and course in different cultures. A world health organisation ten country study.' *Psychological Medicine 20*, 1–97.

Jaynes, J. (1990 first published 1976) *The Origins of Consciousness in the Breakdown of the Bicameral Mind.* Boston: Houghton Mifflin.

Johnston, R. and Magreb, P.R. (1976) *Developmental Disorders: Assessment, Treatment, Education.* Baltimore: University Park Press.

Johnstone, E.C., Crow, T.J., MacMillan, J.F., Owens, D.G., Bydder, G.M. and Steiner, R.E. (1986) 'A magnetic resonance study of early schizophrenia.' *Journal of Neurology, Neurosurgery and Psychiatry 49*, 136–9.

Jones, P., Rodgers, B., Murray, R. and Marmot, M. (1994) 'Child developmental risk factors for adult schizophrenia in the British 1946 Cohort.' *Lancet 344*, 1398–1402.

Kay, J., Lesser, R. and Coltheart, M. (1992) *Psycholinguistics Assessments of Language Processing in Aphasia.* London: Lawrence Erlbaum Associates.

Keith, R.W. and Engineer, T. (1991) 'Effects of methylphenidate on the auditory processing abilities of children with attention deficit/hyperactivity disorder.' *Journal of Learning Disabilities 24*, 630–636.

Kelly, G. (1955) *The Psychology of Personal Constructs.* New York: Norton.

Kendall, R.E. (1988) 'Schizophrenia.' In R.E. Kendall and A.K. Zealley (eds) *Companion Guide to Psychiatric Studies*, fourth edition. Edinburgh: Churchill Livingstone.

King, K., Fraser, W.I., Thomas, P. and Kendall, R.E. (1990) 'Re-examination of the language of psychotic subjects.' *British Journal of Psychiatry 156*, 211–5.

Knowles, W. and Madislover, M. (1982) *The Derbyshire Language Scheme.* Derbyshire County Council.

Kotsopoulos, A. and Boodoosingh, L. (1987) 'Language and speech disorders in children attending a day psychiatric programme.' *British Journal of Disorders of Communication 22*, 3, 227–236.

Koury, L.N. and Lubinski, R. (1991) 'Effective in-service training for staff working with communication impaired patients.' In R. Lubinski (ed) *Dementia and Communication.* Philadelphia: Decker.

Kraepelin, E. (1971) *Dementia Praecox and Paraphrenia.* (R.M. Barclay, Trans.) Edinburgh: Churchill Livingstone. (Original work published 1919).

Kraepelin, E. (1896) 'Dementia praecox.' In J. Cutting and M. Shepherd (eds) *The Clinical Routes of the Schizophrenia Concept.* Cambridge: Cambridge University Press.

Kreitman, N. Sainsbury, P., Morrissey, J., Towers, J. and Scrivener, J. (1961) 'The reliability of psychiatric assessment: an analysis.' *Journal of Mental Science 107*, 887–908.

Kretschmer, E. (1921) *Korperbau und Charakter.* Heidelberg: Springer-Verlag.

Laffal, J. (1965) *Pathological and Normal Language.* New York: Atherton Press.

Laing, R.D. (1966) *The Initial Dysjunction.* Maudsley Bequest Lecture. (January 1966) London: Royal Society of Medicine.

Laing, R.D. and Esterson, A. (1970) *Sanity, Madness and the Family: Families of Schizophrenics* second edition. London: Tavistock.

Lane, E.A. and Albee, G.W. (1964) 'Early childhood intellectual differences between schizophrenic adults and their siblings.' *Journal of Abnormal Social Psychology 68*, 193–5.

Lanin-Kettering, I. and Harrow, M. (1985) 'The thought behind the words: A view of schizophrenic speech and thinking disorders.' *Schizophrenia Bulletin 11*, 1–7.

Lapworth, P., Sills, C. and Fish, S. (1994) *Transactional Analysis Counselling.* Oxford: Winslow.

Leach, G. (1983) *The Principles of Pragmatics.* London: Longmans.

Leff, J., O'Driscoll, C., Dayson, D., Willis, W. and Anderson, J. (1990) 'The structure of social network data obtained from long-stay patients.' *British Journal of Psychiatry 157*, 848–852.

Leslie, A.M. (1987) 'Pretence and representations: the origins of "Theory of Mind".' *Psychological Review 94*, 4, 412–426.

Lesser, R. (1987) 'Cognitive neuropsychological influences on aphasia therapy.' *Aphasiology I*, 189–200.

Lesser, R. and Milroy, L. (1993) *Linguistics and Aphasia: Psycholinguistic and Pragmatic Aspects of Intervention.* UK: Longman.

Leudar, I., Thomas, P. and Johnston, M. (1992) 'Self-repair in dialogues of schizophrenics.' *Brain and Language 43*, 487–511.

Leudar, I., Thomas, P. and Johnston, M. (1994) 'Self monitoring in speech production: Effects of verbal hallucinations and negative symptoms.' *Psychological Medicine 24*, 749–761.

Lewis, B. and Pucelik, F. (1982) *Magic Demystified.* Portland, Oregon: Metamorphous Press.

Ley, P. (1988) *Communicating with Patients.* London: Croom Helm.

Liberman, R.P., Mueser, K.T., Wallace, C.J., Jacobs, H.E., Eckman, T. and Massel, K. (1986) 'Training skills in the psychiatrically disabled: learning coping and competence.' *Schizophrenia Bulletin 12*, 4, 631–647.

Lockhart, M. and Martin, S. (1987) 'The Victoria Infirmary Voice Questionnaire.' In S. Martin (ed) *Working with Dysphonics*. Oxford: Winslow.

Logemann, J. (1983) *Evaluation and Treatment of Swallowing Disorders*. San Diego: College Hill Press.

Lorenz, M. (1961) 'Problems posed by schizophrenic language.' *Archives of General Psychiatry 4*, 603–610.

Love, A. and Thompson, M. (1988) 'Language disorders and attention deficit disorders in young children referred for psychiatric services: analysis of prevalence and a conceptual synthesis.' *American Journal of Orthopsychiatry 58*, 57–64.

Lund, N. and Duchan, J. (1988) *Assessing Children's Language in Naturalistic Contexts*, (second edition). Engelwood Cliffs, NJ: Prentice Hall.

Macdonald, L. (1994) 'I'll be your mirror.' *Therapy Weekly. September 8th.*

MacSorley, K. (1964) 'An investigation into the fertility rates of mentally ill patients.' *Annals of Human Genetics 27*, 247–56.

Maher, B. (1972) 'The language of schizophrenia: A review and interpretation.' *British Journal of Psychiatry 120*, 3–17.

Maher, B. (1983) 'A tentative theory of schizophrenic utterance.' *Progress in Experimental Personality Research (Vol. 12.)*. New York: Academic Press.

Martin, S. (1987) *Working with Dysphonics*. Oxford: Winslow.

Masnik, R., Bucci, L., Isenberg, D. and Normand, W. (1971) '"Coffee and…" a way to treat the untreatable.' *American Journal of Psychiatry 128*, 164–167.

McGhie, A. and Chapman, J. (1961) 'Disorders of attention and perception in early schizophrenia.' *British Journal of Medical Psychology 34*, 103–116.

McGhie, A., Chapman, J. and Lawson, J.S. (1965a) 'The effect of distraction on schizophrenic performance: 2. perception and immediate memory.' *British Journal of Psychiatry 111*, 383–390.

McGhie, A., Chapman, J. and Lawson, J.S. (1965b) 'The effect of distraction on schizophrenic performance: 2. psychomotor ability.' *British Journal of Psychiatry 111*, 391.

McGhie, A. (1970) 'Attention and perception in schizophrenia.' In B. Maher (ed) *Progress in Experimental Personality Research 5*. New York: Academic Press.

McGuire, J. and Richman, N. (1986) 'Screening for behavioural problems in nurseries: the reliability and validity of the pre-school behaviour checklist.' *Journal of Child Psychology and Psychiatry 27*:1, 7–32

McGuire, P., Fairbuison, S. and Fletcher, C. (1989) 'Consultation skills of young doctors. Benefits of undergraduate feedback training in interviews.' In M. Stewart and D. Roter (eds) *Communicating with Medical Patients*. London: Sage Series.

McGuire, P.K., Shah, G.M.S. and Murray, R.M. (1993) 'Increased blood flow in Broca's area during auditory hallucinations in schizophrenia.' *Lancet 342*, 703–706.

McGuire, P.K., Silbersweig, D.A., Wright, I., Murray, R.H., David, A.S., Frackowiak, R.S.J. and Frith, C.D. (1995) 'Adnormal inner speech: a physiological basis for auditory hallucinations.' *Lancet 346*, 596–600.

McManus, I.C., Shergill, S. and Bryden, M.P. (1993) 'Annett's theory that individuals heterozygous for the right shift gene are intellectually advantaged: theoretical and empirical findings.' *British Journal of Psychology 84*, 517–37.

Meehl (1962) 'Schizotaxia, schizotypy, schizophrenia.' *American Psychologist 17*, 827–838.

Meichenbaum, D. (1985) 'Cognitive behavioural therapies.' In S.J. Lynnn and J.P. Garske (eds) *Contemporary Psychotherapies: Models and Methods.* Ohio: Charles E. Merrill.

Meltzer, E., Kemp, P. and Smith, B. (1994) 'Social networks in a cluster of three group homes for the mentally ill.' *Journal of mental Health 3*, 263–270.

Morrice, R. and Ingram, J.C.L. (1982) 'Language analysis in schizophrenia: diagnostic implications.' *Australian and New Zealand Journal of Psychiatry 16*, 11–21.

Morrice, R. and Ingram, J.C.L. (1983) 'Language complexity and age at onset of schizophrenia and linguistic performance.' *Psychiatry Research 9*, 233–42.

Morrice, R. (1995) 'Language impairments and executive dysfunctions in schizophrenia.' In A. Sims (ed) *Speech and Language Disorders in Psychiatry.* London: Gaskell.

Mueser, K.T. and Sayers, M.D. (1992) 'Social skills assessment.' In D.J. Kavanagh (ed) *Schizophrenia.* London: Chapman and Hall.

Muir, N.J., Tanner, P.E. and France, J. (1991) 'Management and treatment techniques: a practical approach.' In R. Gravell and J. France (eds) *Speech and Communication Disorders in Psychiatry.* London: Chapman and Hall.

Muir, N.J. (1992) 'Group encounters in psychiatry.' In M. Fawcus (ed) *Group Encounters in Speech and Language Therapy.* London: Whurr.

Muir, N.J. (1996) 'The role of the speech and language therapist in psychiatry.' *Psychiatric Bulletin 20*, 524–526.

Murray, R. (1994) 'Sanity, madness and the family.' *Paper presented at the Royal College of Psychiatrists Annual Meeting.* July 1994. Cork. Ireland.

Nasrallah, H.A. (1985) 'The unintegrated right cerebral hemispheric consciousness as an alien intruder: a possible mechanism for Schneiderian delusions in schizophrenia.' *Comprehensive Psychiatry 26*, 273.

Nathaniel–James, D.A. and Frith, C.D. (1996) 'Confabulation inSchizophrenia.' *Psychological Medicine 26*, 391–399.

Naylor, C.E., Felton, R.H. and Wood, F.B. (1989) 'Adult outcome in developmental dyslexia.' In G.T. Pavlidis (ed) *Dyslexia Vol II.* New York: John Wiley and Sons.

Neimeyer, R. (1985) 'Personal constructs in depression: Research and clinical Implications.' In E. Button (ed) *Personal Constuct Theory and Mental Health.* London: Croom Helm.

Nelson, H. (1982) *National Adult Reading Test: Test Manual.* Windsor: NFER Nelson.

Nelson, H. and Williamson, J. (1991) *National Adult Reading Test: Test Manual part II.* Windsor: NFER Nelson.

Newby, D. (1995) 'Analysis of language: terminology and techniques.' In A. Sims (ed) *Speech and Language Disorders in Psychiatry.* London: Gaskell.

Nippold, M. (1985) 'Comprehension of figurative language in youth.' *Topics in Language Disorders 5*, 3, 1–20.

Norris, A. (1986) *Reminiscence with Elderly People.* Oxford: Winslow.

Novaco, R.W. (1975) *Anger Control.* London: Lexington Books.

O'Connor, J. and Seymour, J. (1990) *Introducing Neurolinguistic Programming.* London: The Aquarian Press.

Offord, D.R. and Cross, L.A. (1971) 'Adult schizophrenia with scholastic failure or low IQ in childhood.' *Archives of General Psychiatry 24*, 431–6.

Offord, D.R. (1974) 'School performance of adult schizophrenics, their siblings and age mates.' *British Medical Journal 125*, 9–12.

Olson, G.M. and Clark, H.H. (1976) 'Research methods in psycholinguistics.' In. E.C. Carterette and M.P. Friedman (eds) *Handbook of Perception. Vol.7.* New York: Academic Press.

Oltmans, T.F., Murphy, R., Berenbaum, H. and Dunlop, S.R. (1985) 'Rating verbal communication impairment in schizophrenia and affective disorders.' *Schizophrenia Bulletin 11*, 292–299.

Parker, A. (1983) 'Speech conservation.' In W.J. Watts (ed) *Rehabilitation and Acquired Deafness.* London: Croom Helm.

Pattison, E.M., Defrancisco, D., Wood, P., Frazier, H. and Crowder, J. (1975) 'A psychosocial kinship model for family therapy.' *American Journal of Psychiatry 132*, 1246–1251.

Payne, R.W. and Friedlander, D. (1962) 'A short battery of simple tests for measuring over-inclusive thinking.' *Journal of Mental Science 108*, 362–7.

Penrose, L.S. (1991) 'Survey of cases of familial mental illness.' *European Archives of Psychiatry and Neurological Science 240*, 315–24.

Premack, D. and Woodruff, G. (1978) 'Does the chimpanzee have a theory of mind?' *Behavioural and Brain Sciences 4*, 515–526.

Quayle, M., France, J. and Wilkinson, E. (1995) 'An integrated modular approach to therapy in a special hospital young men's unit.' In C. Cordess and M. Cox (eds) *Forensic Psychotherapy: Crime, Psychodynamics and the Offender Patient.* London: Jessica Kingsley Publishers.

Reason, J. and Mycielska, K. (1982) *Absent minded? The Psychology of Mental Lapses and Everyday Errors.* Englewood Cliffs, NJ: Prentice-Hall.

Reason, J. (1984) 'Lapses of attention in everyday life.' In R. Parasuraman and D.R. Davies (eds) *Varieties of Attention.* New York: Academic Press.

Renfrew, C.E. (1966) 'Persistance of the open syllable in defective articulation.' *Journal of Speech and Hearing Disorders 31*, 370–373.

Renfrew, C.E. (1969) *The Bus Story: A Test of Continuous Speech.* Oxford: Renfrew, North Place.

Reusch, J. (1987) 'Values, communication and culture.' In J. Reusch and G. Bateson (eds) *Communication in the Social Matrix of Psychiatry*, third edition. London: Norton.

Reynell, J. and Huntley, M. (1985) *Reynell Developmental Language Scales Manual. Revised edition.* Windsor: NFER Nelson.

Ribiero, B.T. (1994) *Coherence in Psychotic Discourse.* New York: Oxford University Press.

Robertson, S.J. and Thomson, F. (1982) *Working with Dysarthrics.* Oxford: Winslow.

Rochester, S. and Martin, J.R. (1979) *Crazy Talk: A Study of the Discourse of Schizophrenic Speakers.* New York: Plenum Press.

Rogers, C. (1951) *Client Centred Therapy.* Boston: Houghton Mifflin.

Rossi, A., Stratta, P., Mattei, P., Cupillar, M., Bozzao, A., Gallucci, M. and Casacchia, M. (1992) 'Planum temporale in schizophrenia: a magnetic resonance study.' *Schizophrenia Research 7*, 19–22.

Roth, F. and Spekman, N. (1984) 'Assessing the pragmatic ability of children: part 1, organisational framework and assessment parameters.' *Journal of Speech and Hearing Disorders 49*, 2–11.

Royal College of Speech and Language Therapists (1996) *Communicating Quality*, second edition. London: R.C.S.L.T.

Royal College of Speech and Language Therapists (1993) *Audit: A manual for Speech and Language Therapists.* London: R.C.S.L.T.

Rustin, L., Purser, H. and Rowley, D. (1987) *Progress in the Treatment of Fluency Disorders.* London: Taylor and Francis.

Rustin, L. and Kuhr, A. (1989) *Social Skills and the Speech Impaired.* London: Taylor Francis.

Rutter, D.R. (1985) 'Language in schizophrenia: the structure of monologues and conversations.' *British Journal of Psychiatry 146,* 388–404.

Saugstad, L.F. (1989) 'Age at puberty and mental illness: towards a neurodevelopmental aetiology of Kraepelin's endogenous psychoses.' *British Journal of Psychiatry 155,* 536–45.

Scarborough, H.S. and Dobrich, W. (1990) 'Development of children with early language delay.' *Journal of Speech and Hearing Research 33,* 70–83.

Scherer, E. (1972) *Contemporary Community: Sociological Illusion or Reality?* London: Tavistock Publications.

Schneider, K. (1939) *Clinical Psychopathology.* (Trans. M.W. Hamilton). New York: Grune and Stratton.

Schutz, W. (1989) 'In interpersonal world.' In R.B. Alder and G. Rodman (eds) *Understanding Human Communication,* third edition. London: Holt, Reinhart and Winston.

Scott, S. (1994) 'Mental handicap.' In M. Rutter, E. Taylor and L. Hersov (eds) *Child and Adolescent Psychiatry: Modern Approaches,* third edition. Oxford: Blackwell Scientific Publications.

Searle, J.R. (1969) *Speech Acts: An Essay in the Philosophy of Language.* Cambridge: Cambridge University Press.

Shakespeare, W. *Hamlet. Act 2, Scene 2.* London: Michael O'Mara Books Ltd.

Shallice, T. (1988) *From Neuropsychology to Mental Structure.* Cambridge: Cambridge University Press.

Shan-Ming, Y., Flor-Henry, P., Dayi, C., Tiangi, L., Suguang, Q. and Zenxiang, M. (1985) 'Imbalance of hemispheric functions in the major psychoses: A study of handedness in the People's Republic of China.' *Biological Psychiatry 20,* 906–17.

Shenton, M.E., Kikinis, R., Jolesz, F., Pollack, S.D., Le May, H., Wible, C.G., Hokama, H., Martin, J., Metcalf, D., Coleman, M. and McCarley, R.W. (1993) 'Abnormalities of the left temporal lobe and thought disorder in schizophrenia.' *New England Journal of Medicine 327,* 604–12.

Sherratt, S.M. and Penn, C. (1990) 'Discourse in a right hemisphere brain-damaged subject.' *Aphasiology 4,* 6, 539–560.

Shields, J. (1991) 'Semantic pragmatic disorder: a right hemisphere syndrome.' *European Journal of Disorders of Communication 26,* 3, 383–392.

Silva, P.A. (1980) 'The prevalence, stability and significance of developmental language delay in pre-school children.' *Developmental Medicine and Child Neurology 22,* 768–777.

Silva, P.A., Justin, C., Mcgee, R. and Williams, S.M. (1984) 'Developmental language delay from three to seven years and its significance for low intelligence and reading difficulties at age seven.' *British Journal of Disorders of Communication 19,* 149–154.

Silva, P.A., Williams, S.M. and Mcgee, R. (1987) 'A longitudinal study of children with developmental language delay at age three, later intelligence, reading and behaviour problems.' *Developmental Medicine and Child Neurology 29,* 630–640.

Sims, A. (ed) (1995) *Speech and Language Disorders in Psychiatry: Proceedings of the 5th Leeds Psychopathology Symposium.* London: Gaskell.

Sinclair, J. and Coulthard, M. (1992) 'Towards an analysis of discourse.' In M. Coulthard (ed) *Advances in Spoken Discourse Analysis.* London: Routledge.

Skinner, C., Wirz, M., Thompson, I. and Davidson, J. (1984) *The Edinburgh Functional Communication Profile.* Oxford: Winslow.

Sommer, R. and Osmond, H. (1962) 'The schizophrenic no-society.' *Psychiatry 25,* 244–255.

Stevens, S.J. (1985) 'The language of dementia in the elderly: a pilot study.' *British Journal of Disorders of Communication 20,* 181–190.

Stevenson, J. and Richman, N. (1978) 'Behaviour, language and development in three-year-old children.' *Journal of Autism and Childhood Schizophrenia 8,* 299–313.

Stevenson, J., Richman, N. and Graham, P. (1985) 'Behaviour problems and language abilities at three years and behavioural deviance at eight.' *Journal of Child Psychology and Psychiatry 26,* 2, 215–230.

Tallal, P., Dukette, D. and Curtiss, S. (1989) 'Behavioural/emotional profiles of pre-school language-impaired children.' *Development and Psychopathology 1,* 51–67.

Tanner, P.E. (1987) *A Study to Investigate Whether Speech Therapists find it Easier to Re-construct Schizophrenic Monologue and Whether Experience in Psychiatry Influences the Score.* unpublished.

Taylor, P.J. (1987) 'Hemispheric lateralisation and schizophrenia.' In. H. Helmchen and F.A. Henn (eds) *Biological Perspectives in Schizophrenia.* Chichester: Wiley.

Thacker, A. (1988) 'European study will probe psychiatric problems of deaf.' *Therapy Weekly 3,* 8th. December.

Thomas, P., King, K. and Fraser, W.I. (1987) 'Positive and negative symptoms of schizophrenia and linguistic performance.' *Acta Psychiatrica Scandinavica 76,* 144–51.

Thomas, P.H. (1994) *Thought Disorder or Communication Disorder: What can we Learn from Linguistics?* Paper presented at the Annual Meeting of the Royal College of Psychiatrists. (July 1994) Cork. Ireland.

Thomas, P. and Fraser, W.I. (1994) 'Linguistics, human communication and psychiatry.' *British Journal of Psychiatry 165,* 585–592.

Thornton, J.F. and Seeman, M.V. (1991) *Schizophrenia Simplified.* Canada: Hogrefe and Huber.

Tomblin, J.B., Freese, P.R. and Records, N.L. (1992) 'Diagnosing specific language impairment in adults for the purpose of pedigree analysis.' *Journal of Speech and Hearing Research 35,* 832–843.

Trower, P., Bryant, B. and Argyle, M. (1978) *Social Skills and Mental Health.* London: Methuen.

Urey, J.R., Laughlin, C. and Kelly, J.A. (1979) 'Teaching heterosocial conversational skills to male psychiatric patients.' *Journal of Behaviour Therapy and Experimental Psychiatry 10,* 323–328.

Van den Bergh, O., De Boeck, P. and Claeys, W. (1985) 'Schizophrenia: what is loose in schizophrenic construing?' In E. Button (ed) *Personal Constuct Theory and Mental Health.* London: Croom Helm.

Vetter, H. (1968) *Language Behaviour in Schizophrenia.* Springfield, Ill: Charles C. Thomas.

Von Domarus, E. (1944) 'The specific laws of logic in schizophrenia.' In S. Kasanin and N.D.C. Lewis (eds) *Language and Thought in Schizophrenia.* New York: Norton.

Walker, E.F. (ed) (1991) *Schizophrenia: A Life Course Developmental Perspective.* California: Academic Press.

Walker, M. (1979) 'The Makaton: in perspective.' *Apex 7,* 12–14.

Ward, D.J. (1975) 'Therapeutic groups and individual treatment in psychiatric out-patient clinics: a controlled study.' *Journal of the Irish Medical Association 68*, 486–489.

Watt, N.F. (1978) 'Patterns of childhood social development in adult schizophrenics.' *Archives of General Psychiatry 35*, 160–5.

Watt, N., Anthony, E.J., Wynne, L. and Rolf, R. (eds) (1984) *Children at Risk for Schizophrenia*. New York: Cambridge.

Wechsler, D. (1974) *Manual for the Wechsler Intelligence Scale for Children. Revised*. New York: Psychological Corporation.

Wechsler, D. (1981) *Wechsler Adult Intelligence Scale. Revised*. New York: Psychological Corporation.

Weinberger, D. (1995) 'News letter of the Ontario Friends of schizophrenics.' *National Schizophrenia Fellowship. Hampshire Borders, Aldershot Carers News Notes*. February 1996.

Whitehurst, G.J. and Fischel, J. (1994) 'Practitioner review: early developmental language delay. What if anything should the clinician do about it?' *Journal of Child Psychology and Psychiatry 5*, 4, 613–648.

Whurr, R. (1974) *An Aphasia Screening Test*. London: Whurr.

Wigan, A.L. (1844) *A New View of Insanity: The Duality of Mind*. London: Longman.

Willis, J.H. and Bannister, D. (1965) 'The diagnosis and treatment of schizophrenia: a questionnaire study of psychiatric opinion.' *British Journal of Psychiatry 111*, 1165–71.

Wing, J.K. and Brown, G. (1970) *Institutionalism and Schizophrenia: A Comparative Study of Three Mental Hospitals 1960–1968*. Cambridge: University Press.

Wing, J.K., Cooper, J.E. and Sartorius, N. (1974) *The Measurement and Classification of Psychiatric Symptoms*. Cambridge: Cambridge University Press.

Winter, D. (1987) 'PCP as a radical alternative to social skills training.' In R. Neimeyer and R. Neimeyer (eds) *Personal Construct Therapy Casebook*. New York: Springer.

Wolfensberger, W. (1972) *The Principle of Normalisation in Human Services*. Toronto: National Institute on Mental Retardation.

Wong, S.E. and Woosley, J.E. (1989) 'Re-establishing conversational skills in overtly psychotic chronic schizophrenic patients.' *Behaviour Modification 13*, 415–430.

World Health Organisation (1994) *ICD 10: Classification of Mental and Behavioural Disorders*. Edinburgh: Churchill Livingstone.

Woolis, R. (1995) 'News letter of the Ontario Friends of schizophrenics.' *National Schizophrenia Fellowship. Hampshire Borders, Aldershot Carers News Notes*. February 1996.

Wykes, T. (1981) 'Can the psychiatrist learn form the psycholinguist? Detecting coherence in the disordered speech of manics and scizophrenics.' *Psychological Medicine 11*, 641–642.

Wykes, T. and Leff, J. (1982) 'Disordered speech: Differences between manics and schizophrenics.' *Brain and Language 15*, 117–124.

Zangwill, O.L. (1960) *Cerebral Dominance and its Relation to Psychological Function*. Edinburgh: Oliver and Boyd.

Contributors

David Abrahamson is the Consultant Psychiatrist for the Mental Health Rehabilitation Team of Newham Community Healthcare Trust.

Vivian Burden is a research psychologist at the child development clinic of Addenbrokes Hospital, Cambridge and was previously part of the Cambridge Language Project team.

Elaine Chaika is Chair of Linguistics at Providence College, Rhode Island, USA.

Timothy Crow is a research psychiatrist at the University of Oxford Department of Psychiatry at the Warneford Hospital.

John Done is a senior clinical and research psychologist at the University of Hertfordshire.

Martin Duckworth is course leader in speech and language therapy at the College of St Mark and St John, Plymouth.

Jenny Forge is a clinical lecturer in child and adolescent psychiatry in the University of Cambridge Developmental Psychiatry Section.

Jenny France is Specialist Speech and Language Therapist at Broadmoor Hospital in Crowthorne, Berkshire.

William Fraser is Professor of Psychiatry at the University of Wales College of Medicine Department of Psychological Medicine in Cardiff.

Christopher Frith is Professor at the Wellcome Institute of Cognitive Neurology and University College London.

Ian Goodyer is Professor of Child and Adolescent Psychiatry at the University of Cambridge, Developmental Psychiatry Section.

Carmel Hayes is a speech and language therapist for the mental health service of Camden and Islington Community Health Services NHS Trust.

Joseph Joyce is a Senior Psychiatric Registrar at Ely Hospital in Cardiff.

Sarah Kramer is a speech and language therapist and a research fellow at University College London.

Laurie Macdonald is a speech and language therapist and a psychotherapist.

Niki Muir is a freelance speech and language therapist specialising in consultancy and training in all aspects of mental health.

Carol Stott is a research psychologist in the University of Cambridge Developmental Psychiatry Section.

Philip Thomas is Senior Lecturer in Psychological Medicine and Honorary Consultant Psychiatrist at the University of Wales College of Medicine, the Hergest Unit, Ysbyty Gwynedd.

Irene Walsh is a lecturer at the School of Clinical Speech and Language Studies, Trinity College, Dublin.

Subject Index

References in italic indicate figures or tables.

Author Index